Corner on Main Street

DEDICATED
with all due respect
to
Harry (Red) Sinclair Lewis
and
Another man from Main Street
R. J. Schwartz

Al Tingley

Published by:
Dauntless and **CREATIVE CONCEPTS, INC.**
St. Cloud, Minnesota 56301

Many of the names in this book have been changed for their own protection, as well as mine. Other characters appear as composites. However, the events are as real as Richard and myself.

Al Tingley

The true story of two innkeepers on the Corner of Main Street and Sinclair Lewis Avenue.

Library of Congress Catalog Card Number: 84-90203
ISBN   0-9613811-0-8

TABLE OF CONTENTS

INTRODUCTION

In July of 1982, I had the pleasure of being summoned to Sauk Centre as a guest of Al Tingley, Richard Schwartz, and the Palmer House. The occasion was the annual "Sinclair Lewis Days" celebration, and John Hamerlinck's delightful play, **Ole Doc Lewis's Younger Boy Harry** was being presented at the Palmer House. Following dinner and the performance, Mr. Tingley (but you'd better call him Al) and I swapped stories until dawn, or at least until the night clerk was relieved by the day clerk, or by Richard himself, who never sleeps.

At some point before our mutterings turned into yawns, and the last cycle had farted in front of the Short Stop Bar just down the block, Al suggested I take a walk in the park to gawk at Sauk Lake; that is, to capture the flavor of nocturnal Sauk Centre and how Sinclair Lewis and Myra Hendryx would have seen it as they rowed out from Orvaar's Boat Livery. Having nearly been mugged once in New York's Central Park, AND IN BROAD DAYLIGHT, I was a bit hesitant, but Al assured me the streets of Sauk Centre were safe well beyond the bewitching hour. "Go ahead," he urged, "this isn't Minneapolis. People don't get mugged in Gopher Prairie." He was right.

Circa 4:00 a.m. I retired but I could not sleep that night. The thrill of it all. My hosts had put me up in a room that Sinclair Lewis may have slept in, and as I glanced across the street at Centre Jobbing, formerly O'Gara's Garage, where Sinclair used to party, it all came back to me. The Palmer House and Sinclair Lewis...

For two weeks during the summer of 1902, Harry Sinclair Lewis had been employed as a night clerk at the Palmer House from six in the evening until six in the morning, earning five dollars per week plus room and board. Now it just so happened that Sauk Centre was served by a dozen trains per day, and the Palmer House was always filled with salesmen. One of these drummers had requested that young Sinclair awaken him at two in the morning so he could catch the three o'clock train. The dozing clerk overslept, but did manage to roust his customer sometime later to inform him that he had missed his train. Despite this disaster, Lewis returned to work at the Palmer House the following summer and was slightly more adept this time around.

And then there was the time in 1920, shortly after the publication of **Main Street** when Sinclair was honored with a reception at this same Palmer House. During the course of that dinner (I wonder if it could have been half as good as the one I would enjoy sixty-two years later) one Sauk Centre resident queried Lewis about his opinion of Eugene Debs, controversial labor leader and founder of the American Socialist Party. When Red Lewis insisted on comparing him to the Messiah, all those present at the table went into a state of shock, heads bobbing mechanically, all eyes on the floor.

Suddenly the headlights of a passing motorist, no doubt lost and looking for the interstate, brought me back to 1982. I was glad I hadn't slept, for I had gotten to know Sinclair Lewis, Sauk Centre, and the Palmer House that night. Best of all, I had gotten to know Al Tingley.

You see, before Al actually wrote **Corner on Main Street**, he merely wasted his best anecdotes on people like me. Now, he has written a delightful book, and with the likes of Sinclair Lewis and Jim Hendryx (not to be confused with the rock musician of the 60's) Sauk Centre can boast a third author, Al Tingley. And with **Corner on Main Street** Tingley has done something unique. While most authors go to New York or as they say on television, "Space; The Final Frontier," Tingley has stayed home and written about what he knows best, Sauk Centre. And in the tradition of Sinclair Lewis, Zona Gale, and Sherwood Anderson, he is not afraid to hang out America's "dirty laundry," or in Al's case, America's dirty coffee cups.

Al Tingley will make you laugh, and if you are the sentimental type, he will make you cry. One of his anecdotes even gave me goose bumps. **Corner on Main Street** is really an old-fashioned love story, a man in love with a hotel and all the people that have made it what it is today. The Palmer House is not made of brick and mortar, but of flesh and bone. And it certainly has heart.

Some people may not like everything Al Tingley says in **Corner on Main Street**, especially if they, like all of Sinclair Lewis's acquaintances find themselves in a book. There is certainly no tinsel, absolutely no frosting in Tingley's typewriter and he wouldn't have it any other way. You see, Al Tingley tells it like it is. To fib, to fabricate, to resort to euphemisms would ruin the idea behind **Corner on Main Street**. Main Street is far removed from the yellow brick road.

I have known Al for two years now (he says it is actually five) and I am proud to be his friend. Never once does he pretend to be the next John Steinbeck; only Al Tingley of the Palmer House who will give you the shirt off his back, and if he isn't wearing one, a good cup of hot coffee. He is a man who sees life first-hand, from eight to five and from five to eight. The good, the bad, and the ugly. Yet, somehow, and he must be given credit, he is able to laugh about it, and better yet, he makes us all laugh with him.

Sinclair Lewis once said that **Main Street's** Gopher Prairie was really a composite of Sauk Centre, Fergus Falls, Mankato, Winona, and a score of other communities scattered across the country. I think it is fair to say that Al Tingley writes not only about Sauk Centre's Palmer House, but of all those Palmer Houses tucked away in all those sleeping little communities across America. No, perhaps sleeping isn't the correct term (unless you are spending a night at the Palmer). I should interject instead, Small Town America, the authentic backbone of our nation.

I would think this book would be especially interesting to those of you who, like Tingley and Schwartz, have actually renovated and operated a historic inn not unlike the Palmer House. These trials and tribulations are certainly not unknown to you. Thank goodness Tingley had the guts to put them on paper.

Of course, most of us do not own such a hostelry and may or may not want to after reading this book. But if you've ever passed up the convenient newer motels with television and swimming pool in favor of eldritch renovation — the Palmer House, the Anderson House, the St. James, then this book's for you too. And for those of you who are only familiar with all the 8's, Super 8, Regal 8, Thrifty 8, and Crazy 8 chains and have never been exposed to the Red Carpet treatment of overnight accommodations a'la Palmer House, this book will make you wish you had been.

All of the characters in **Corner on Main Street** are very real. During a conversation with Al, I once referred to them as "living, breathing entities." But Al corrected me: "No, they're just people." And he writes about them better than most. He's qualified, you see. He makes people his business. And when I say this I mean he is more interested in personalities than he is in dollars.

I guess it's safe to say that some of the characters in this book actually live in Sauk Centre while some of them don't. Whether you live in Rockport, Maine, or on Crater Ridge in the Sierras, you'll find them living next door, delivering your mail, or hitch-hiking on a country road. It takes all kinds to fill a hotel, and I'm glad it does, or this book would not have been possible.

For those of you reading this book for the first time, there is a wonderful experience just ahead. I certainly envy you, for you will soon discover all those lovable characters who suddenly come to life in **Corner on Main Street**. And what a discovery it is: the cooks...the waitresses...Pauline...Alice...the kid from Atlanta...Chris, the friendly dog...the Faceless Soup Lady...the Naked Lady...and of course, Sauk Centre's own deadly duo of Tingley and Schwartz, armed only with a sense of humor, who must confront them all. Holy Cow, Batman, you thought you had it tough.

So what's the soup of the day? I'd better let Al Tingley tell you. He can do so much better than I....

John J. Koblas
Minneapolis, Minnesota
9 July 1984

ACKNOWLEDGEMENTS

I wish to express my thanks to the many persons and loved ones who contributed to the completion of this book, those who listened to me rant and rave over a two-year period as the book moved toward reality.

- **My Partner, Richard J. Schwartz**, without his faith in me, this never would have come to pass.
- **My Daughter, Donna**, who inspired me to write the story after receiving a few letters containing incidents.
- **Lucille McClain**, who suffered through the first rough, rough draft. Later, she volunteered to type copy.
- **Joe Bartch**, the first person to read the material.
- **My Mother, Mildred**, who called after reading the first draft and said it was a GO, but fretted over the drinking situations.
- **My Sister, Carol**, who never said a word.
- **Kathy Beste**, who never had a cup of coffee in the restaurant without my shoving papers in her hand.
- **John Koblas**, who's telephone call about the chapter he read sent me to seventh heaven, and his wonderful job of editing and introduction.
- **Ed Shannon**, who saw it as a dramatic production and began adapting before it was even a book. He also edited.
- **Sharon Kowski**, for copy editing.
- **Virgil Sieben**, who must have listened in a thousand times as I read various passages to people.
- **The Staff and Management of the Sauk Centre Herald**, for ten years of reporting and supporting.
- **Bea Knoll**, who's love and concern has always been a joy to both Richard and myself. She suffered through the first draft and came up with encouragement.
- **Roselea Hostetler**, who's book *Roselea's Hotel, Bible Belt Oasis* was my inspiration.
- **Roderick Nordell**, of the *Christian Science Monitor*, for his faith and suggestions.
- **The Patrons of the Palmer House Restaurant**, and even the coffee crowd without whose irritation would have given me nothing to be angry about.
- **The Staff and Management of Creative Concepts, Inc.**, for continuous support and concern.
- **Eva Sieben**, who helped with original typing.
- **Polly Jaeger**, who helped type the final copy.
- **Jeanne Wentland**, for helping with final copy.
- **Donna and Larry Hartigan**, faithful and loyal for ten years, always flowers for anniversaries, ready and willing to work.
- **Sinclair Lewis**, and the book *Main Street* and *Work of Art*. I humbly present this book.

Did Lewis Really Work Here?

"**D**id Sinclair Lewis really work here?" The question came from a young lady who was standing by the front desk of the Palmer House Hotel. She had long, flaming red hair which looked like it hadn't seen a comb in a month of Sundays. Her face was flushed as though she had just finished the Boston Marathon. Her baggage consisted of a long, rather wrinkled trench coat, the style which was popular in the early '50's. A wide strap was hanging from her neck and if one's eyes followed the strap to the end, one would see a very expensive 35 MM camera. Tucked under one arm were a number of books and magazines plus a Rand-McNally road atlas. She removed her very wide-lens glasses and was chewing on the end of one of the ear pieces.

"He certainly did," Richard proudly proclaimed in answer to her question.

"Golly," was her incredulous reply.

"How long did he work here?" her male counterpart asked.

He, too, was a typical tourist. His hair, not so long as hers, was also in need of combing. One ear sported a long, dangling rectangle of gold swaying gently above a short and wrinkled genuine *Fingerhut* jacket. Faded Levis that had once been *tie-dyed* many years earlier completed his attire. He too had an armful of books and papers. However, his camera was held in one hand. No doubt a strap was not necessary, it wasn't that expensive. They were colorful, congenial and curious.

"He worked here in 1902, before he went to Yale and one summer thereafter. And where are you people from?" Richard answered, then asked.

I was sitting in the lobby and I could hear their accents. *"New Joursey,"* I announced.

They both turned, stared and spoke in unison, "How'd you know?"

"He's originally from the east coast," Richard added quickly.

"Oh, whereabouts?"

"Maine," Richard and I stated simultaneously. And we all shared a great laugh.

"How about a cup of *coiffy*?" I asked, mimicking their Jersey accent.
Sounds like a great idea to me," she piped.

I headed into the restaurant which had been closed for about two hours. The coffee pot, however is never off, nor empty.

"Well, Sinclair's boyhood home is just three blocks west of the hotel," Richard pointed, carrying on an animated conversation. If there is anything Richard loves to do is to talk about Sauk Centre. I have never met anyone prouder of Sauk Centre than he. I handed the coffee to our guests as Richard continued. "Then there is the Episcopal Church just four blocks south on Main Street. It was the first church built in Sauk Centre, and is made of manure and grout. A captain from the fort and a Miss Nellie Barrows were married on Christmas Eve in 1869."

"Do you have any rooms for rent?" the girl interrupted, thinking he'd never ask. "We have been sleeping in the car for the past few nights and brother could we use a shower."

"Well," Richard said as he put on his glasses, and puffed on his cigarette. Then looking over the top of his glasses at the registration board, he asked. "Do you want a room with bath or without?"

"Oh how quaint," she replied. "Rooms without bath, just like

England." She poked her partner then asked, "What's the difference in price?"

"About four dollars. That would be fifteen dollars for a double without bath."

"That's all?" he remarked. But, the tone in his voice said, "Can't be much for only fifteen bucks."

"May we see the room please?" she asked, again implying their concern.

Richard took keys from slots numbered six and eight and handed them to me. "Al, you want to take them up? Here is six, and you might as well show them number eight too."

*　*　*　*　*

"Oh, look at the wainscoating on the staircase," she cooed as we headed up the stairs.

"Well, notice also the automatic sprinkler system we have throughout the hotel. We have spent nearly $70,000 on just fire safety alone," I stated pompously as I opened the fire door to the first floor of the hotel. I noticed them staring at the pictures hanging on the wall just ahead. "All these people have stayed at the hotel, most of them since we have been here," I continued as I unlocked the door to room number six. I swung open the door and stepped inside to turn on the desk lamp.

As the light illuminated the room she exclaimed, "Oh, this is lovely. Look at that bed and dresser, and the old wardrobe trunk!" He poked her to restrain her exuberance.

"This is my favorite room," I remarked, "even though it doesn't have a bath, it reminds me of sleeping in Grandma's attic."

"I just love it," she answered.

"And it is only fifteen dollars a night, plus tax," I added quickly. I moved out the door and down the hall. "Here is the bath." I called to them.

She was the first to notice the original claw feet on the bathtub. "Oh, look," she exclaimed. "My grandmother had one like that years ago."

"You will notice all the inside rooms have a skylight," I explained proudly. "When Mr. Palmer built the hotel in 1901, he had four skylights on the roof to let in the sun. They leaked and soon after, they were closed off. When we put on a new roof in 1979 we reopened them. Now we have plexiglass domes. Of course you can't notice it tonight but in the morning they are beautiful." I stepped smartly out the door as they remained to admire the oval mirror hanging on the wall. "Would you like to see the room with the bath?" I asked.

"Oh, no," came their immediate reply. "Room six is just what we want. Oh, I just love it here," she squealed. And as I headed down the stairs, I noticed that they had paused to study the pictures of our more notable guests.

"Well?" Richard inquired as he looked up from the desk.

"They love room six. They didn't even look at room eight."

"You try and figure people out," he mused. "Last night a couple wouldn't stay because we had no rooms left with a bath."

"Well Richard, it's guests like this that make all the work and heartache worth it. Don't you think?"

"Yeah, but there are not enough of them to go around."

"Oh, it's just great," a voice echoed from the stair landing. "I'm so glad we stopped here."

"It's like out of a page of a Lewis novel," he added as they descended the stairs to sign the registration card.

"Are you hungry?" Richard asked.

"Not really," she answered. "We stopped down the road and had some Kentucky fried chicken, but I bet you have all home cooking."

"Yes, and even our own baker," I responded.

"About this big," Richard added holding his arms out as far as he could stretch them. We all laughed.

"Then the food must be good," her companion stated as he licked his lips.

"Restaurant opens at 7:00 a.m. with homemade cinnamon and

caramel rolls." Richard strolled from behind the registration desk and Christopher the *dog-gondest* thing in the Palmer House followed.

"Oh you have a little doggie," she cooed leaning down to pet Chris. But, the dog ignored her and headed out the front door.

"He's not little anymore," Richard remarked, "He's almost twelve-years-old, and he's got a mind of his own. Now where are you parked?"

"Out front."

"Well, you will have to park in the lot behind the hotel. They tag cars on the street after 2:00 a.m."

"Fine. I'll move it now," he lamented, leaving the lobby.

She remained, casually looking around the lobby.

"Where are you two heading?" I inquired.

"West to California and back to New York in two weeks. But I would just love to stay here the rest of the vacation. It is so relaxing."

"How would you like to buy it and stay here forever?" Richard responded.

She laughed. "I would if I could. It's just charming."

Charming to her. Chaotic to us, I thought.

The conversation was stopped by the commotion at the door. The lad was struggling with luggage, and the dog was barking to get in . For a moment it was situation normal. Six hours of boredom interrupted by thirty seconds of potential catastrophe. "Here, let me help you," Richard insisted as he grabbed a suitcase, then nearly fell from the weight of it.

"What's in here, pure gold?" he asked, dragging the huge suitcase to the stairs.

"You know women," the lad answered. "They pack everything but the kitchen sink."

"I don't think she forgot that this time," Richard mumbled as he stumbled up the steps, stopping instinctively as the telephone rang.

"Good evening, Palmer House. May I help you?" I answered.

"Yes, I am calling long distance from New York City and need some information."

"Well, I will try to be of help."

"I teach English in a private school and I am planning on coming west this summer. One of my stops will be in Gopher Prairie. Er, I mean Sauk Centre. I understand that you have rooms for rent?"

"Yes, ma'am, we do," I replied, wondering why people can't call during normal business hours.

"I am planning on flying to Minneapolis and taking the bus to Sauk Centre," she continued. "They told me it was about a two hour ride."

"That's right," I answered.

"Would you have any rooms with bath open for July 15?"

I ruffled through the reservation book. "Yes, I have one room with double bed and bath open that evening."

"Oh great, why don't you reserve that for me. I teach Lewis' **Main Street** and I am just dying to walk Main Street just like Carol Kennicott did."

I chuckled to myself. If only the locals knew how the rest of the world admires Sinclair Lewis. "What time do you arrive in Minneapolis?" I asked.

"Nine in the morning."

"Well, you would be smart to take a taxi to downtown Minneapolis and catch the noon bus to Fargo. That will get you in here about 2:30 or 3:00 p.m. We could plan on meeting you at the Sauk Centre bus depot."

"Oh, that would be sweet of you. I can hardly wait. Why don't you reserve that room for me now? It's Miss Catherine Zooz, that's Z-O-O-Z, and I will send a deposit."

"That will be fine Miss Zooz. I have it down for July 15. And we will meet you at the bus stop at 2:30."

"Oh, I can hardly wait. Oh sir, not that it makes any difference, but what is the cost of that room for one night?"

"One person. One night. Fifteen dollars plus tax." There was a long pause. "Miss Zooz. Is there anything wrong?" I was just about to check to see if we were cut off when:

"What did you say was the cost of that room?" Her voice was rather distant.

"Fifteen dollars plus tax," I repeated loudly.

"Well sir, you must be running a dump so, forget it." CLICK!

"What was that all about?" Richard asked as he re-entered the lobby. He was holding a cup of coffee and I was holding a buzzing receiver.

"Reservations from New York," I stammered. "It was all set, confirmed and everything. Then she asked the price and when I told her she canceled and hung up."

"Well, what did you quote her?" he asked.

"The regular price, fifteen dollars plus tax."

"Then what turned her off?"

"It's too cheap," I shouted. "I should have quoted her fifty dollars. Then she would have probably smiled and said, 'That will be fine. See you on the 15th of July.' What's wrong with people today. Are they not happy unless they are getting ripped off?"

The young couple had overheard our conversation. "We can't believe your rates for such lovely rooms," she commented. I was appeased but not amused. I wanted to say we made a mistake. They are really fifty dollars instead of fifteen but Richard immediately changed the subject. "The night clerk comes on soon. Would you two like to go uptown with us?"

"That would be great," the young man responded. "We were just talking about taking a walk. How far is the Lewis grave from here?" he questioned, noticing the old photographs on the lobby wall.

"Just a mile east of town," Richard replied, pointing out the window. "We could have a drink and then we could walk by his boyhood home if you would like."

"A great suggestion," she answered. "We have to leave very early in the morning. We've got to be in Jamestown, North Dakota, by noon tomorrow. Some of our friends are teaching school there. So we would not have time to go see his home tomorrow and I could take pictures tonight," she added, holding up her camera as if ready to shoot.

"Evening, Matthew," Richard called as the night clerk entered from the east, with Bible in hand as usual, right on the stroke of ten.

"We're going to take this couple to see the sights. We'll be back later," I reported as Matthew positioned himself behind the desk. He did not answer. Perhaps he was meditating .

"Did you take the dog upstairs, Richard?" I asked.

"Yes. While you were on the phone."

"Okay, let's go."

Little did we know that at midnight, we would all be plowing through the soggy spring snow at Greenwood Cemetery to allow our guests to get a picture of Sinclair Lewis' grave. This is not the first time we have taken guests to the cemetery, but it was the first time we scraped snow off the marker. One guest we took to the grave site actually knelt down and kissed the granite marker which has engraved on it *SINCLAIR LEWIS — AUTHOR OF "MAIN STREET."*

And, yes, I would like to add, he did work at the Palmer House. And was fired, it is rumored, for reading and daydreaming.

No Vacancy!

L ittle did we know what we were getting into when we bought the hotel. It was a romantic adventure. We were sure we would be making money hand over fist, in a couple of years. The great American dream: own your own business. And here we were, owners of the largest building in Sauk Centre, with not one iota of business experience, much less any knowledge of the restaurant and hotel business.

We had a dream. This was going to be the greatest and most historical undertaking Sauk Centre had ever seen. They couldn't help but be impressed. They would back us with heart, soul and wallet. Reality hit the first day we moved in, as we began to meet the permanent residents of the Palmer House Hotel.

First there was Merlin. Merlin had just returned from the Merchant Marines and came to live here because his mother and other family members were nearby. He is a straight-forward looking man, with balding head and horned-rimmed glasses. He walks very erect, almost to a fault. Merlin is neatly dressed and soft spoken. A very cordial man.

He was very helpful as we unpacked the U-Haul trailer, and the three carloads of household goods we had chosen to bring with us to the Palmer House.

My prized possession is a huge Everett Orgatron, which I had purchased a few years before in St. Paul. It is an old reed and electronic device that weights of a thousand pounds including the speaker system. We unloaded this first, finally wrestling it to its temporary resting place in the large lobby. That was something else again: the lobby.

It was a large, ugly room, about twenty-five feet by forty feet, flooded by long, tubular florescent lights reminiscent of the office buildings of the late forties. The original tin ceiling had been painted brown; later we found out why. It was to cover the rust spots which had developed from the various sink leaks, overflowing from above. The lobby was dominated by the front desk, taking up about half the room. There was an antiquated table lamp near the teller's cage. Behind the front desk was a large square of pigeon holes with various and sundry keys. An old kitchen clock with a checkerboard background was tilted on the wall above the mailboxes. An old twenty-one-inch black and white television set sat on the desk blaring out a ball game. And there, halfway across the room, was the audience — our residents — about eight old men, some smoking, some chewing, others sleeping. One was coughing to the point of gagging, another was staring into space beating out a non-rhythmic tune with his fingers on a battered standup ashtray. There were no drapes on the huge windows facing east and the panes needed to be washed so badly that you could write "wash me" on them. As I turned to the east, facing the sun, I reddened as I saw the residents and the furniture upon which they were seated.

The furniture was tubular steel, that's right, the patio type, each one different from the other. In the center was the seat, leather of course, but from an old 1940 Ford station wagon. Naturally, its low proximity rendered it ornamental rather than operational. An old, bedraggled bridge lamp hung aimlessly in the middle of the room in case someone wanted to read the evening paper, assuming it was available, or one was disposed to reading it.

The south lobby door opened just as I was going out to bring in some more boxes and an elderly man, perhaps in his 100s, entered the lobby. At first, I thought he might be ill, he was shaking so badly. He could hardly stand up. Little did I know that he was stricken with palsy and alcoholism. I stopped and paused. It was a sight to behold, all these elderly men just wasting away in "our" lobby. There was one exception. Merlin came forward, extended his hand and introduced himself saying, "Welcome aboard. I'm Merlin and I moved in here about two months ago. Can I help?" I pointed to the U-Haul trailer, then rushed behind the desk, calling out to Richard.

"Let's look at the rooms we now own."

On our previous visits, the former owner had shown us only a couple of rooms. "I can't show you most of the rooms," he said. "They are rented to permanents and that would be an invasion of privacy." I swear those were his exact words and we never thought to question him. Privacy or not, we now owned the building and had the right to inspect our property. So up the stairs, two at a time, and down the hall to room number three, we ran. Richard was shaking as he unlocked the door.

It was a corner room overlooking Main Street and the parking lot to the rear of the hotel. "WOW, two windows!" Standing in awe our eyes perused the small twelve by fifteen sleeping room: A double bed with a sleazy khaki blanket muddled on top; a sink with both faucets dripping a considerable stream of water; one half of the plaster on the ceiling was already gone and the other half appeared ready to drop at any moment; half-painted walls looked like they had been decorated by a cycloptic child; a threadbare rug lay on the floor; and the room smelled of dampness and mold. Income per month $30.00. Reasoning of the former owner? "Fill all the rooms with old men, they will be so happy to have a place to live and a roof over their head. They will never complain, and you will never have to do any repair work." WOW! What a shock to see this room compared to the few we were shown. Nor did it stop here. All the way down the hall, door after door, floor after floor, revealed the same neglect and disrepair.

* * * * *

"Didn't you know there is an American Legion Convention in town this weekend?" Merlin asked as we both stood behind the desk holding the keys from the rooms we had just inspected.

"A what?" Richard exclaimed.

"Didn't he tell you? All the rooms have been reserved this weekend, about three-hundred people will be in town." Merlin could sense our bewilderment. "There's a book there somewhere with all the reservations. I am surprised he didn't tell you."

"He didn't tell us anything," I pouted. "He just gave Richard the keys and said good luck."

Merlin was getting anxious by now. "Get him on the phone and tell him to get over here," I commanded angrily.

"No," Richard replied emphatically. "He has already lied to us enough. We'll see it through somehow." He shook his head and stared at the reservation book.

*   *   *   *   *

The first guests for the convention started arriving two days after we arrived. We worked 'round the clock to get the rooms presentable.

"Hi, and welcome to the Palmer House," Richard said with a smile.

"We are Mr. and Mrs. Bancroft and we have a confirmed reservation for a room with a bath," the gentleman announced as he shuffled a valet bag on his arm.

"Well, Mr. Bancroft, I am sorry. My partner and I just took over this hotel on Wednesday and I have no rooms with bath to give you. I can, however, give you a room without bath. The bathroom would be located down the hall."

"Don't tell me that," he interrupted. "Here is the letter I received:"

'This is to confirm your reservation for a room with one double bed and bath for the nights of June 6 and 7, 1974. We have reserved room number seven for you and Mrs. Bancroft.'

"I am terribly sorry. I just can't imagine him promising you room number seven. That room has a permanent renter already living there." The couple looked at one another in disgust.

"Could you see if there is room in any other hotel or motel in town?" Mr. Bancroft inquired politely.

"There isn't sir, every available space has been filled to capacity. I'm sorry but I would like to have you stay here. We have nice rooms and a full-service restaurant, plus you can walk to the legion meeting. It's just one block north," Richard pleaded.

"I'm not happy about this. But I guess it is not your fault. Where do I sign?" the customer had capitulated.

"Right here sir," Richard sighed, handing him the registration card.

The same pleading and explaining procedure was Richard's lot for the next few hours as more than thirty people arrived with "confirmed" reservations. And with all the check-ins in the hotel, the restaurant was busy as all get-out for the next few hours. I had little time to talk to Richard or anyone else until after we closed.

"Well? How did it go?" I asked as I headed behind the desk. Richard was still knee-deep in registration cards and letters of confirmation.

"I hope to hell every weekend isn't like this one. I felt like a goddamn fool, telling all these people I didn't have any rooms with bath. I must have sounded like a complete idiot."

"You must have done a good job of convincing them. I heard a lot of them talking in the restaurant about how sorry they felt for you on the mix-up. Besides, most of them will be so drunk when they get home tonight they won't remember what room they had anyway," I laughed.

"I hope not. I can see me staying up all night directing drunks to rooms I don't even know myself. Why did I ever let you talk me into this project anyway?" He nervously lighted another cigarette.

At 1:30 a.m. I was still awake, struggling to sleep in a strange room with a dog that refused to settle down. Richard was still in the lobby, greeting the guests as they arrived home from the festivities. The cloudy, damp sky had been getting heavier as the night wore on until a clap of thunder BOOMED so loud, that it nearly blasted me out of bed. I ran to close the window as the downpour fought its way in. It continued to rain harder and harder, blotting out the street lights below. I dressed and ran down to the lobby. People were standing everywhere, staring out the windows. Main Street looked more like Sauk River.

"What are you doing down here?" Richard barked from behind the desk as I stretched to look out one of the windows.

"My god, is it raining! It was pouring in through our window. I hope most of the windows are closed or we'll all be drowned," I answered, joining him behind the desk. "Much trouble tonight?" I asked, bumming a cigarette.

"Not too bad, most of them are a little tipsy but no one is obnoxious — yet." More loud thunderclaps and lightning shook and lighted the lobby. "When is it going to stop raining?" he demanded.

"SIR, SIR, OH MANAGER!" a visitor shouted from the first landing. Looking up, we saw two people, one in a night gown and one in a bathrobe, both doing their *Chicken Little* routine, holding their hands over their heads as if the sky were about to fall.

"Yes, what is it?" Richard nonchalantly called up to them, as he walked toward the staircase.

"I know you can't help it, since you just took over," the distraught voice droned, "but the ceiling in our room just caved in all over the bed."

"Oh my god!" was our joint reply. "What's your room number?" Richard queried.

"Number...number..." He turned to his wife, "Where's the key?" She begun fishing around in the pockets of his robe. Finding the key she announced, "Number twenty-two."

"That's on the top floor," I called to Richard, "on the corner by the parking lot." But Richard was already up the stairs.

"That son-of-a-bitch told us he just had a new roof put on the hotel last year," he said as we stood at the door of room twenty-two.

"What a mess. What can we do tonight?" I wondered. "Have you got any vacant rooms at all to put them in?"

"I don't know, but we'll have to do something. They can't stay in this mess." Water was still dripping from the open lathes on the ceiling, most of the plaster was on the floor, a little had fallen on the bed.

"Thank God they aren't hurt. Think of the lawsuits," I mentioned completely dazed while picking up some of the larger pieces of plaster. Richard was patting his pockets for a cigarette when the occupants of the room finally caught up with us.

"Sure is a mess. But nobody got hurt," the gentleman said in a more resigned voice.

"Our friends have offered to share their room," his wife added, "they have an extra bed."

We apologized and thanked them. Then we humbly headed for the lobby.

As we descended, we met a number of the guests on the stairs.

The rain had let up slightly. They were tired, but we were exhausted. "Good night."

"Good night."

"Sleep well."

"Looks as though the worst is over for now."

"Golly what a downpour."

"Good night," we answered with a smile.

The lobby was nearly deserted by the time we returned. Only one legionnaire lay snoring loudly in a lobby chair. There was no need to disturb him. God with his lightning and thundering couldn't and I didn't have the energy.

"You got any cigarettes Allan? I'm out," Richard asked placing his head in his hands behind the desk.

"Here, take one," I offered. "What do you say we call it a day or night or whatever it is."

"Yeah," Richard sighed. "And to think I once had a job where I looked forward to weekends."

* * * * *

Not only did the ceilings fall in on the third floor, but it seemed like *Murphy's Law* was in full force throughout the entire summer.

"But we can't afford to put a new roof on this summer," Richard argued as we cleaned up the mess in room twenty-two.

"I know. We've got to get that kitchen cleaned up first. It's a disgrace," I answered. So we decided to have a cleaning party and invite all our friends, enticing them in with a couple of cases of beer.

That following Sunday some of the staff, some of our family, and a few friends showed up in their *grubbies* to help clean the kitchen. There was grease you wouldn't believe, including under the stove and seeping through the floor. When we pulled the exhaust fan from the back of the building it was so thick with grease it couldn't breathe, much less spin. The fan assembly was removed, cleaned and set out on the back porch to dry. The whole day was spent washing walls, steam tables, freezers — you name it, we washed it. And when the time came to install the fan assembly, it was gone. We looked high and low, but the fan was nowhere to be found.

"How in the hell can we open the restaurant tomorrow morning without an exhaust fan?" I moaned.

"We really didn't have one before," Richard responded.

Now Richard's brother-in-law is a genius when it comes to creating makeshift devices. A fixed-up fan assembly was installed, intended to serve us until the original was found. It has been ten years now and the original has still not shown up.

* * * * * *

"Good morning, Palmer House. May I help you?"

"Yes, this is the street department calling to inform you that we are going to be tearing up your sidewalk this week."

"You'll be doing what?" I exclaimed.

"The city has decided that a new sidewalk should be installed by the Palmer House this summer!"

"Yes, but do you have to do it during our peak tourist season?" I questioned.

"We have the time and the manpower available this week, so we will be starting early tomorrow morning." CLICK.

The former owners had been told to install a new sidewalk over four years ago. But today they decide to do it tomorrow. I guess it was their way of welcoming the new owners. When Richard arrived, I told him of the city's decision to tear up the sidewalk.

"For Christ's sake, we're not ready for such a project. I want to plant trees along the curb and block off that dangerous second alley." He lighted another cigarette and continued, "I think we should have the basement windows filled in with glass block and remove the grates. I had been thinking about this for some time, but to start tomorrow morning — holy cow, who do they think they are?"

The noise and pounding of the machines tearing up the sidewalk the next morning made us believe an earthquake had struck each time the cement crusher collided with the concrete. I dressed and came down to the lobby. "What's going on out there?" one of the coffee regulars asked.

"Oh, the city is putting in a new sidewalk at our expense," I answered. "And I'm trying to find someone who is in charge." That was difficult, for there were seven men leaning on shovels, watching one man break up the sidewalk. "Who's in charge?" I asked the first worker I saw.

"Huh?"

"WHO'S IN CHARGE?" I screamed over the diesel engine.

"He ain't here," was the reply.

"Tell him," the worker cupped his ear toward me, "TELL HIM I WANT TO TALK TO HIM; ASK FOR AL INSIDE." He nodded his head. The noise wasn't much better inside the building, but at least I could talk to the man in charge.

"I have asked to talk to the boss," I reported to Richard as he poured a cup of coffee.

"Why do you want to talk to the boss?"

"We want tree holes, don't we?"

"I'll call the park commissioner and see if we can get permission to put the holes in," I answered, storming off.

"Yeah, but I doubt if we'll get them," Richard was a little discouraged this morning.

"I can't understand why you would want to plant trees downtown," the commissioner argued. "As they get bigger they will just bust up the sidewalk. And besides, they will get so tall no one will be able to see the traffic lights." Thus, we listened to the various anti-tree arguments. For almost a week we fought for trees, and all the while the work was progressing. They were getting ready to pour cement and still there was no official word about the trees.

"Well, Al," the head shovel-holder said. "We are about ready to pour the sidewalk. What about the tree holes and what about the back alley?"

"We have our lawyer looking into the closing of the second alley, and the park commissioner is trying to decide about the trees," I answered.

"OK," he shrugged. "In the meantime, I have five cement trucks on their way here with fresh cement to pour this afternoon." It was clear the construction company needed some answers.

For the past who-knows-how-many-years, the public has had access to the back doors of all businesses on Sinclair Lewis Avenue, via an alleyway which ran just five feet behind the back door of the Palmer House. Many a time an employee of the Palmer House had almost been run-down by an automobile while exiting via the back door. Since there was already an official alley just twenty-five feet beyond, we could see no reason for another dangerous right-of-way so close to our building, which incidently also dissected our land. Our lawyer was trying to get more information as to the existence of the questionable alley, but the cement trucks were coming! We decided to put in tree holes anyway. We could always fill them in if they were not approved. And as the trucks pulled up to dump the first load of cement, the street commissioner, standing near the back of the building, uttered the famous words which solved the problem of the double alley forever. "Curb the bastard up," he said. And it was done.

The next morning, I was again awakened early by the tremendous pounding of heavy machinery in the parking lot. I sleepily got out of bed to seek out the cause of such sleep-disturbing noise. There, at the west end of our lot, was a post hole digger working furiously, placing huge poles evenly spaced so that cars would not be able to have access to the lot next door. Well, I thought to myself, the guy next door didn't like the commissioner's decision to block off the second access to his business. He was punishing us with a series of ugly poles. Needless to say, if I had known ahead of time, I would have lined that, too, with a series of trees just like those that now flourish along the side of our hotel.

"Hi, I'm The Health Inspector"

" I f you want my advice, and I guess that's what you are paying me for, I suggest you contact the State Health Department and ask for a report or an on-site inspection before you go any further." Pat was our lawyer. He was helping us with our decision, as to whether we should or shouldn't purchase the Palmer House.

"Sounds like a good idea to me," I replied.

"Well, I can't get off work for a trip to Sauk Centre in the middle of the week," Richard broke in.

"But I can," I retorted.

"I think it would be worthwhile to make such an inspection," Pat answered.

"But I wouldn't know what to look for."

"That's why I suggest you call the health department and have a qualified inspector go with you. You are making a big investment and I'd hate to see you get stung."

So it was decided. The plans were set for me to meet Mr. Webber of the St. Cloud Health Department at the Palmer House.

When I walked into the lobby of the Palmer House, an older, rather distinguished looking man stood up and greeted me. "Hi, I'm Mr. Webber from St. Cloud." He extended his hand and clenched it firmly and sincerely around mine.

"Hi, I'm Al Tingley. They said you would be prompt."

"Let's sit down for a moment and talk." He motioned to a large leather chair by the window. I turned to it and sat down.

"Well, son," he began, "if I were your age, this is the place that I would buy. It is the only decent place in town to eat. When I am in the area, I always make it a point to stop here come lunch time. The food is not only excellent, but the kitchen is one of the cleanest around. And I should know, because I have seen them all." He sounded more like a realtor than a health inspector. But I was already excited about owning the Palmer House, and this guy was just adding frosting to the cake.

He rose and said, "Let's take a walk through the kitchen and I will show you."

"Now take that old stove," he began." It is a gem. I bet it will last another hundred years."

The small kitchen contained two chest type freezers of the home variety, a Vulcan stove with a grill section measuring two feet by two feet, four burners and a warming shelf above the deck of the stove. I noticed a lot of dirt and grease on the old stove, but Mr. Webber noticed other things. Beside the greasy stove stood a gas-fired deep-fryer. It also was soaked with grease and I wondered, how this could be the cleanest kitchen around, for if this was clean, then what was dirty? The tour of the kitchen ended as abruptly as it started. As we were getting ready to leave, Mr. Webber said, "Well, son, good luck. I will be retiring shortly and a new inspector will be taking my place."

He extended his hand. As I shook it, he finalized the sale. "I think if you buy this place," he said, "you will be making a good investment. It's a money maker. I wish my wife and I were younger. We would snap it up. Well, son, I'm very glad to have met you." With that he was out the door.

Needless to say, he told me exactly what I wanted to hear. I was elated. I couldn't wait to tell Richard what Mr. Webber had said, for Richard was still in the midst of indecision about returning to his home town and entering into a business as his own boss. My report was just one of many that funneled us toward the final decision.

Two weeks into ownership I had the opportunity to recall Mr. Webber's remarks. The ice machine quit working, so I called the supply house and asked them to send out an representative. A few days later a young man arrived. It was good timing, for by now one of the freezers had stopped working also. I took him into the kitchen, and he was shocked by the what he saw. "Didn't anyone tell you that home chest-type freezers are illegal in restaurants in the state of Minnesota? All restaurant equipment today must be NSF approved."

I soon learned that NSF stood for National Sanitary Foundation and I also relearned the meaning of the phrase *buyer beware*. I, too, discovered that the add-on walk-in cooler was not insulated, and was also illegal. It over-heated in the summer and froze-up in the winter. In fact, by the time we were done, there were only two pieces of purchased equipment that were up to code. My mind flew rapidly in rage back to the walk-through inspection when Mr. Webber said: "Son, if I were younger this is the place I would buy, it's a gold mine." What did P. T. Barnum say? "There's one born every minute?" This time there were two.

I asked the representative from the supply house to draw up kitchen plans and make suggestions as to how we could best bring it up to code.

"Gut it," he answered.

* * * * *

I was working in the kitchen when a staff member handed me a calling card which told me the health inspector was in the lobby. It had already been one of those days, and I was in no mood to be told again how much work had to be done to bring this kitchen up to code. I angrily strutted into the lobby to find a young man, his early twenties, dressed in white shirt and tie.

"Hi," he said as he extended his hand to me. "My name is Tim Fredricks. I am with the State Health Department." I shook his hand rather coldly. "I am replacing Mr. Webber. He just retired," he continued.

"It's a good thing," I said, "I am furious with that man." I couldn't help but wonder how much money he got paid when Richard and I bought this place. But I bit my tongue.

Our friend, Mr. Webber, told me just a few months ago that this was the cleanest kitchen he had seen and that everything was up to code. Now I found out we will have to replace everything: put in new drains, a new ceiling, exhaust fans, stoves...." I was getting carried away. Mr. Fredricks stepped back, sensing my anger.

"I'm sorry, sir," I continued. "I know you have your job to do, but I don't want you inspecting this place now. We're not ready for it. If your predecessor had been honest with us, I doubt that we would have purchased it anyway."

The young man was very polite, even understanding. "Why don't you and I walk through the building unofficially. Because of the circumstances, and the fact that you are just getting started, I will only make some suggestions."

"O.K. That sounds fair enough," I replied.

He handed me a book on Minnesota health regulations and I lead him toward the kitchen. I realized that our kitchen was a long way from receiving a clean bill of health but when our informal inspection had finished, I needed to make an appointment with a doctor — to check *my* own health.

"Get The Buckets,
Get The Buckets!!"

"Get the buckets! Get the buckets!" The cry came from the clothing store manager. He was leasing the former Palmer House barroom which was located southwest of the lobby. I was talking with some tourists when I heard his screams.

I ran quickly to see what was happening, and I was nearly knocked down by the store manager who was running equally as fast, but out rather than in. He was heading for the kitchen. I looked into the room and was dumbfounded. From the ceiling there was water dripping everywhere. No wonder his clothing racks were placed so irregularly throughout the store; the dripping must have occurred before. And it didn't take a genius to figure the water was from one of the rooms upstairs.

I was interrupted by the store manager, the cook, and the baker who were thundering toward me with an assortment of large buckets, pots and pans. They immediately began strategically placing them beneath the now rapidly flowing water. I jumped out of their way and ran up the stairs, three at a time, and headed for room seventeen. I had calculated it to be directly above the clothing store. Stopping to listen at the door I could hear the water running. I tried the door. It was locked. I looked up at the open transom above the door and decided that it was the quickest way to enter the room without destroying the door. With one gigantic leap, which one can only do when the adrenal glands are in full operation, I reached the transom and splashed to the floor on the other side. I landed flat on my stomach surfacing immediately in about three inches of water. I skidded my way to the sink where both the hot and cold taps were pouring water onto the floor with full surge. I shut off the faucets and not having a key with which to unlock the old fashioned dead lock, I exited the same way I came in.

Back downstairs, the commotion had turned to chaos. Nearly everyone from the restaurant and the hotel stood in the little doorway trying to get a glimpse of the excitement going on in the store. Richard had arrived also, and with him came an explanation.

It seems that Glen, the one man who was singlehandedly helping us restore the Palmer House, had shut off the water in the morning to repair another leak, but had neglected to inform all the residents that the water was turned off. So, when the guy in room seventeen tried to get water in his sink and failed, he left the faucets open and toddled off to work. When the water was turned back on...well, you get the picture.

It wasn't long after this latest catastrophe that the storekeeper turned in his notice. He was not planning to renew his lease. He was instead quite matter-of-factly moving out. That evening Richard lamented to me as we sat in the apartment.

"What are we going to do without the rent money from the store?"

"I think it's great," I replied enthusiastically. "We can now have The Minniemashie Room."

"The WHAT room?" Richard quizzed.

"The Minniemashie Room," I laughed. "A banquet room for private parties, receptions, gourmet dinners and lots of things."

"Well, how can we make any money on that? Besides, look at all the work involved. And what the hell is Minniemashie?"

"You know, in the book **Main Street**, Lewis called the downtown hotel in Gopher Prairie the Minniemashie House. We already have The Kennicott Room, why not have The Minniemashie Room?"

"You gotta be dreaming already," Richard rasped. "Good night. I'm going to bed."

(On August 8, 1974, the following article by Purdy Johnson appeared in the **Sauk Centre Herald**.)

The sun rose brightly on the beginning of a new day and a new aspect of life for a young couple about to be married and for a Sauk Centre landmark.

For a while sunbeams danced through the stained glass arch windows, focusing on the refreshed decor of the first stairway landing. It was a promise of fulfillment of all good things.

There was an immaculate freshness, an air of expectancy in the contemplating "Minniemashie Room." The organ in the foyer was polished and open in readiness for the maestro, who would set the mood for the reception honoring the young bride and groom.

Time ticked along rapidly, and rosey-faced cooks in the kitchen painstakingly and lovingly prepared delicious home-made rolls and old fashioned, mouth-watering entrees for the wedding feast.

The hour arrived, and so did the wedding party. Suddenly the building's years of descent appeared to do an about face, and the Palmer House was transformed with a new life and an atmosphere and popularity that it enjoyed in 1901 when R. L. Palmer opened one of the outstanding hotels in the Midwest.

Like many Americans, with nostalgia reigning supreme and a trend toward preserving nearly unobtainable and enduring properties and design, the new owners, Allan Tingley and Dick Schwartz, have a dream of restoration and a disdain for synthetic contemporary materials.

They are already well-launched on an eight-year plan to complete recovery, which will be reminiscent of the days when important social affairs were catered at the Palmer House, as salesmen made it their home away from home, and a boy named Harry Lewis served as a desk clerk and part-time bell-hop.

Slowly but surely, or perhaps (considering the progress made in three months) it is more accurate to say "with giant steps," the hotel is being transformed to the days when its solid oak lobby and guest room floors, bordering bright floral area rugs, glistened with a clear lustre. Then heavy velvet drapes hung just beneath the leaded glass arches, allowing warm light rays to escape into the dark evening hours as a welcome beacon to weary travelers.

Inside, a guest sank comfortably into the leather chairs in the lobby or penned a line to the family back home at the large varnished oak desks in the lobby, which were appointed with red, green and yellow glass shaded electric lamps, dip pens, and ink bottles that fit into slots.

Upstairs in the renovated guest rooms, a clean freshness greets the guest, and he enjoys the turn-of-the-century period furniture. With a full-time reconditioning crew at work, the natural butternut, birch, and maple casings and floors are being stripped of paint. Crisp curtains and cool light pull-down shades hang at the windows. Blocked skylights are being opened and covered with glass domes, admitting light and warmth into ample walk-in closets and inside spaces.

At times, we as citizens "can't see the forest for trees." There is a recentness about the traditionalism of the Palmer House that is good for Sauk Centre. Hundreds of visitors are being attracted to the "Gopher Prairie" landmark.

A Touch Of Class!

In mid-summer, Minnesota nights are hot and muggy. It's the height of the construction season in Sauk Centre and eight construction workers are registered in the hotel while working on a new sewer system in town. This group did not seem to be as rowdy as those who stayed here last year. Yet, like all transient workers, they labored hard during the day and they certainly played hard at night. From the first summer we owned the hotel, I've marveled at how these guys can get up at 4:30 or 5:00 a.m., work all day, come back, shower, go out drinking 'til the bars close at 1:00 a.m. and then up again the next morning for a repeat performance.

They were hard at work when the 3:00 bus pulled in. A few minutes later a very elegant lady entered the lobby. Her silver hair was finely coiffured and she wore a shiny black dress with a rope of pearls around her neck, emphasizing a rather low-cut neckline. Hearing the bell at the desk, Richard immediately raced to greet her. "Good afternoon. Rather warm out today. May I help you?"

"Yes, I would like a single room with bath, if possible." Her voice was low but distinct. Her enunciation and diction were perfect, befitting perhaps an English or speech teacher. She appeared to be in her mid- to upper-40s and very sure of herself. After registering her and receiving her money, Richard immediately dashed around the desk to assist her with her luggage.

"Here, let me help you," he offered, as he instinctively reached for her suitcase. "You'll be in room number seven, right at the top of the stairs. We had just installed an air conditioner in this room. Even if you don't like air conditioning, it would be wise to turn on the fan since it helps drown out the street noise. Here we are. I'll open the door for you." Doing so, he flipped on the light and turned on the air conditioner. "Would you care for a pot of coffee? I'll be glad to bring one to you."

"Why that would be nice, thank you very much," she replied with a slight gleam in her eye. She handed Richard a dollar bill and closed the door.

I was in the kitchen getting the evening special ready to put in the oven when he came through with a pot of coffee and a cup on a tray. "You should see the elegant lady who just checked into room seven. She was off the bus from Fargo. She is beautifully dressed with a very chic hairdo. It sure will add some class if she comes down and sits in the lobby." And out the back door he went. We were so used to having old men, salesmen, or construction workers checking into the hotel that it was like a breath of fresh air to have a lady guest.

It was Friday night and, as usual, I was making scalloped potatoes and fish for our "all you can eat" fish night. Believe me, in this area, when you announce an "all you can eat" night, expect the unexpected. People who we have never before seen suddenly appear. One evening last spring *Mr. & Mrs. Salad Bar*, along with their family, consumed nearly seventy-five pieces of fish. On another occasion one of our waiters ate eighteen pieces of fish by himself.

Somehow this evening seemed more hectic than usual. A lot of *lake people* came in to dine. Also, a number of tourists heading north stopped for a meal. We have a growing reputation around the state for serving good food at reasonable prices, yet the locals still complain. They like to compare us to the King Kong Kafe. They can't seem to understand that we are a historic restaurant.

Finally the restaurant is closed. I can breathe easier, and take some time to talk with Richard. "Tell me about the lovely lady in room seven," I asked Richard as I joined him behind the desk.

"I haven't seen her since she went upstairs. She probably has an early bus to catch in the morning and went directly to bed, I'm bushed too," he continued. "I bussed too many tables this evening and

I've got to be up all night at the desk." He took a long drag on his cigarette and uttered dejectedly, "I hope it won't be too hectic with all those construction guys upstairs. Especially if they go out drinking."

I was putting my sweater on when he asked, "Are you going out? Don't you open the restaurant in the morning?"

"Yes," I answered. "Is it okay if I go for a couple of drinks at the Corner Bar? I'll be back shortly." He looked at me with his typical omniscient grin, as though he was saying, "Yeah, I know, you won't be back for a couple of hours."

"Now don't get drunk," he called as I opened the south door.

The Corner Bar is unique in its own way. Both Richard and I respect the owner and his wife. Like us, they have worked hard to build a business in Sauk Centre. They purchased the bar a few years ago. They worked side-by-side and have built a good clientele. None of the rough gangs hang out at the Corner Bar. The owners wouldn't put up with it. Last year they built and stained all new booths. The focal point in this establishment, however, is the beautiful mahogany back bar. It is especially meaningful to us because it was originally built for the Palmer House barroom in 1901, and later sold and moved to the Corner Bar.

The unit consists of huge, round, carved pillars with pedestal tops, a beveled mirror in the center, and hand-carved shelves. It stands out like a collector's dream. The large round globes of light cast rich multi-colored shadows, reflecting on the various liquor bottles on the shelves around the bar.

Richard and I used to frequent this bar long before we purchased the Palmer House. I can remember an old-fashioned, hand-carved, wooden orchestra hanging above the center of the back bar. When the jukebox played, the semi-circular velvet curtains around the orchestra would slowly open. The wooden figures would come to life and play until the song was finished, then the curtains would close. We have asked the owners and others about the antique music piece, but no one seems to know what happened to it. It is still a mystery to this day.

One thing certain about the local bar scene in Sauk Centre is that it never seems to change. Once in a while I might see a new face downtown, but usually I know before I enter who will be sitting on a certain stool or in a certain booth. The faces begin to transform like ours with age, but the same persons are still sitting in the same places, at the same time, and sorry to say, talking about the same mundane matters. This perhaps is true about any town, anywhere: New York, Chicago, Los Angeles; it's the continuation of Main Street.

"Brandy and sweet," I called out to the bartender, as I sat near the middle of the long bar. I didn't immediately notice one local, further down the bar. Had I noticed him soon enough, I doubt that I would have sat down. It was too late now, my drink was already before me.

"Well, hi stranger," he mumbled as he slid his beer down the bar toward me, "haven't seen you in a long time." He continued to stagger from stool to stool, following his beer. "How 'er ya been," he slurred.

"Busy, as usual," I answered, not being overly friendly.

"Hear ya' gotta lot a 'struction workers at the hotel."

"Yes," I replied, "they are working on the sewer system out by Hickman Drive."

"There was a bunch of 'em in here last night. Quite a bunch of 'em," he continued, pushing his glasses up off the end of his nose. "They shur had a ball, playin' the jukebox an' drinkin'."

"I'll bet they did," I answered, finally glancing at him. "I heard them when they returned to the hotel. But they aren't as rowdy as that PARKO group we had last year." He rolled his eyes to the back of his head and smiled weakly.

"Boy, do I 'member that crew, yah, they were wild. Buyin' me drinks all night."

"Yeah, that was some crew," I commented, disgustingly disinterested.

I was nearly finished with my drink when the bartender returned with another. "This one is on your buddy here," he said, pointing to my companion.

"I was only going to have one," I said.

"Ya, ya, ya, I've heard that before. I haven't seen you for quite awhile," my buddy bellowed.

"Well," I answered rather sarcastically, "you know where I work and I don't see you there very often either." One of my major peeves was surfacing: I see these people all over town, but they never stop in my restaurant. So I smile and conciliate, but it does irritate me. I'm in business in this town, right on Main Street. Yet they have the audacity to ask, "Where have you been? Haven't seen you lately." For God's sake, I'd like to shout, I'm less than a block down the street. If you are my friend, come meet me there.

I finished the second drink hurriedly and left. Standing outside, I looked up and down Sinclair Lewis Avenue. I heard the jukebox blaring inside the Sportsman Bar just two doors away. There are a number of motorcycles parked out front. The decibel level of the music is enough to drive anyone to drink, but, for me, not in there. I slowly crossed the street and as I passed the service station on the corner, I saw three guys in the parking lot taking a leak in unison by one of the parked cars. I turned east and walked past the Water and Power office, the Tile Company and the dentist's office, and stood in front of the Tic Toc Bar. This I call the "Medicare Bar" due to the age of the patrons and the tranquilizing atmosphere.

Behind me I heard the sound of motorcycles. The noise was earsplitting as they revved up their engines. I watched as the sign on the Avenue shook with vibration. "Why in hell don't they make them muffle that noise?" I asked, shaking with anger.

I peered in the front window of the Tic Toc. Yep, same crowd every night. I noticed the T.V. and the news broadcast in progress. I entered and found a stool near the T.V. "Hi Al, brandy sweet?"

"Ya, I suppose so."

"And now for a look at the presidential hopefuls in this years' election. With Hubert Humphrey out of the presidential picture, it should give Gerald Ford some leeway in possibly defeating the unknown Jimmy Carter." The T.V. droned on just like the bar crowd. Same thing every night.

I became aware of movement down the bar. Glancing over, I saw a woman, glass in hand, watching me. As soon as I noticed her, she started to move in my direction. "Hi," she said, as she struggled to sit on the stool next to me. "I haven't seen you around before. Are you a local?"

"Yeah," I answered, keeping my eyes glued to the T.V.

"Not much action around here," she continued. Her voice possessed a squealing quality that ran up and down my spine like fingernails on a chalkboard. "Didn't want to go to my room alone. Just thought I'd have one beer," she commented suggestively.

"'Nother drink, Al?" the bartender asked, interrupting the senseless chatter.

"No, that's enough for now, I'll catch you later."

"See you later," was the bartender's reply.

I knew I should go home since I was opening in the morning. I walked east on the avenue. I felt the warm breeze on my face. A perfect night for window shopping.

Slowly strolling down the Avenue I came to John's Place. Through the open door I could see a few old-timers playing cards. The place usually closes at 9:00 p.m. Because of the summer evening and the guys playing cards, John must have decided to remain open a little longer.

John's Place is a classic small town card hall. It serves coffee, 3.2 beer, a few breakfasts and is famous largely for hot beef sandwiches.

Looking through the dingy windows I see bare bulbs hanging down from the very high tin ceiling. The ceiling fan is slowly rotating, trying to keep the smoke-filled air moving. A mixture of old kitchen and dining room chairs were carelessly set around three old, battered dining room tables. A few dirty mugs were stationed on one of the tables. John probably hadn't had time to pick them up. Four elderly men, deeply involved in their card game, were seated at the far table. Coffee cups and a couple of beer bottles were scattered amid them. The wood floor was stained and covered with ashes and cigarette butts. The counter, with eight stools in front, was worn, and desperately in need of varnish.

The long, narrow building is reminiscent of the early 1900's. I peered straight through the building to the back door. A built-in partition was added years ago to block off the kitchen area from the main room. On the back bar there were old and cracked restaurant dishes and mugs, probably handed down from family to family. Candy and other odds and ends are for sale near the front door. As I started to move on past the open door, my nostrils were assailed with the smell of grease and stale cigarette smoke being carried out the open door.

John's Place is an integral part of Sauk Centre. What would the old men do all day if they didn't have a card hall to while-away the hours? And what boy in town doesn't remember the first time his dad took him into John's Place for a *hot beef*.

The card hall was started by Richard's uncle at the turn of the century. He made a lot of money with 5ᶜ coffee and 10ᶜ hot beefs. His wife baked pies at home every day and brought them in to be devoured by the patrons. Even Sinclair Lewis looked back with fondness at the card hall. Woe be to the one who ever destroys John's Place.

Walking east past the Gambles store and the insurance office, I stopped in front of the drug store. It stands on the corner of Main Street and Sinclair Lewis Avenue, directly across from the Palmer House. Glancing back at the hotel I noticed the light in the *Window on Yesterday* still on. It is the only window on the first floor of the hotel which faces Lewis Avenue. We try to be imaginative with the displays and this week we are featuring a "Gourmet Dinner" setting. I wonder what some of the locals must think as they count nine eating utensils positioned at each place setting.

Turning away from the Palmer House and looking south on Main Street, I glanced into the windows of the drug store. I thought of the many times Sinclair must have walked this way. Back then it was called the Corner Drug and his dad, Ol' Doc Lewis, maintained offices on the second floor of this lovely old brick building. On down the street I'm greeted by the heavy smell of popcorn issuing forth from the Mainstreet Theatre, one-half block away. Personally I dislike popcorn, yet the smell of it popping brings to mind memories of Christmas, ball games, parties and movies. I remember sitting in the third balcony, holding my breath, and hoping Gene Autry would catch all the robbers.

I wandered on past the dentist's office, J.C. Penney's, and the jewelry store. Suddenly, just ahead of me, a violent brawl spilled onto the sidewalk. They came tumbling out of the Short Stop Bar and from the number of cycles parked in front I could tell that *the zoo* was hopping full tonight. I've missed the best part of the fight for I can hear the police siren wailing down from city hall. This is not an uncommon occurrence, especially on weekends. If Richard or I had tolerated these shenanigans in the Palmer House, we would have been run out of town years ago. I decided, definitely, against another drink. I turned and headed for the hotel.

I sensed something was wrong as soon as I entered the lobby. Richard was very upset. I assumed it was because I had gone out for a drink. As I approached the front desk I could tell it wasn't me with whom he was upset. He was flushed, while mumbling and shuffling papers in an anxious sort of way. And Richard, generally, is not the nervous type.

"What is it?" I asked as I removed my sweater.

He couldn't wait to answer.

"That elegant lady that checked in this afternoon, remember? Well, I went upstairs and you wouldn't believe it." He started to stutter as he sometimes does when he is upset or tired. "Well, I h-h-heard all -a-all this w-w-walking back and forth f-f-from the rooms at the s-s-south end. I th-th-thought it was the construction w-w-workers going to the b-b-bathrooms or using the sh-sh-showers. B-b-but there was so much of it, I decided to g-g-go up and check." He put out one cigarette and reached for another and never stopped talking. "When I opened the door to the landing, there she stood, in front of room seven, stark naked, and fondling herself. Imagine, with all those construction guys walking by! God, was I embarrased. She looked at me and motioned for me to come forward. I shouted at her, 'YOU GET BACK INTO YOUR ROOM OR I WILL CALL THE POLICE!' She glared at me a few seconds then turned and slammed the door."

He struck another match. "You already have a cigarette burning," I commented.

Ignoring my suggestion, he continued, "I hadn't been downstairs five minutes when all the commotion began again. I ran up the stairs and there she was again, still naked, and standing in her doorway. The guys were all in the hallway, gaping and laughing. I yelled at her again to get into her room, then I ran down here and called the police. They still haven't arrived. Of all the kooks that check into old hotels, this one is too much. He snuffed out his cigarette and lighted yet another one.

"Get me a cup of coffee," he implored. I grabbed his empty cup and headed for the restaurant. While I fumbled with the coffee pot in the dark, I heard the policeman come into the lobby. I didn't go out, but instead listened as Richard related to the officer the entire series of events. They both headed up the stairs and I entered the lobby with his coffee and sat down.

"Now if this happens again, call me, and we will take her to detox," the officer ordered as they descended the stairs.

Richard, still visibly shaken by the whole ordeal asked, "Why don't you take her now? She's definitely been drinking."

"I can't, I have to have a matron when there is a woman involved," replied the officer. "She will probably settle down now that I have been up there," he concluded, encouragingly, as he exited by the east door.

Richard took his coffee and sat in the chair next to me. "What happened?" I begged.

Richard took a deep breath and started, "W-w-when w-we got to the top of the stairs and opened the landing d-d-door, th-there she was again. S-she looked right at the officer and m-m-motioned for him to come into the room. He turned to me and said 'What do we do now?' 'How do I know?' I said, 'you're the policeman.' He told her to get back into her room and stay there or he would have to place her under arrest. All she did was smile defiantly and close her door."

He paused, taking a sip of his coffee, "My god, why did we ever buy an old hotel and bring all this grief on ourselves? I didn't want to buy the place anyway. I didn't want to come back to my home town." He was really upset. He was searching for a cigarette but he had obviously left them someplace else. He took one of mine and as I struck a match he continued shaking his head. "Of all the dumb things to have happen. People will think we are running a cat house now."

"Oh, I don't know," I countered compassionately, "she will settle down now that you have had the police talk to her." Wrong again. The stirrings upstairs started anew. And I could plainly hear the footsteps, back and forth.

"Oh, Christ," Richard muttered, "she's out again."

"Hello, this is R-R-R-Richard at the Palmer House. Tell the officer to get over here and get that woman out of here. Thank you." CLICK!

It seemed like an eternity before the police returned. The footsteps upstairs were intensifying, as though every male in the hotel was arriving for the show. Finally, the officer appeared and with the police woman, reluctantly headed upstairs to room seven. Richard paced back and forth, back and forth, until they finally appeared on the stair landing with the scantily clad — formerly elegant woman — who was scratching and screaming about her right to rent a room. As the police departed, with our super stripper and her suitcase, Richard sighed and then lamented *"Damn! She was such a classy lady."*

"Listen, I Need A Job!"
(Part 1)

I t certainly has been a weird day at the Palmer House. I overslept until 9:55; when my usual get up time is 7:30. I came downstairs quickly to go through the mail and was immediately surrounded by residents and guests grouping for their mail. It was as though they were all expecting free money, when in fact it was only junk mail. But junk or no, each day they eagerly await the arrival of the mailman. It has become a ritual.

I know very well not to use the letter opener, because without a *please* or a *thank you*, Lester will jerk it out of my hand. So, I instinctively hand him the letter opener to avoid the growling, hand waving and screaming, "Opener, opener, goddamn it, opener." It's much easier to hand it over, stay calm and wait to open my own mail.

Only rooms twenty-three, twenty-four and twenty-five get something of substance, namely their government checks, and that only occurs on the first of the month. But they all wait anxiously each morning for the mail. I find it interesting how important the mailman, perhaps today it should be mailperson, is in the lives of people, both young and old alike. Perhaps it is their only form of acknowledgement or recognition. Even junk mail seems to fulfill this need. The realization that they are important or even exist, that they are an individual with a name, even if that name is *resident* or *occupant*, seems to reassure their troubled souls.

Lester finally finishes with the letter opener and I can open our mail. Again there is no check for the $1000 account which is way overdue. Our checkbook is at a -$900 with more suppliers demanding money daily. Today happens to be Wednesday and American Linen, Coke, Randy's Meat, and who knows who else, will be standing at the front desk waiting for their money. I am bemoaning our fate when the phone rings.

"What's your soup today?" the voice asks, as if I knew this early in the morning. I remembered seeing some chicken bones on the side table in the kitchen so I replied, "It's chicken something or other," having no idea what the cook might add to it. The party hung up and the phone rang again. "Could you give me some information on your van that goes to the Cities each day?" More talk, more conversation, another CLICK.

"Do you have any rooms to rent?" demanded an overpowering voice next to my ear. I turned to find a tall, heavy-set man who had stepped up to the front desk.

"Yes, I do," I answered.

"How much are they?" he asked loudly and I proceeded to recite the complete rate rundown. He turned his back and said, "Thanks, I might come back."

"I doubt it." I thought to myself. "They never do." Oh, maybe once in a while a few will stay, but as a general rule most never return.

The phone rang again, "Hello."

"May I speak to the manager, please." The voice on the other end was pleasant.

"This is he," I replied.

"Congratulations, sir, you have just won a $50,000 lottery and I am delighted to pass on the good news. Now, let me tell you about our company..." CLICK. This time I hung up. "I'm so sick and tired of these come-on sales pitches, I sometimes hate to answer the telephone," I announced to no one in particular.

"Al, Al," a voice boomed from the kitchen, "could you come here a minute?"

"What is it now?" I asked, knowing full well that someone couldn't find the celery or the peppers or some other insignificant thing.

As I arrived in the kitchen, I found out it was just as I thought. Well, no not really. This time they couldn't find the tomatoes. Naturally, they were in a box under the celery, which was under the strawberries. We call it: *Palmer House Blindness.*

"Al, telephone."

"Palmer House. May I help you?"

"Yeah. What is your special today?"

"Chicken breast plate. Deep fried chicken breast with dressing, vegetable, bread and butter, and jello for dessert."

"Ah, ah, ah. Why don't you gimme a grilled ham and cheese and, ah, ah, maybe some french fries and a large Coke."
I repeated the order.

"No, make it a cheeseburger instead and could you deliver it?"

"Sure, we have *Meals on Wheels* at the Palmer House."

I called in the order and watched as the waitress wrote it up for the cook. Then I poured myself a cup of coffee and sat down at the end of the counter.

The counter is a very poor place for Richard or me to sit. The customers and staff believe it is a signal to *share* their frustrations. It's as if we turned a light on in a confessional. First it's Diane, who reminding me of her seniority, begins a tirade about the cook who she claims has been hassling her all morning: refusing to put her orders up correctly, throwing towels at her and teasing her about her son being out the night before. Simultaneously our dishwasher, who is subject to seizures, expounds in his own special brand of non-sequiturs about the events at his latest family reunion. These reunions seem to occur as often as the sun sets in the west. Then a local clerk sits down beside me to talk about the recent retail trades committee meeting; whereas Merlin, our now unofficial assistant manager, summons me from the restaurant door. He tells me there is someone to see me at the front desk.

I grabbed my coffee and cigarettes, and left the entourage that had surrounded me at the counter.

"Come back here," Fred yelled as I made my way past the cash register.

"Just a minute," I replied, ignoring him as I headed for the lobby. "May I help you?" I asked the young man standing at the front desk.

"Yes, sir. My name is Jeffery and I was told that I might be able to find a job here. Are you hiring? I'm a very good cook and waiter."

Jeffery is a handsome lad, in about his mid-twenties, with well-groomed, coal-black beard and hair, deep set, dark and penetrating eyes. He stands five feet ten inches tall, well built, with legs of a runner, broad shoulders and a commanding stance disposed to military training. There was something about Jeffery that I liked immediately.

"I don't have any full-time openings at the present moment, but I am sure there might be one shortly. Why don't you tell me about yourself."

Jeffery had met a Sauk Centre girl who was in Atlanta on a vacation a few weeks earlier and had spent some time with her and her girlfriend. As a passing remark the girl said, "If you ever get to Minnesota, look me up." And he did. I smiled. I knew the girl; she would be overwhelmed by his arrival. It seems she had inadvertently forgot to tell him she was engaged to be married.

I was impressed and I could just see him in our male waiter uniform. White shirt, red and white checkered vest, black bow tie, and black pants. "Why don't you fill out an application?"

"O.K. I'd love to," was his immediate reply.

He took the application, left and I wished he had taken the phone with him. It was ringing and of course no one answered it.

"Good morning, Palmer House. May I help you?"

"What's your soup today?" asked a familiar voice.

"Chicken Noodle," I retorted very curtly, having become more knowledgeable by this time.

"Thank you." CLICK.

Every morning for the past four years I have heard the same voice with the same question and have yet to put a name to the voice. I doubt that she has ever been in the Palmer House. With the fifty-two soups that we make in the restaurant, I can't help but wonder just what kind of soup would strike her fancy.

"Al, Al!" a voice called from the restaurant, "someone wants to talk to you."

"Naturally," I mumbled. "That is all anyone wants to do, is talk, talk."

Her name was Mary and she represented a new printing company in Glenwood. "I would like to show you some of our prices, especially on menus, placemats and things like that," she closed.

"Well, we have all our menus printed in town, since that's where our trade comes from," I concluded.

"Al, come into the kitchen for a minute. Someone at the back door wants to see you."

"Excuse me."

I am relieved for the moment but exchanging one sales person for another is like going from the proverbial frying pan into the fire, or in this case from the lobby to the kitchen.

"What can I do for you?" I asked the short, fat and rather dusty farmer standing at the kitchen door.

"What are you paying for potatoes right now?"

"I don't need any potatoes," I answered.

"You should see these, six dollars a hundred and they're real nice. Got three bags left and I hate to take them back home."

"But I don't need any right now."

"But look at 'em, six dollars a hundred and they'll last a long time."

"No, thank you." The phone is ringing and I quickly spin to answer it.

"Just three bags left at six dollars a hundred."

"Hello, Palmer House. May I help you?"

"Is Jon Jacobs there?" a voice asks.

"Just a minute."

I stepped back into the restaurant just as the dishwasher dropped a cup and saucer, making enough noise to cause the entire clientele to stop their gossiping and quip, *There go the profits.* I have heard that phrase so many times I could throw up. I located Mr. Jacobs, as usual, shaking dice with the coffee crowd. It's another Palmer House ritual which has such a following that no one dares to miss it. Of course, one reason no one dares miss is because the absentee would become the next victim, of gossip, that is.

"Jon, excuse me, you have a telephone call. Please take it at the front desk."

I can't stand to have a customer walk in the kitchen to use the phone as if he or she owned the place. It's one of the petty irritations that goes along with owning a business. I could add "in a small town," but I wonder if it is really different anywhere else? I don't know. Red Lewis didn't either. But the thought, that things are the same everywhere, helps me make it through the day.

"What is it?" I ask the cook who I sensed standing behind me.

"That potato man says he'll give you those last three bags for five dollars if you will take them."

Tell him to take his damn potatoes and plant 'em. I don't want to buy them. Besides, the last potatoes we got from him were just good on top. By the time we got to the bottom of the sack they were all rotten. You remember that don't you?"

"I guess so," he muttered as he shuffled back to the kitchen.

Jon had finished with the phone. He returned to the dice game which was so rudely interrupted. Which comes first, business or the daily dice game? I don't know. As I walked away, it was a horse apiece. Whatever that means.

"Telephone, Al, telephone!" they were shouting from the kitchen.

"O.K. I'll get it." I ran to the front desk. "This is Al," I replied rather abruptly into the receiver.

"Oh my god," an alluring, feminine voice exclaimed breathlessly, "you'll never guess who just got into town, OH MY GOD!"

"That wouldn't be a handsome young man from Atlanta, would it?"

"How did you know?"

"He has already been here and applied for a job," I said tauntingly.

"What am I going to do? He wants to see me after work."

"Guess you'll just have to see him, after all, you're the reason he came all the way up here. Call me and let me know how you make out. By the way, I think I am going to hire him. Our female trade should increase by leaps and bounds." I laughed and hung up. Then picked it up again.

"Good morning, Palmer House... No, he isn't; can I take a message?... He'll be here around noon..." CLICK. I looked into the receiver. Richard's mother is quite a woman. She never says 'good bye,' the conversation just ends. A strange custom. I will never get used to it.

As I walked back into the kitchen, I almost get clobbered by a flying counter cloth, which I'm sure the cook had certainly intended for one of our waitresses. "All right, enough of this horse-play. Turn that damn radio down or I'll take it away again."

The radio was immediately unplugged and all was quiet in the kitchen. Oh what power! It is not even 11:00 and I am trying to imagine why I am already tired, when the phone rings again.

"Good morning, Palmer House. May I help you?"

"Could you tell me what kind of soup you are having today?"

"Chicken Noodle," I answered.

"O.K. Thank you very much."

This was not the faceless soup lady. I recognized this voice. This lady had been a good customer, but lately we haven't seen her. I have no idea why she stopped coming in and it's all I can do to fight the beginnings of paranoia. Suddenly I remember my *Meals on Wheels* order.

"Write me up a ticket for a cheeseburger and fries to go," I shouted to one of the waitresses, "I'll deliver it."

"I'll be right back," she answered as she sailed out of the kitchen.

"Never mind, I'll do it myself." Oh, what happened to that power, I wondered.

"Al, Al, come here a minute," Fred called again.

"Yes, what is it?"

Fred stood beside the till. He had that familiar — *what the hell causes this?* — look on his face.

"The till is short two dollars and ten cents. Look here, I've gone through all the breakfast tickets and we are short two dollars and ten cents. How can that be?" It's a ritual we repeat most every day.

"I don't know, Fred, maybe it's wrong change or a ticket not rung up. What difference does it make anyhow? If it is not there, it's not there. I've got to go and deliver this order." I turned abruptly and walked out the door. My, but it was nice to get outside.

I enjoy take-out orders. At least I can escape the madness for a few minutes. Especially just before the lunch hour, which is hectic. As I stand on the corner waiting for the light to change, at least four passing cars honk at me, their drivers wave and I wave back, but not too enthusiastically, for not one of those who have honked have ever been in the restaurant.

When I returned from the delivery, I stopped at the entrance to chat with another businessman. I knew Richard was downstairs because the dog was whining inside the front door. Richard opened the door and away Christopher ran. God knows where. Probably to clone his way around town. There is a dog-leashing ordinance in our town, but Christopher hasn't heard about it and frankly, if he had, he wouldn't adhere to it. There were times when we had to scour the town looking for him. He was making a nuisance of himself, howling after some female, generating some real sons of bitches. Chris, however, has managed to clone himself so often, that there are now many replicas running 'round town. Now when irate people call we just say, "It can't be Chris. He's here behind the desk, sleeping."

"Why are you up so early, Richard?" I asked. "I was going to let you sleep. You work tonight, you know." If there was a reply I didn't hear it. Richard isn't very talkative this early in the morning.

The phone rang and he answered it in his inimitable style, "Palmer House." Then a pause. "Just a minute." With a long sighing, resigned attitude, he called to me. "So, what's the special?"

"Chicken breast plate with dressing, vegetable, bread and butter, with jello for dessert."

He repeated the special into the phone. Then, looking up in disgust he asked, "What's the soup?"

"Chicken Noodle," he grumbled then slammed the receiver down. "I need a cup of coffee," he announced and I couldn't have agreed with him more.

By now the dining room was filling up and I spied a couple of dirty tables. I grabbed a bustray and begin removing dishes. Before I got back to wipe it off, a party of four had already seated themselves. There were clean tables, but it never fails. Customers will invariably seat themselves at a dirty table. I have always marveled at this phenomenon. If I try to say anything, the curt answer usually will be, "Well, you'll have to clean it anyway." Three more tables filled as I entered the kitchen with the dirty dishes. The orders were stacked up over the steam table. "What is this — free food day?" I asked. I emptied the bustray then noticed the dishwasher scrubbing the wall as hard as he could, even though there were five full bustrays sitting beside him. He was having a seizure, I put my arms around him and held him tight and he began to scrub my face with the dirty cloth in his hand.

"It's O.K., it's O.K.," I reinterated. His eyes rolled as he struggled to get free of my grip. "Let's sit down for a minute. Come on now, let's sit down." I consoled.

He is a rugged farm boy, weighing about 160 pounds, and used to heavy work throughout his whole life. I weigh only 115, so I have a lot to contend with. Finally I move him to a chair by the staff table. Looking up at me with a most quizzical look, he asked, "What's the matter?" I left for a minute to get him a glass of water and in the process I almost got ran over by two busy waitresses. As I entered the dining room, I noticed that Richard has taken my place busing tables. Customers were standing in the lobby.

"Damn it, where are they all coming from?" he growled passing me with a full bustray heading for the dishwasher. He stopped.

"Where the hell is the dishwasher?" he asked.

"He's having a seizure."

"Well, we are out of cups and spoons."

Richard began immediately to wash dishes and when the phone rang, he grabbed it. "Palmer House," a pause then "Just a minute." He slammed the phone down on the microwave and headed for the front desk. "Someone wants room information," he stammered as he passed me. "It never fails. Every damn time we get busy, someone wants information."

I took over washing the dishes. Glancing at the clock, I saw that it was not quite 12:30. It seemed like it should have been quitting time.

"We're out of spoons," a waitress yelled.

"They're coming," Richard answered, running from the lobby.

"What was that all about?" I asked.

"Oh, somebody inquiring about room rates. They said they will call back. They wanted to know how large the rooms were and whether or not we had a pool. I get so tired of stupid questions."

"I know," I nodded as I carried the spoons and cups into the dining room.

"Ticket! Ticket!" Fred was yelling from the cash register. Someone was waiting to pay their bill and the waitress forgot their ticket. Another daily occurrence. I spun and retraced my steps into the kitchen.

"Who had the table under the sculpture?" I inquired.

Everyone turned their heads, looking dumbfounded. Our tables are numbered, but no one uses the numbers. So we have the pole table, the corner table, the window table, the table by the door and, of course, the coffee table. And now we have the sculpture table.

The restaurant emptied out just as fast as it filled up. The dishwasher is back at his post. The tables are filled with dirty dishes. The noon rush is over and all our nerves are a little frayed. It was a very good lunch hour, considering the season and circumstances.

Richard has finally poured himself a cup of coffee and is now sitting at the counter. He lights a cigarette. As I sit down beside him, I notice someone at the front desk. "There's someone at the desk, Richard," I offer.

"Damn, why didn't he pay me when he was standing there talking to me an hour ago?"

"Maybe he didn't have his checkbook?" I spouted spontaneously. Richard picked up his coffee and cigarette and headed to the lobby.

"Won't be long before coffee hour," a waitress commented. "It's almost 2:00." I picked up the morning paper and scanned the headlines. Just then the faint sound of a siren swept down the street. I waited, and as soon as the noise reached the kitchen, the cook dashed for the telephone. Almost all the locals have a scanner and his mother is no exception. He called to ask her where the ambulance was heading.

Everybody has a pattern. Richard turned to the front door. People in the restaurant scurried to the windows. Everyone wants to be first to know who died or who was in an accident. I guess it's no different in the big city, except here everyone knows everyone else. The news becomes the topic of conversation for the next day or at least until the next siren.

Frankly, I couldn't care less.

There has got to be something more to think and talk about than the latest scandal or death. I can't get used to people who seem to dwell on the trials and tribulations of their fellow human beings. The newspaper that I was scanning offered more of the same: death, destruction, violence; augmented by Ann Landers and the myriads of problems that she solves and readers commiserate with. I was not in a commiserating mood.

"Telephone, Al."

I ran into the kitchen.

"Al Tingley, may I help you?...Just a minute, I'll get him... Tell Richard he's wanted on the phone," I shouted to a waitress. I was getting tired of walking and running around all day. Besides, it was probably his mother with the news about the latest ambulance run. Out front I heard Fred grumbling about something. I made a mental note to avoid him. I was sure that the 2:00 p.m. register reading was at least two dollars off. He would spend the day looking for the mistake.

Fred is our volunteer worker. He is 78-years-old and a retired businessman and farmer. He is also Richards' father. He is the salt of the earth when it comes to honesty and hard work, but a son-of-a-gun for me to get along with. To me he is stubborn, even bull-headed and he rarely admits to making a mistake. When Richard was growing up, Fred worked in his gas station eighteen hours-a-day. In later years, he ran the station and farmed as well. A taskmaster of note, a workaholic of the extraordinary proportions. He did this not so much for the money nor for *good life*, but merely for the love of work. When he retired a few years ago he became bored at home, so one day he announced: "I'm going to be your cashier. I'll come in at 11:00 a.m. and run the till for a while, then go home." Now he comes in at 7:00 a.m., stays most of the day, and balances the till 'til all hours of the night. I always know where to find Fred, even when I have trouble locating his son.

When I finally found Richard, I sat him down with a cup of coffee. I wanted to tell him a few of the day's events, especially about Jeffery. He already knew that Pam had met this guy in Atlanta. She was laughing about it a few weeks ago when she returned. Little did she suspect that he would take her up on her offer and come to Minnesota. I described him to Richard as best I could, and mentioned his warm personality. I felt that he would add a lot of class to our dining room. Besides, our head waitress was leaving in a few months to have her first baby and we would need someone full time to take on her responsibilities. I felt he could do the job. Richard was not so easily convinced. As usual, he lead with his mind, not with his heart. We finally agreed to talk with Jeffery and sound him out.

"Telephone, Al," the call came from the kitchen.

"Hello, this is Al. May I help you?"

"I understand you occasionally have a gourmet dinner. Could you tell me about it?"

"Certainly. It is a nine-course dinner which begins at 7:00 p.m. and lasts until 10:30 p.m., with a twenty-minute intermission. This month we are featuring Poached Walleye Pike and Chicken Breast in Cumberland Sauce, plus seven other courses. The cost is fifteen dollars per person, wine and gratuity not included. We limit the seating to twenty or thirty people. If you have a reservation for two, then you are seated at a table for two. It is not banquet style. The date of the next dinner will be May 21."

"Well, thank you very much. How soon must we have reservations?"

"As soon as possible, they fill up fast. I think we have about five openings left."

"Thank you very much. Good-bye."

"What was that all about?" Richard asked as I entered the fireplace room.

"Oh, just some questions about the gourmet."

"Another big waste of time, they never show up. I wish you would cut out all that extra work. It's nothing but grief and then you're grumpy for a week afterward."

"I know," I replied, " but I enjoy preparing for it and it does bring in a little extra money. We make more money in one night of gourmet than in two days of winter-time restaurant business. Besides, it's my play time."

"Yeah, you go to bed half-smashed and I stay up all night and finish dishes, clean the kitchen, and put the Minniemashie room back together again. I don't think it's worth it. You never know if you'll get enough reservations and you never see any of the locals unless it's a freebie from **The Herald**."

It was Richard's standard gourmet-skepticism speech. He considered gourmets too high class for the area. And granted, through years the Palmer House has not exactly been a gathering spot for the elite.

* * * * *

I was pounding down the stairs about 8:45 a.m. I had made an appointment with Jeffery for 9:00 a.m., so I wanted to be down a little early. As I approached to the lobby floor, I noticed Jeffery entering through the east door. He was smiling and immediately extended his hand. "I know I'm early, but I can't stand arriving late for an interview."

"Good morning," I answered, extending my hand. The shake was firm and commanding. I was not only impressed by his being early, but by the way he shook my hand. He was wearing a pair of dress slacks and sportshirt with a dark navy-blue sport jacket. I could not help but notice his wide smile, even though the sun blinded me as it glistened through the stained glass windows. He radiated personality. "Let's get some coffee and go into the Kennicott Room," I said as I entered the restaurant. The coffee hour was in full swing. The same fourteen men were at the table for six. The dice boxes were banging on the tables and the noise was reminiscent of the Kentucky Derby. Why not, they were playing horses, weren't they? The ladies' table in the back was already overfilled, and they were busy discussing someone or something, in hushed tones. I nodded to two ladies who had both suddenly looked up and waved. As I went behind the counter to get a black thermal pot of coffee, our head waitress asked if we were out of napkins.

"Is this a quiz?" I asked, answering her.

"Just thought I'd ask," was her reply, "I can't find any."

"Ask Merlin. He probably put them in a different place," which was highly unlikely. "Forget the napkins for now," I said as I poured the pot full of coffee. "I want you to come into the Kennicott room shortly and interview Jeffery. He's applying for a job and I think he will make a tremendous addition to the staff. He seems to have a great deal of experience. Come in when you can, O.K.?" She nodded her head yes and hurried off with a coffee pot to refill the coffee table with undoubtedly their fourth cup. I could also hear someone at the ladies' table calling for more hot water. I grabbed a couple of cups and some cream and sugar, not knowing how Jeffery liked his coffee. Since he was from the southeast, I guessed that he used cream and sugar. I didn't learn to drink coffee black 'til I had been in the midwest for nigh on three years.

As I entered the lobby heading for the Kennicott Room the phone rang and I ran behind the desk to answer it. "Good morning, Palmer House."

"Could you tell me the soup of the day?"

This time I was unprepared, not knowing the soup, nor wanting to go out into the kitchen to find out, and recognizing the voice of the faceless soup lady, I said "Mullagatawny." There was a pause on the other end which I interrupted by adding, "You wouldn't like it anyway," and I hung up.

The Kennicott Room, build in the late '40's, was used as rental space until we took over. It is a rectangular room, about fifteen feet by ten feet, with a dropped ceiling and a corrugated florescent light in the center. The plywood walls have a greenish grain and the huge front window, removed by the former owners, is now filled in with glass block. The dining room set, Richard purchased for our home in St. Paul, a large expandable trestle table with six ornately-carved oak chairs sits inside. And on the west wall is a hand carved wooden sconce and picture set we had purchased at a recent Methodist Church bazaar.

"I bet you use cream and sugar in your coffee, Jeffery," I said as I sat down.

"How did you know?" he replied questionably.

"Well, if you're from the east and especially the southeast, that's the only way to drink it. *Coffee regular,* they say when you order it in a restaurant."

"Golly, makes me almost homesick. Yeah, coffee regular," was his smiling reply. After pouring coffee and watching him doctor it up with powdered non-dairy product and sugar, I sat down.

"I knew who you were as soon as you walked in yesterday," I began. "Pam told me all about you. She described you to a *T.*"

"I'm flattered, to say the least. I didn't know if she would even remember," he answered, with a pale blush rushing to his cheeks.

"Just the opposite. I think you made quite an impression on her. You are the first thing she talked about when she returned. Did you see her last night?" He remained silent for a moment.

"Yes," he answered hesitantly, "but I didn't know she was engaged."

"I doubt if that subject would come up in a chance meeting with a young man in a campground a thousand miles away from home."

"She's a wonderful girl."

"To say the least," I replied. "She has a super personality and I can see how you might have followed her all the way to Minnesota. Were I a bit younger I think I might have followed her also." There was a long pause as we both sipped some coffee. I lighted a cigarette.

"Well," I finally said, breaking the silence, "tell me more."

"I hardly know where to begin. I was born in a small town outside of Atlanta. My dad was a fireman and by the way, still is, even though we live in the city of Atlanta now. I have three brothers and two sisters. I am the youngest. I graduated from high school four years ago and enlisted in the Navy. I ended up cooking and waiting on tables. When I got out I realized I liked restaurant work and started working in some of the finest restaurants in Georgia. Being young and adventurous I had trouble at home, so I moved out. This past summer I took a job as a guide in a campground and that's where I met your Pam. We bummed around a couple of days together and I really got to like her. She was such fun to be with, I just wanted to get to know her better. After she left, I got to thinking about going somewhere after the campground closed, and then one night I packed up the car and said to myself, 'I'm going to Minnesota. So here I am." He took a deep breath and then a sip of coffee.

"Well, I can see you are a man of determination. Have you ever been married?"

"Haven't had time. Too busy working I guess and trying to find out who I am," he answered pensively.

I remember noting the answer "trying to find out who I am."

"You wanted me?" our head waitress asked, knocking on the door.

"Oh, yes. I want you to meet Jeffery from Atlanta. He is applying for a job here. Jeffery, this is our head waitress." Jeffery stood the moment she had entered the room. It was a courtesy I had rarely seen, since moving to Sauk Centre. As they shook hands I could already see she was pleased, not only with his manners, but with his very presence.

Just then there was another knock at the door.

"Al, sorry to bother you, but there is a salesman at the front desk."

"Thank you, I'll be right out." I turned to the waitress. "Why don't you talk to Jeffery for a few minutes and see if we could use him at the Palmer House. I'll be right back."

I left the Kennicott Room to be confronted by Mr. Obnoxious.

"Hi, my name is Rex, and I'm with the Blando Food Company. Now let me show you some of our great buys in steaks and chops this week." He was so overbearing that I would have probably been knocked off my feet by his booming voice except for the fact that my little hand was encased by his, preventing any movement.

"We have all the meat suppliers we need, sir," I said, hopping around to try and free my hand.

"But you haven't seen our prices. We can beat any price on meats! And I am going to show you how you can save a bundle." This guy came on like gangbusters. He just wouldn't stop talking and he was so loud, I was getting shell-shocked.

"I don't have the time to talk with you now, sir, I am in the middle of an interview."

"Just look at some of the specials we have this week," he continued without even listening to my reply. He threw a large sales book open in front at me, nearly knocking me off balance. "We have boneless pork chops, quarter pound hamburgers, hamburger steak and chicken breast all on sale this week. I can have them in your freezer by tomorrow afternoon and you could be making money by tomorrow night." By now, even the old timers were looking up from their newspapers, the first time in several years. I was getting more angry by the moment. I have dealt with some pushy salesmen before, but this guy was pushing for the top of the list.

If Richard were here he would probably say my eyes were flashing. "Sir," I said, "I do not want to hear about your specials, nor do I want to hear about your company. I am happy with the suppliers I have. I am busy and I do not have time to talk to you now." I turned and spun on my heels as I headed back to the Kennicott Room.

"I'LL DROP IN TO SEE YOU NEXT WEEK," he hollered across the lobby.

"Don't bother," I replied and slammed the door, startling both our waitress and Jeffery.

"Another one of those salesmen?" she queried as she looked up with a knowing grin. She had seen my temper flare before at salesmen who just happen to walk in the back door of the kitchen trying to catch me at work.

"That bastard acted like he was God's gift to the restaurant business." I was trying to cool down but to no avail, so I took a swig of coffee instead.

"I know how some of those guys can be, Mr. Tingley," Jeffrey stated breaking the silence.

I turned to look at our head waitress. I have always trusted her judgement, almost more than my own. Richard felt I gave her too much authority, but she was my right hand, and a real asset as head waitress. She was tough but fair. Some of the high school help would stop at the front desk before work and ask: "What kind of mood is she in today?" which I believed showed their respect for her. And I could always count on her for the parties, the gourmets, and special events. She took extreme pride in the Palmer House and in the reputation we were trying to establish.

"I believe Jeffrey will be a great addition to our staff," she said.

"Well, when does he start?" I asked, regaining my composure.

"I'll start training him in tomorrow on my nine to five shift, if that's alright with you. Has Richard met him yet?" she asked knowing that there is little that we do at the Palmer House without consulting one another.

"No, he hasn't, but we talked at great length about it last night."

Jeffery rose and extended his hand. I shook his hand then carried the tray of dirty cups through the lobby and into the restaurant.

"Who was that HUNK that just left the Kennicott room?" a waitress asked as I walked into the kitchen.

"Me," I reply nonchalantly.

"No, What's his name? Tell me!" she inquired eagerly.

"Jeffery. He's from Atlanta and keep your paws off him," I smiled. Already the staff was buzzing about him. It never takes long for word to spread in small towns. The addition of Jeffery would breathe new life into the the Palmer House Hotel.

* * * * *

It was almost lunch time and the customers were beginning to file into the restaurant, table by table. Alice, the cook, was ready for the onslaught, but she was also apprehensive. Business had indeed increased since we took over. She was a holdover from the previous owner and her workload was a far cry from when she first started here. Back then, she would prepare about twelve noon specials, such as meat loaf, and the staff would eat right along with the customers. Soon we were preparing thirty to fifty orders of the noon special and still running out. Finally I ran an ad in **The Herald** saying, "WE PROMISE WE WILL NOT RUN OUT OF THE NOON SPECIAL."

She specializes in soup. Her soup of the day is without a doubt the best in the land. She has a way with spices and seasonings which is unsurpassed, if only she could find one which would please the "faceless soup lady" my dreams would be fulfilled. She is about fifty-five years old, rather heavy set, and has a large family with just one boy left at home. All the rest have married and left the nest except when it comes to weekends and holidays. Then they all show up hungry and eager for Ma's home cooking. I remember many a Monday morning when she would come to work and say:

"Boy, am I bushed. Had the whole family home this weekend and baked ten loaves of bread, six apple pies and served dinner for twenty-two."

"How come they don't invite you and your husband over for dinner once in a while?" I'd ask.

"Oh, they just like my cooking," she'd reply.

She cooked both at home and at work and I learned many of my kitchen techniques from her. To watch her grind up leftover ham for a ham loaf was an art in itself. A little of this and a little of that, poke it here, poke it there and put it in the oven. There it was. Alice's ham loaf, fit for a king. In reflecting back, I am sure that this style of cooking is well on its way out, with the hustle, bustle, hurry, scurry America of today. It is still a mystery to me, how Alice could produce such succulent dishes in such a short time. Oh how I want to be able to take a little of this and a little of that and make a Yankee Pot Roast that would taste like hers. I guess I did learn something, for as the years passed she began to let me take her shift. As she grew older, she finally had to leave the Palmer House because of ill-health. But all of us will remember Alice and her great contribution to our culinary art.

*   *   *   *   *

It seems that everyone in the whole world has to eat at exactly noon. I can understand why the clerks and workers, who are given exactly one-half hour for lunch, have to eat at noon; but please tell me why the owners and managers who could take off for lunch at their convenience also have to eat exactly at noon. They arrive and are perturbed if we are a little slow at getting to their table. And then, they want a rush order. We bust our asses to get the food out to them, then watch as they sit for nearly another hour leisurely sipping coffee, reading the paper or becoming involved in a discussion about the latest national or state news. It galls me, especially when there are people waiting to sit down. But that's show business, folks.

It is 1:15 and the restaurant has nearly emptied. The tables are filled with dirty dishes and the kitchen looks as if a tornado has just spun through heading north. Richard lights up a cigarette and sits at the counter in front of his now cold cup of coffee. I remove my apron and leave the clean-up work for the next shift. I pour a cup of coffee, reach for a cigarette, and sit down beside him. "We hired Jeffery this morning," I state matter-of-factly.

"Who?" he says, without looking up from his coffee cup.

"Jeffery. The guy I told you about yesterday. You know, the lad from Atlanta."

"Oh him. What do we need more help for? We're heading into winter. You know how slow it gets after Christmas." He took a drag on his cigarette.

"Matra is leaving shortly to have her baby. And Lois is leaving for school. We have got to have someone around who knows what's going on. I think Jeffery will be a great addition to the staff. Anyway, he is starting tomorrow morning. I think you will be impressed. The girls love him already. He will be great for business."

"But what do you know about the guy? What is his background? Where does he live?" Richard was being very practical, and somewhat pugnacious.

"I explained all that yesterday." I answered.

"We'll see," was his final remark. The conversation was inter-rupted by a two-pronged attack; the telephone and another salesman coming through the restaurant door. "I'll get it," Richard grumbled as he headed for the kitchen phone. I had no time to run and hide. The salesman stood before me with an outstretched hand. Some days I get to the point where I don't want to shake hands with a salesman even though I know they are just trying to make a living. I was still fuming over the great obnoxious one.

"Hi there. My name is Rob and I am with Continental Bulb and Light Company. How many light bulbs do you use around here in a year?" He smiled.

"As many as we need. How should I know how many light bulbs we use? Besides, we buy them locally." I took a drag off my cigarette and sipped my coffee.

"Do you realize how much you pay for light bulbs when you buy them over the counter?" he snapped back at me as though I was go-ing to be overwhelmed by his lightning bolt.

"Do you know how many times the Coast to Coast manager and his family, and his staff, have eaten meals at the Palmer House?" I retorted. "I have never before in my life seen you and I know for a fact you have never spent a dime here."

"I get your point," he replied, " but our bulbs will last longer and save you even more money in the end."

By this time the salesman was sitting beside me at the counter and, as they all do, had opened his big book which knocked the salt shaker to the back of the counter, which in turn hit my coffee cup, which knocked a menu into my lap. I can never figure out why salesmen have to be issued oversized and underpriced sales aids. They monopolize all available counter and desk space within a four block radius. And it all appears suddenly whenever the word "No" is implied or spoken.

He had no sooner stretched out his humungous offering, when Richard returned from the telephone and stood behind the counter. Pouring himself another cup of coffee, he said sarcastically, "Not another salesman? I just hung up on one who wanted me to buy five gross of pens with our name on them. We would receive a free tran-sistor radio. What are you giving away?" he snarled at the man whose wares were festooned all over the counter.

"Light bulbs, sir," the man said as he immediately stood up and extended his hand to Richard. "Rob Nalar, Continental Light Bulb Company."

Richard sort of touched the outstretched hand and said, "We don't need any. Besides, we buy all our bulbs in town. That's where our business comes from."

"Your partner was just telling me that, but I would like to show you the savings you could make if you bought them from me."

"We are not interested," Richard said. Then, as an afterthought, he asked. "How many light bulb companies are there anyway? You must be the fifth one this month."

The phone rang and Richard turned toward the kitchen mumbling "God let there be light," as he disappeared through the swinging doors.

"No, sir, we are not interested, but thank you for stopping. Come dine with us sometime." Suddenly he got the message and quickly packed up his huge book and headed out into the lobby.

"More coffee, Al?" a waitress asked as she bubbled by the counter with a half-full pot of coffee. She started to fill my cup, then smiled and asked, "When does that cute guy start? Is he going to work here?"

"Tomorrow morning," I told her.

"Oh, he's too much," she exclaimed as she bounced off, filling cups along the counter.

"Allan," Richard called from the kitchen, "telephone."

I got up and entered the kitchen. "Hello, this is Al. May I help you?"

"Well, I hope so. We are planning a little get-together for some of our friends and we were wondering what you charge for a nice dinner in the Minniemashie Room?"

"Well, that depends on how many people and what you want served," I announced. "Our plate-style dinners run anywhere from three-fifty for roast beef to two-seventy-five for a complete chicken dinner, to fifteen dollars per person for a gourmet dinner. What do you have in mind?"

"Well, I don't know. They put me in charge and I was to find out the various prices for a nice ladies luncheon."

"How many are you planning for?" I asked.

"Oh, there is about fifteen of us. We really would like something real nice and different and not too expensive."

"What date do you have in mind?"

"Oh, we don't know. We are just checking around at various places."

"Well, the most important thing is to set the date so we can reserve the room, then we can decide on the meal. When you have the date, why don't you give me a ring and we will arrange a meeting where we can decide on the food."

"O.K. Thank you very much." CLICK.

"Did she want a party?" Richard asked, standing beside the dishwasher.

"Just an inquiry as to what it would cost for a dinner party, real fancy but very cheap," I answered.

"Typical. They all want something real fancy, but cheap." Richard echoed as he headed back out to the lobby. "Just like our salesmen; We have the best for less. Ladies and Gentlemen let me tell you it don't compute," he grunted. I picked up my coffee and walked after him.

*   *   *   *   *

I arrived downstairs earlier than usual this morning. I was anxious to get a first-hand customer reaction to Jeffery. I wasn't disappointed. The coffee ladies in the back room spotted me as I entered the restaurant and waved me over to their table. They are yet another tradition at the Palmer House.

I remember the first day we walked into the place. The former owner immediately took us over to their table and introduced us to every last one of them. "They are a wonderful group of ladies and very good customers. They come in here every morning for coffee and conversation. You had better be good to them." he ordered. I smiled and greeted each one of them. Every morning, without fail, just as he promised, they gather for their coffee and "conversation," although through the years some of them have switched to drinking hot water.

As I approached their table "the leader of the pack" whispered loudly to me, "Who is the handsome new waiter you just hired?"

"His name is Jeffery and he's from Atlanta."

"I thought I noticed an accent. My is he handsome. I wish I were fifty years younger."

Then the questions came fast and furious. "Is he married?" "Is he engaged?" "Does he have a girlfriend?" "Is he staying here?" "Where is he living?" After giving his life history, I begged off from the conversation and entered the kitchen.

*   *   *   *   *

Jeffery was well into his first day of training. He was an imposing picture of masculinity, especially when he walked out of the kitchen with a tray full of food balanced on one hand high above his head. "Wow," said Alice, the cook, "he sure is handsome and so polite. He says 'thank you' to me every time he picks up an order. Where did you ever find him?" And so it went on throughout the day. "Who is he?" "Where's he from?" It was peculiar, since the Palmer House had male waiters before.

We started with young men during our very first summer in Sauk Centre. The first man we hired was tall and very good looking. He came to the front desk one day and said "Listen, I need a job."

"Just what kind of a job are you looking for?" I asked.

"Anything, I just need a job. I am living in a foster home here and am a senior in high school." The idea hit me right there. How about a waiter. I knew it would set a precedent in this small town. But what the heck, I loved being a trend setter. This young man was going to be in for a lot of ribbing, if he was to become the first man to wait on tables in Sauk Centre. "Do you think you could be a waiter?" I asked very seriously.

"I don't know. Never thought about it before," he replied.

"Well, I could use a waiter. One of our girls just quit. I can't promise you many hours, and you will have to take a lot of kidding and grief."

"I think I could handle it," he replied very firmly.

I knew the coffee ladies might like it but the men at the coffee table would go crazy. "Why don't you let me talk it over with my partner and the staff and I'll get back to you."

Within two days he was hired and it was just as I thought, "Hey waitress, er... I mean waiter, could I get some more coffee. Ha! Ha!" Nice set of legs honey...and so on throughout the first week. What a novelty to have a man waiting on tables. He handled himself admirably throughout the ordeal and soon we began hiring more and more waiters until at one time we had four men on our dining room staff. I must comment on the hiring of a waiters, at the risk of being overwhelmed by the new wave, ERA. When our waiters came to work, they didn't bring their family, or girlfriend problems. Consequently, there was much less gossiping in the kitchen, and fighting among the employees. This is not to say the waitresses were not good workers, but there was a tendency for them to create more uneasiness in staff relations.

As Jeffery's first day wore on and some of the school girls came to work, you could imagine their excitement upon being introduced to him, and likewise, Jeffery's enthusiasm for his young and lovely co-workers. In fact, one of our younger and very attractive waitresses was already hinting that she had no plans for this evening.

Pam showed up that evening, bubbly as usual and wanting to know all about Jeffery's first day. When I told her about the ladies at the coffee table this morning and how their rigormortis left them, she said "I can believe it, he's such a hunk."

"And Dana has been hinting all day that she is free this evening and would love to show him around the town."

"Yeah, Dana would," she laughed.

"What really surprises me is the way Rama is carrying on about Jeffery."

"Rama! I thought she was planning on becoming a nun or something."

And then I realized that I, too, had fallen into the small town gossiping trap. It's amazing what chemistry takes place when a young lad comes on the scene, especially if he is a new guy in town.

The weeks went by and business continued to pick up, and I'd like to believe it was because of Jeffery. We were getting into late fall when business usually starts to slow down. I had delegated a lot of authority to Jeffery and he was taking it very well. The staff and customers had settled back into their normal routines. He was no longer the "Adonis from Atlanta" but rather just Jeffery. The classiest waiter that the Kennicott Room ever had.

A Study In Contrasts.

The Palmer House is a study in contrasts. Throughout the eighty years since its grand opening, the world has moved at a rapid pace while the hotel seems to have stood as a silent sentinel to times past Yet with the ever changing tide of progress I can see great similarities and contradictions. One day, while I was relaxing in the lobby after lunch and before the hectic coffee hour, I was contemplating the wonderful, methodical tic of the old regulator clock above the front desk. Tic, tic, tic. Think of the years that clock had ticked away for mankind.

As I sat mesmerized by the old clock, my reverie was interrupted by a shrill *Beep, beep, beep.* I was startled back into reality and knew instantaneously that it had to be Monday. Monday was the day one of our salesmen would sit in the lobby, possibly for an hour or so, and enter all his daily orders into his pocket computer. *Beep, beep, beep,* the sound seemed to fill the air of this ancient structure. But when I listened intently I sensed the time warp between the *tic, tic, tic,* and the *beep, beep, beep.*

After all the daily orders had been entered the salesman would walk over to one of the pay phones and dial the operator for a credit card call. When the party, or should I say *data bank,* was on the line, he'd plug in his portable unit and push another button. All the daily orders would then be *beeped* into the home computer. Throughout the night the orders would be processed and early the next morning a truck would arrive to deliver an order to the Palmer House and possibly a hundred other places along the route. Yes, the lobby was indeed a place of contrasts.

Not infrequently we have requests from schools and groups desiring to tour the old hotel. We have developed a pattern for tours. It's easier than a random, walk-through trip. I remember one such occasion with a group of Explorer Scouts. I asked the group to come to the south end of the lobby. On the lobby walls we have a number of photographs depicting the early days of the Palmer House. I began with the wedding picture of Mr. and Mrs. R. L. Palmer, the original proprietors, then proceeded to pictures of the original building, the old barroom and the restaurant as it appeared in 1901.

Then I directed their attention to the red oak woodwork spread throughout the first floor. I pointed out with pride the ripple stained glass windows which were imported from Vienna, then related a story told by a local lady who lived to be ninety-four. She remembered when the Palmer House was being built. She and her family lived in a house directly to the east, where the First Bank now stands. She was five-or six-years-old when she witnessed the construction. She and the other children in the family had watched the installation of the stained glass windows and *knew* it was going to be a church, since in those days no one had ever heard of a commercial building displaying stained glass windows.

With pride I informed the group, "This was the first hotel outside of the Twin Cities to have running water and electric lights in every room. In fact, there is a story told that Mr. Palmer had to replace most of the light switches within the first year. The salesmen were apparently so fascinated by this modern miracle, they wore them out by constantly switching the lights off and on."

I continued my narration. "Staying at the Palmer House in 1901 could be compared to staying at a Holiday Inn today." And invariably, one of the youngsters would squawk, "So where's the pool?"

When we arrived at the front desk, I called their attention to the buzzer system which was installed by Mr. Palmer. Powered by dry cell batteries, it consists of a series of buttons at the front desk, a buzzer in each room and corresponding brass arrows located in a display case at the desk. When someone desired to speak with a house guest, the desk clerk would push the button and the corresponding buzzer upstairs would sound. If the guest was in, he would reciprocally push a button in his room and the arrow would move to indicate that the caller would be received. This was quite a step saving system in a pre-telephone era, and not unlike the *beep, beep, beep* of the salesman in the lobby today.

M*A*S*H Isn't The Only Place!

It was a warm, late summer afternoon. Richard was sitting in the lobby talking with his cousin. I had just gone on duty in the kitchen. The coffee rush was over and the waitresses were setting up for the evening dinner hour. It had been a busy day and I could see Richard was tired from busing tables through the hectic lunch hour. As he sat relaxing, the east door opened and a rather tall, thin, construction-worker-type entered. He was carrying a large, brown paper bag, which possibly could have contained all his worldly possessions. As he approached the front desk, Richard got up, went behind the counter and politely said, "Hi. Can I help you?"

"Yes," the man answered with a slight smile. "I'd like a room on the top floor, the one overlooking the parking lot. I think it is number twenty-two?"

"O.K., that will be eight dollars," Richard replied as he passed the registration card and a pen to the man.

"Prices have gone up here, haven't they?"

"So has everything else," Richard reported.

Obviously the man had stayed here before, but it must have been pre-Tingley and Schwartz, as Richard rarely forgets a face or a name and often recalls an entire episode. I remember one time in the '60's when Richard and I were on a bus trip to the west coast. We had to change busses in Tulsa, Oklahoma so we were having a drink at the bar when Richard spotted a person he thought he knew. After thinking about it for some time, he finally walked over and said, "Aren't you Joe from Moorhead, Minnesota? Didn't we meet at a bowling alley about six or seven years ago?" The man's jaw opened and you could see he was desperately searching his mind for past recollections in order to respond to this stranger's questions. "Oh, yeeeaaahh, I seem to remember, you're a-a-a printer, or ah, no, a typesetter, right?"

"I thought that was you," Richard replied, "I have been watching you for a long time. You haven't really changed much…"and he was off again on an animated historical conversation. He never fails to amaze me with his ability to recall.

"If you have a car, you will have to park in the lot behind the hotel," Richard stated, hoping to extract more information from the tall, thin man. The man handed Richard a ten dollar bill for which he received two dollars back. He then headed up the stairs, two at a time. Richard sat back down beside his cousin, "He signed in from Fargo. I bet he just got off the Fargo bus. It just came in."

"Wonder what he's got in the bag?" his cousin asked, "Clothes or booze?"

"I don't know, but somehow he looks familiar." This time Richard was wrong.

Now, Wednesday evenings are normally slow. Even the phone rings only a couple of times with just the usual people inquiring about evening specials. I was busy scrubbing potatoes to put in the oven when Richard hurriedly called me from the hallway door. "Allan, come here, you got to see this. That construction worker that just checked in? He just came downstairs dressed as a woman and is heading for the bars. Hurry."

As I sped around the corner I saw him standing in the lobby. He was dressed in a blue denim skirt, long black net stockings, purple spike-heeled shoes, yet he still wore a white T-shirt and the face of a man. Richard stood chiding him, "Where do you think you're going dressed like that?"

"To the bars," he flipped back haughtily.

"Well, dressed like that you may get raped," Richard replied.

"I hope so," he chirped, flinging his wrist at Richard. He headed for the south door, and he was very obviously wiggling his posterior.

As soon as he had sauntered into the street, Richard, his cousin and I ran to the door to see which bar he would first choose. "My god," said Richard recreating the events. "He just checked in no more than ten minutes ago, and went up to his room. I was sitting here when I heard the click, click of high heels coming down the stairs. So I said to cousin Norm, 'That's a woman's heels making that noise, but there are no women on the third floor and Rosie is working in the kitchen!' When he came down to the first floor, I saw him and I jumped up before he reached the lobby floor. 'What the Christ do you think you're doing????' I asked. He stopped half-way down the staircase and flipped his wrist at me. 'This is a public place and I can dress anyway I want to and you can't stop me.' He proceeded down the stairs, then turned and said, 'Wait till you see the gown I will be wearing for dinner this evening. I'll be dining in the restaurant around 6:00.' 'Like hell you will,' I said. Then I came out into the kitchen to get you. What are we going to do? Should I call the police? I wonder if he escaped from Fergus or something???"

Cousin Norm was flustered. And the loudness of his voice is directly proportional to his state of excitement. "I never saw anything like it," he bellowed. "And he's going to the bars dressed like that?"

This outburst drew the waitresses and what few people there were in the restaurant to the lobby where they all talked at once. Who saw whom and who saw what and who said what to whom.

"My god, right here in downtown Sauk Centre. And he said he was coming back for dinner tonight dressed in a long gown," Richard repeatedly reported.

"I've gotta see this," one customer exclaimed. "I'll be in for dinner tonight," and then he left through the Main Street door, no doubt to get on the telephone and begin calling everyone in town.

The news must have travelled fast for it wasn't long before the tables started filling up with people I had never seen in the here before. We were not prepared for such a large dinner crowd. By 4:30 there must have been forty people all chattering and discussing what they saw or what they heard about the new stranger in town. We were the talk of the town. Or rather he/she, or whatever, was staying in room twenty-two at the Palmer House was.

Richard became very nervous by the end of the afternoon. In and out, up and down, continuously looking out the door and windows to see if and when our star attraction would be coming back. The orders kept piling up in the kitchen, and I finally called in someone to help get rid of the backlog. I knew the customers wouldn't leave until they saw what they came to see. Interesting isn't it? A similar individual could check into a hotel in Minneapolis or St. Paul and no one would bat an eye, but in Sauk Centre all eyes and ears turned. Suddenly some residents were even willing to sample our sandwiches. Surely this event will be the topic of conversation at the coffee table for some time to come. One consolation, it will take the heat off the latest local, due to be roasted tomorrow.

Richard rushed into the kitchen. "He's coming back to the hotel. He just left the Short Stop Bar. He's walking down Main Street towards the hotel. You should see the looks he's getting from people in cars. Hurry, come on out to the lobby." In one door and out the other, Richard ran. He was as hyper as I have ever seen him.

Our guest arrived. He had entered the lobby and swaggered his way to the staircase, hardly pausing to notice the many pairs of eyes pondering his every move. Just as he started to ascend the stairs, he turned to the now clustered curious crowd, and flipped his wrist haughtily and announced, "I'll be down for dinner shortly. Reserve me a table." And with a flip of his head, he proceeded to click his way up the stairs and into his room.

The restaurant was at fever pitch now and I believe Richard also had a fever. "What are we going to do?" he wondered as we walked back into the kitchen.

"Well," I said, "it certainly is good for business. We haven't had a crowd like this on a Wednesday for a long, long time."

"Christ, I'm embarrassed. All those people out there and he's staying at the Palmer House. We've only been here a short while. What will people think?" He was noticeably disturbed.

"Well, they'll think some kook checked into our hotel!" For once I was the one who was calm and philosophical, strange as it seemed. But not for long.

A waitress came bursting into the kitchen and announced, "He's here! He's here! Oh, I hope he doesn't sit in my section. I don't want to wait on him." I peeked out the door and sure enough, he had entered the restaurant. But not with a long gown as he had promised. He wore the same denim skirt he had on in the afternoon. And sure enough, he took the only table available, the pole table which just happened to be in the beleaguered waitress' section. She stood in the kitchen and covered her face. "Oh, no! OH, NO! I don't want to wait on him."

"Don't worry, He won't hurt you. Make believe he is just another customer," I reassured.

The restaurant was suddenly very quiet. Just a few whispers as he was seated. I remember Richard saying, "Turn up the music Merlin, do anything to stop the silence."

Our guest placed himself at the north end of the room with his back to the pole. He was facing south which allowed him to look out the entrance of the restaurant and into the lobby. Since we had not yet replaced the sliding glass patio doors with the original oak doors, he could easily see the crowd in the lobby.

With some more words of encouragement, our shy waitress collected her courage and took a glass of water and a menu to his table. "Our special this evening, sir, is Beef Burgundy on rice and it comes with, with your— —choice— —of— —soup or salad. Oh, I'll be right back," she gasped. She was hyperventilating when she made it back into the kitchen. "O my god, I'm not going back out there, I'm not," she shouted.

By now more curious patrons had entered the lobby and the kitchen staff was way behind with the orders due to the ongoing excitement. "O.K. O.K. Let's get the show on the road, we got orders to get out. Let's get these dishes done up," I barked. Our waitress recomposed herself and returned to take his order. I watched from the kitchen. He must have been talking very softly for she leaned down over him, I presumed, to hear what he was saying. The music in the restaurant was now quite audible, yet I could *hear* the tension among the other diners mounting. It seemed like an eternity before she returned to the kitchen. She was in tears. I didn't know what he had said to her, but it certainly had affected her.

"Oh my god, O my god," she wailed as she burst through the swinging doors. "He's going to kill himself. He said he was going to kill himself. He's got a big knife and he's cleaning his fingernails with it." She put her arms around me for protection. "He says nobody loves him and nobody wants him, O my god!" Her voice got higher and higher. "He's got a knife and he's going to do it. I know it! I could see it in his eyes." She was out of control so I shook her a bit.

"It's all right. We'll take care of it. He's been drinking all afternoon and he's probably drunk." The rest of the staff gathered around trying to calm her down and I ran out the back kitchen door to the lobby.

"Richard! Richard! He told Jean he was going to kill himself." I screamed as I arrived at the front of the lobby where Richard stood talking to a policeman.

After reviewing the situation, the policeman kindly entered the restaurant and said something to our star attraction who quietly got up and left the Palmer House, never to be seen or heard from again. Many of our guests also departed that night, never to be seen or heard from again.

"It's Showtime!"

"**D**o you have any opening?" The voice startled me for a second as I was busy reading the mail. Looking up, I saw a tall, dark haired lady standing in front of the desk.

"Yes, may I help you?" I smiled.

"I hope so," she smiled back. Her voice was strong and forceful. She had a pleasant smile, I was impressed. "Are you hiring?"

"Hiring what?" I laughed.

"Anyone for anything. I need a job and I have tried every place in town."

"Well, the only possiblity here might be a waitress. Have you ever done waitress work?"

"A little," she replied. "When I was in my first year in college."

"Do you mind being a waitress?" I asked. I had a feeling that this girl was not the waitress type, but she impressed me with her style. "Are you from town?" I continued.

"Not really. My husband and I were living in the Cities, but his father could no longer live alone so we sold everything and moved up here to take care of him."

"Oh. What is his name?"

"Whose, my husband's or my father-in-law's?"

"I guess both," I replied, realizing the stupidity of my question.

"My name is Dorita Graff. I'm married to Ed Flichauer and we are living in his father's house. His name is Don."

I did a double take with that answer. It was a little too upbeat for Sauk Centre. "Your name is Graff and your husband's name is Flichauer?"

"Certainly. I kept my maiden name."

Letting the obvious pass, I fumbled through the filing cabinet to see if we had any applications left. Not finding one, I grabbed a piece of paper and a pen and said, "Here, we are out of applications at the moment, but why don't you take this and give me the vital statistics." She began to grin at my phraseology. I also blushed. "I mean, tell me about yourself, all the ordinary things you would put on an application. There is a desk over there by the window and I will have the head waitress talk with you when you have finished."

A new *era* was launched at the Palmer House with the addition of Dorita to the staff. She quickly adjusted to the routine and the customers, or should I say, the customers adjusted to her.

"You must be new in town," one of the coffee men said as Dorita was refilling his cup for the third time. "What is your name?" he asked politely.

"Dorita. Dorita Graff," she replied with a smile.

"Who do you belong to?" he continued.

"I don't belong to anybody, but I am married to Ed Flichauer."

"Old man Flichauer's boy?"

"Yes. Ed and I have been married about two years."

"Any children yet?" another voice piped up. It was the third degree. I had warned her, yet I think she underestimated the inquisitiveness of the locals. She finished the third round of refills and headed for the ladies table. They, too, were equally curious about our newest addition.

"What is your name, dear?" the "leader of the pack" inquired.

"Dorita Graff," she replied warmly, refilling the two pots on the table with hot water, for some of the ladies had switched to hot water when we raised the coffee to forty cents a cup. "And I am married to Ed Flichauer." A heavy silence fell around the table. As Dorita walked away, the conversation began anew.

"I can't imagine a girl marrying a man and not taking his family name."

"What are they going to do when the baby comes. She will have to change her name."

"Well, if you ask me, this younger generation is too independent. They have no respect for tradition."

"I would just die if my child married a girl like that." Thus, the coffee table had a new load of grist for the mill.

The staff in the kitchen were not without comment either. The baker, who herself is very overspoken and outgoing, could not accept the fact that a woman could choose to keep her own name in today's society. And so began a series of arguments which went on for months about a woman and her right to maintain her maiden name.

One morning after a very heated argument on the subject, I was standing by the steam table. The baker was ready to leave work when Dorita entered the kitchen to pick up an order of ham and eggs. The baker railed at her, calling out in a loud voice, "I bet it's Flichauer on the church records." The baker retreated and slammed the door, thus ending the debate once and for all.

Working with Dorita was a real joy. She was very creative and always came up with challenging suggestions. The Medieval Feast and Follies was a gem of an idea and a great success, thanks to her hours of work. Designing dinner theatre menus, calligraphy, art work, you name it, she could do it all. Planning and executing a gourmet is seventy-five percent good food and twenty-five percent presentation. So whenever an event was about to begin in the Minniemashie Room, Dorita would burst into the kitchen and with a great sweep of her arms announce, "Al, it's showtime."

How true it is. I would whip off my apron, don my suit coat and tie, open the kitchen, and bowing low, while extending my hand to her, reply, "And the show must go on."

About thirty people were seated in the Minniemashie Room for this particular gourmet dinner. The wine and champagne had been served. The waitresses, all decked out in their long dresses, had finished serving the hors d'oeuvres and the Sesame Chicken in Cumberlin Sauce. The intermission was over and the guests were waiting for the final entree. Tonight we were featuring our famous American House Potato Balls, a house favorite for the past four years. They are made with mashed potatoes rolled up into balls about one inch in diameter. They are stuffed with cheese, rolled in egg and bread crumbs and deep fried. On cue, I'd run into the kitchen and call out to the cook, "Drop the balls." But today as the trays were being prepared and the girls were clearing the last round of dishes from the tables, the cook came running out instead.

"Al, Al, help! The balls, help! They blew up!"

I heard her panic from the lobby and hoped to heavens the guests hadn't heard it. "O.K. Take it easy. I'm coming," I cried. I rushed through the restaurant into the kitchen. The entire staff was standing around the deep fryer making all sorts of comments. I could hardly get through the throng.

When I finally worked my way up to the vat, there was nothing left but a layer of crumbs and bits of cheese floating on the top.

"I'm ready to serve them, Al," Dorita said in a frantic voice. "But what are we going to do. We can't serve them like that!"

"Relax. Get me your serving bowls," I commanded.

"I'm not going in there with those things," another waitress protested. I reached for the bowls while at the same time lifting the baskets of crumbs from the fryers.

"Listen, I will take care of it. Here, put some of the crumbs in each of the bowls. Where are your pinchers?" I called out to Dorita.

"You don't expect us to serve those things, do you Al?" she questioned.

After filling all the bowls with crumbs and bits of cheese, I headed for the Minniemashie Room telling the girls, "Follow me and when I finish, I want you to give some to every guest." My heart was in my throat as I entered the room. The music of Bach was playing softly and all eyes were on me. I felt that the guests were about to cry out,

"Where's our food?" I rang the Swedish dinner bell, which I always use to attract their attention, and suddenly the room was silent.

I placed the bell on the waitress stand and folded my hands. "Ladies and gentlemen, this is a first. Never before have our guests been so fortunate, or unfortunate as the case may be, to have such an unusual thing happen. To be honest with you, the American House Potato Balls blew up! But because they were so good, we want you to at least taste the crumbs!"

There was a sudden dramatic pause then suddenly the entire room was filled with applause and some of the guests even rose to give us a standing ovation. The crumbs were served. The show goes on.

Minnesota, A Winter Wonderland.

It was four o'clock on a Friday afternoon in early January. The sun had been obscured by the clouds all day and there was a feeling of dampness in the air. The customers in the restaurant were continually talking about the unusually warm January weather. Some said it looked like snow, but most discussed the weather just for the sake of discussion.

A customer entered from outside and said it was beginning to rain. The next report said it was getting colder and the rain was freezing as it hit the ground. We were just getting set up for the supper hour when the phone rang. Richard answered, "Palmer House, may I help you?"

"This is the Truckers Inn. Trucks are beginning to come in off the freeway. Drivers say the roads are really slippery. There are already cars in the ditches. Do you have any rooms available?"

"Sure, what do you need?" Richard asked.

"Just a single for tonight."

"O.K. I'll hold one for you."

As he hung up the telephone, four people entered the lobby and asked if we had any rooms. "Two doubles would do, preferably with bath." Richard smiled, and anticipating a rush on the rooms he decided to reserve one room with bath for someone perhaps more elderly. These young people could easily take a room on the top floor. They signed the registration form and Richard showed them to the third floor.

This was our first winter in the Palmer House and we had not yet begun to restore the rooms on the third floor. But they were clean, warm, and cheap. When Richard returned to the desk two more people were asking for rooms. "What is this, anyway?" he questioned.

"It's snowing so hard up by Alexandria the police are closing the freeway going north," one of the guests replied. "We counted twelve cars in the ditch so we took the first exit and called it quits."

"We have some very nice rooms," Richard said. "They don't have private baths, but the restrooms and shower room are just down the hall."

"Anything will be just fine. We don't want to get stuck out on the freeway," the gentleman replied. They signed the register and again Richard made the trek upstairs.

The phone rang and I answered it, "Palmer House, this is Al, may I help you?"

"This is Mary Kentwoods. I came to town today from Fargo and I think I would be stupid to try and get home tonight. I'll be busy for an hour or so, but I doubt if you'll have any rooms left by then. Have you looked outside lately? The snow is really coming down. If we should get a wind with this, it could be treacherous."

"Just a second." I laid the telephone down and headed for the lobby. Richard already looked harassed as he scurried behind the desk, filling out the registration cards and putting them in the respective room slots. "Richard, a Mary Kentwoods is on the phone and wants to reserve a room for tonight."

"Mary who?" he snapped.

"It's a lady from Fargo. She's on the phone now. Why don't you talk to her."

"Hello. Yes, I have one on the third floor but it's not very presentable. Part of the ceiling has come down, but it's clean." There was a slight pause and then Richard said, "O.K. I'll hold it for you, bye."

He hung up and turned to me. "Boy, is this going to be hectic if it keeps up."

The telephone continued to ring incessantly. "Hello Palmer House. "

"This is the Hillcrest Motel. Do you have any rooms left? We are booked solid."

"Yes, I have a few but they don't have baths," Richard replied. There was a slight pause, and then, "Send them down. I'll see what I can do."

The restaurant was also filling up with nervous and anxious travelers. The atmosphere felt electrically charged, as if it were about to explode. The radio had been turned on and everyone was listening for weather reports. "NO TRAVEL ADVISED," boomed the voice from the radio. "THE HIGHWAY PATROL HAS WARNED THAT THE SLEET AND SNOW HAS MADE THE HIGHWAYS IN CENTRAL MINNESOTA NEARLY IMPASSABLE. THE FREEWAY IS CLOSED FROM ALEXANDRIA NORTH AND NO TRAVEL IS ADVISED." This type of report naturally set the tone for the frantic conversation in the restaurant. The waiter and waitresses, the cook and the dishwasher kept running to the windows, peering out, and returning to the kitchen with reports of, "Golly, you can hardly see across the street. It's really snowing. And you should see how it's blowing." It all added to the frantic fever in the Palmer House.

In the lobby, people were still coming in off the highway. A young couple had just entered. They were wearing lightweight nylon jackets. They looked nearly frozen, shivering down to their toes. They offered more information. "It was so nice when we started from Fargo. We were hitchhiking to the Cities." Neither had enough money to take a room so we agreed to let them sit in the lobby till the storm subsided. From the looks of things outside that would not happen soon.

The crew in the kitchen remained very busy making sandwiches, dishing up soup, and filling dinner orders. The waitresses were trying to seat the customers and serve them as rapidly as possible. There seemed to be people everywhere.

It was 6:30 p.m. Someone had brought in a police scanner. It was broadcasting aloud in the lobby. It did little to calm people down, with its constant barrage of conversation as truckers still on the highway talked about the wind and snow.

Richard had rented just about everything rentable in the hotel except for the one room with a bath, which he was saving. Why, I will never know, but Richard often has shown a sixth sense when it comes to the hotel business.

A group of the younger people had gathered in the Minniemashie Room. One member of the group had his guitar with him, so a sing-a-long started up. They kept asking the waitresses for beer, wine, or anything to make it a full-fledged party.

The restaurant was overflowing and the novelty of the situation was wearing off for the waitresses. Some of the ladies offered to help make sandwiches in the kitchen. Everything was in a state of chaos.

The phone rang continuously with people and motels looking for more rooms. The pay phone in the lobby had a long waiting line, with stranded people trying to call home to tell their loved ones that they were safe. The scanner was screaming out distress signals and the radio blared cancellations and warnings. The lobby housed more than fifty people, all raising their voices to be heard over the din of the radio, the scanner, and each other. Richard hurried and scurried around, offering blankets to some of the older folks who would be staying in the lobby overnight.

It is raging outside and the snow is blowing furiously up and down Main Street. I cannot see the bank building across the street. The wind is from the northwest and the snow is drifting in between the cracks in the exit door of the Minniemashie Room. It is impossible to keep the room comfortable. Richard is still scurrying about, rounding up blankets and pillows from the various storerooms. In all the confusion someone is banging on the call bell at the front desk. "Just a minute. I'll be there shortly," Richard calls from the first floor landing.

We are running out of bread in the kitchen; we have already served some two hundred sandwiches. I call the bakery down the street one block away. As luck would have it, the baker is stranded in the shop. I ask if he has any bread available and if so can he bring some over to the Palmer House. "Yeah, if I can find my way," he replies. The storm is that severe.

The phone starts ringing again. It is Richard's mother asking for his father.

"No, I haven't seen him," I reply.

"My gosh," she said, "he left the house about a half hour ago. Where could he be?"

"It's so bad out, maybe he got lost," I answer. "I'll call the police department. Maybe he stopped to get warm." The temperature has started to drop and the wind chill is approaching fifty degrees below zero.

I call the police station.

The police officer informs me there is no sign of Fred, but there are approximately fifty people stranded in the city hall and they have no food. He asks if we can feed them at the Palmer House.

"Sure, but not right now. The restaurant is full. Maybe I can make a hot dish, a pot of soup, or something that would warm them up. When it's ready I'll call and you can send them over."

The hectic pace continues. Richard finally gets back behind the desk to take care of the man who was banging on the call bell. He is yet another truck driver. His truck is parked at a service station on the freeway. The police have given him a ride into town to look for accommodations, "Have you got a room?" he asks hopefully.

"We haven't got a thing left," Richard replies, obviously very tired and upset.

"Is there a couch or something I can lay down on? I've been up for two days and I'm completely exhausted."

Always the compassionate person, Richard enters the kitchen and asks me if I'd mind if he'd let the truck driver *crash* in his bed in our apartment for a couple of hours, since he is going to be on duty all night anyway. "No, I don't mind," I reply. It's clear every available space in the hotel is taken. Then I remember room seven, with bath. I ask Richard about putting the truck driver in there.

"No, I'm saving that. I just have a feeling." Richard replies.

He escorts the truck driver up to our apartment. When he returns downstairs, the phone is ringing, as usual. It is the police department. "Do you have any rooms left?" they question. "We have an older gentleman here who has kidney problems. He and his wife are on their way to Minneapolis for his weekly dialysis treatment, and there are no rooms or beds left at the local hospital."

"Yes, I have one room left. It has a bath and is on the first floor." Richard smiles. Once again his intuition pays off. He comes out to the kitchen to relay the story. He is glowing with self-satisfaction. After living with Richard for ten years, I still get a thrill when his face lights up as he knows he has made the right decision.

Suddenly Richard's father stumbles in. We are all thankful he has arrived safely. He is chilled to the bone trying to travel the three blocks from his home. His appearance reminds me to get food over to the people stranded at City Hall.

The evening wears on and more people continue to arrive. Some of them have began to bed down in the fireplace room. In the Minniemashie Room, the Christmas decorations are still up. Some ingenious individual has taken cotton from the decorations and stuffed it in the cracks around the west door. It helps keep the snow and the biting wind outside. One couple has placed six chairs, face to face, in a row and made a sort of couch to lie on, rather than make contact with the cold floor. There are three or four groups in the restaurant playing cards and getting very excited about their luck, both good and bad. In the lobby the lucky ones, who were able to land one of the old-fashioned benches, are snuggling down in their blankets and drifting off to sleep.

I have dismissed the staff and they have retired to a waitress's room on the top floor. One of the dishwashers had stashed and now retrieved a bottle of vodka. So now even they are ready for the "Blizzard of the Century."

The scanner is still beeping and the radio is still droning out the weather report, but the hectic pace begins to slow. The truck driver has finished his sleep in our apartment. He is sitting in the restaurant sipping a cup of coffee. Mary, from Fargo, is preparing a sandwich for him. She serves the sandwich and then sits down behind the counter to chat with the truck driver.

Richard begins turning off the lights. He dims the lobby and turns down the radio, in an attempt to calm the masses. He turns off the scanner, it was driving him up a tree. He has all the people and problems he can handle right here in the hotel.

I am bushed. It's late and I want to go to bed, but I am so wound up I know I can't sleep. The wind is still howling outside and even with the street lights on I can't see across the street.

The noise level has finally diminished. Snoring can be heard coming from the Minniemashie Room. There are giggles heard from some of the people on the benches in the lobby. Mary and the truck driver are sitting in the darkened restaurant, whispering and holding hands. Deep breathing, assorted moans and groans, and an occasional cry can be heard from the fireplace room.

Outside, a snowmobile roars down the main highway, probably on an errand of mercy. We have heard reports on the radio that the local snowmobile club has been rescuing stranded motorists.

I finally give in and go up to bed. I don't know whether or not the truck driver will be coming back to the apartment. I find out the next morning that he didn't. He had been invited to share Mary's room. I'm sure it was more comfortable.

Our apartment is on the north end of the building. I can hear the wind whine and feel the cold through the windows. We didn't get the storm windows on before this winter set in. There seems to be hundreds of them in the basement but the thought of carrying those oversized, heavy, old-fashioned storm windows up a ladder tall enough to reach the third floor is more than either Richard or I can bear.

It is hard to turn off my thoughts. I lie there thinking about all the people stranded in the hotel and wonder how long the storm will last. I guess I must have drifted off to sleep out of sheer exhaustion. It isn't long, however, before someone wakes me by licking my face. Thank God, it's Chris. He has to go out. I glance at the clock. 4:00 a.m. Not unusual. Chris keeps odd hours. I slip on my pants and slippers and head down the back stairs. Now the back stairs at the Palmer House are something else. They wind in a tight circle, and the steps are narrow on the inside and wider on the outside. Chris has a rough time descending them and so do I.

Opening the door to the hallway I hear the sound of breathing throughout the lobby and the banquet room and sense the smell of

human beings in the state of sleep. There is something heavy about
the smell of sleep. Chris heads for the front desk and nuzzles up to
Richard. He is seated on the stool with his brown corduroy coat pulled over his shoulders. A drunken gentleman is leaning over the desk
talking in a harsh whisper about the last snowstorm he had been in. I
call to Chris and let him out the door as quietly as possible. I don't
want to disturb any of the weary travelers sleeping in the lobby. He
stays outside only momentarily.

I turn from closing the door. I can see that Richard is bored to tears
by the earbanging he is receiving. I plan my rescue. "Richard, will
you help me in the kitchen, please?"

Richard breathes a sigh of relief, "Excuse me," he says. "My partner needs some help in the kitchen." As he enters the kitchen he tells
me he has been trapped behind the desk by the drunk for almost an
hour. Compassionate Richard; is there no end to his mercy?

We hear footsteps on the stairs and return to the lobby to see who
is up and about. It isn't the drunk. He has fallen asleep in one of the
lobby chairs. A waitress is coming down the stairs. "What are you
doing up at this hour?" I ask. "You have got to open the restaurant in
two hours."

"Well, we really haven't been sleeping. The dishwasher had a bottle of vodka and we have been having a party...."

At this point Richard enters the conversation with, "God, a chance
to sleep and they're having a party."

"But Richard, it's not our fault," she continues. "You should see it.
That lady from Fargo and that truck driver are carrying on, with the
door wide open. I think it's disgusting, but the others keep sneaking
down the hall to watch."

I take two and three steps at a time to get to the third floor. I can
now see what the waitress is talking about. I storm up to the open
doorway and explode, "At least you could close the damn door.
What you do is your business but you don't have to perform for the
entire hotel." She lay there with her new friend, the truck driver.
There they were. Together they were big as life but twice as natural. I
wondered how they would feel when they faced the staff in the morning...

Back downstairs, I started checking supplies in the kitchen. What do we have left for food? What can I make for a special? How are we going to feed all these people?

It was still snowing heavily and the wind seemed even stronger. Richard looked beat. I wanted him to try to get some sleep, now that I was awake. "No," he said, "I'm too excited to sleep. I want to stay with the desk and the registrations. We don't know how long the storm is going to last."

We went into the darkened restaurant, poured two cups of coffee, and sat down at the counter. He told me about an old man who had come in after I had gone to bed, who just had to have a room. Anything, just so he could get some sleep. Only a storage room was left and Richard didn't want to rent it. He believed that renting such a room could ruin our reputation. A reputation of being a comfortable, pleasant, restored hotel with reasonable rates. The old man was relentless in his insistence on needing a bed. He didn't care what the room looked like. Richard, against his better judgement, gave in and rented him room thirty-six. Now room thirty-six is an inside room without windows. Today it is actually illegal to rent an inside room. But this man created quite a disturbance. So Richard was relieved when he finally picked up the man's worn valise and headed him upstairs.

The next morning Mary from Fargo met the old man in the hallway.He was grumbling as he walked down the hall, "Flea bag hotel. Lousy room. No windows. Too hot. I couldn't turn down the heat. Couldn't sleep a wink."

Hearing his soliloquy, she replied, "Who Cares? Didn't get much sleep myself last night either."

Confusion is rampant downstairs this morning. The storm has not abated one iota. I still cannot see across the street. The radio is blaring out warnings and the scanner is again squealing and squawking. Richard is still on duty. He looks pretty rough — having been up all night — even though it is his normal shift. I'm sure it's all the hassling he put up with throughout the stormy night and again this morning. People haven't slept well. They are tired and irritable. Rendezvous have been missed, plans changed and appointments cancelled. Loved ones can't be located. They seem to be taking their frustrations out on Richard, as though the storm is all his fault. In spite of this, he stays up, helping throughout the day, going nearly forty-eight hours before finally retiring.

As I expected, the staff is practically worthless after partying most of the night. People in the restaurant are hungry and impatient, even though they know they can't go anywhere. Our truck driver is really making himself at home. He looks rested and well cared for. He and Mary sit by a window table and order steak and eggs for breakfast. He follows it with a couple bottles of beer. When he approaches the cash register he announces that he has left his wallet in the truck. He wants to know if he can charge his room and meals until he can get back to his truck and his money. What could I say? He has to eat. And, of course, he also wants to pick up Mary's ticket. Sure, fella.

There is one bar in town that is open and it's doing a land office business. A number of our stranded patrons have already found it. The snowmobilers are also using it to fortify themselves for the frightful outdoor conditions. There is a city ordinance that prohibits running snowmobiles on the city streets except under certain conditions. Apparently we are under those certain conditions. Supposedly they are on the lookout for stranded motorists and people who might be having a problem. I wonder how many they found in the bar. However, snowmobiles are the only vehicles able to move about, so today they are using Main Street.

We can't use the lobby's south exit. There is a six-foot drift blocking the door. The snow on the east side of the building has drifted so high that the parking meters can no longer be seen. Last night a station wagon stalled on the bridge which crosses Sauk River, two blocks to the north. The driver walked to safety but didn't notify anyone about his car. Snow drifted around and on top of it. Since there was no way to keep up with the drifting snow and intense wind, the snowplows had been taken off the streets. When they tried to reopen the road later in the day, they collided with a crystalized object. It was the stranded and now smashed station wagon.

People are always discussing weather. This day they had a reason. Some are still discussing it. Many are comparing it to the famous Armistice Day blizzard of nearly thirty years ago. The medias are already hyping it as the "blizzard of the century." I keep circulating among the tables, offering light conversation, reassurance, and general chit chat, trying to keep everyone somewhat content.

"Al, Al," the call comes from the kitchen.

"What is it now?" I answer as I head back with a bustray full of dirty dishes.

"We're out of milk and eggs and the orders are piling up. What are we going to do?" the cook asks.

He had been cooking all day yesterday and is now back on duty. He is a very tall, extremely thin young man. His longish blonde hair often hangs down over his eyes like a shaggy dog. He wears wire-framed glasses which slip down his nose, giving him the appearance of a worried school teacher. His grandmother has been a cook here since we bought the hotel. As business began to increase and we needed more help, she suggested hiring him. He had some cooking experience and appeared to be a good worker. We all liked him, but at eighteen his youthfulness often displayed itself in horseplay and tom-foolery. Regardless, he is a good cook and right now I was thankful that he was stranded in the storm. Otherwise, I would have had to do all the cooking for this restless bunch.

"Call Ken Mart, see if they are open," I answered. Ken Mart is a discount grocery store across Main Street and a very convenient place for us to pick up groceries when we run short. Our regular egg man lives out in the country and there was no telling when he would be able to get back into town.

"No answer at Ken Mart," one of the waitresses replies.

"Well, just tell the customers we are out of eggs," I said flippantly.

"You tell them yourself. Some of them have been waiting a half hour and I'm not going to have them yelling at me," came the response.

As a waitress this one is a little too outspoken and occasionally downright tactless. Many of our customers didn't like her and have made that point clear to both Richard and me. But we know she is loyal and dependable. And if one of the high school kids can't make it to work, we can call her at the last minute, She has never let us down. Occasionally her temper flares. When it does, she gets tongue-tied and her face goes from very red to a dead white, almost simultaneously, like right now for instance.

She has a sixth sense about tipping. She can spot a tourist or a big tipper almost as soon as they enter the lobby. I like to watch her cleverly manipulate a new waitress when the restaurant gets busy.

"You take the four at the pole table and I'll take the table by the window." The new girl is unaware of the local poor-tipping custom.

As I head back into the confusion of the restaurant I can still hear her complaining, "All those customers can do today is bitch, bitch, bitch." I know it's going to be a bad day.

Richard is busy busing tables and explaining to the customers that we are running short of food. The storm has caught us off guard and our supply is diminishing. The phone rings and I hurry over to answer, "Palmer House."

"City Hall here" comes the reply. "How are you fixed for feeding about fifty people this noon? We have no supplies here and they haven't eaten since last night. We can string a rope over to the Palmer House so they don't get lost in the blinding snow."

I stop to think for a minute, then answer, "Why don't I prepare a hamburger hot-dish and cole-slaw and call you when it's ready. The restaurant is full right now. I don't know how many we have in the hotel but it's close to two hundred." My mind is scrambling around trying to think of ways to prepare the food we do not have for people we do not know.

"O.K., we'll wait for your call."

I hung up and explained the situation to Richard, who was now helping the dishwasher catch up on the dishes. "I hope they aren't as bitchy as the people here," he replied. I could tell he was getting very tired, but he refused to give in and go to bed.

"Richard, Richard," a voice rang through the restaurant and into the kitchen, "someone's at the front desk."

"Jesus Christ," he muttered, "I just left the desk." He grabbed a tray of cups and headed back into the restaurant. There was a line at the till so he stopped and started taking money from the customers who had already eaten. "We need to keep everything moving — a lot of people are waiting in the lobby to get into the restaurant," he shouted.

It was a typical situation. It seems whenever one person stands up to pay a bill everyone follows. Many-a-time a waitress will have an order up in the kitchen, but will get stuck at the till. She had planned to help one person but the line never ends. Meanwhile, the food is getting cold, the cook is banging on the bell, and customers are growing more irritated.

All day long the storm rages. Some of the guests busy themselves with cards, while others sing in the Minniemashie Room. The faces change but the singing goes on. Others remain in their rooms, taking advantage of the privacy. But many are bound and determined to sit in the lobby and bitch.

The forty or so people from city hall have arrived by following a rope which a police officer has tied to the Palmer House. Holding onto the rope they have all made the trip safely. Fortunately the restaurant has emptied out sufficiently to accommodate them. I have prepared a hot dish for them, but naturally they look at our extensive menu and start ordering Reubens, hamburgers, hot beefs and other sundry items. It keeps the kitchen hopping just telling them that this isn't build-your-own-sandwich day.

Several of the people who had crossed the street to the bar wander back to the hotel. They seem well on their way to putting the worries on hold. They are hungry and need food to sober up, so the action starts anew.

The weather reports are not very encouraging, although it does sound like the snow is letting up somewhat. I can now get an occasional glimpse of the bank across the street. This seems to be a sign for our anxious lobby guests to renew their restlessness. The group paces from window to window, peering out and discussing, what else, but the weather.

Our truck driver friend has returned from across the street and is fairly well-lubricated. He is in a very spendy mood. He orders steaks for himself and a new found playmate. Richard and I both wonder, if he doesn't have money to pay for his food and lodging, what is he using to pay for the drinks? Hmmm.

"Hope he doesn't run out on us," Richard whispers.

A young man who was fortunate enough to get a room last night approaches Richard and says he doesn't have enough money to pay for his room and food. He explains to Richard that his dad is a highway patrolman and will send a check. In fact, his dad is on the pay phone in the lobby, waiting for the innkeeper, so that he can reassure him that he will cover any charges his son incurrs. "Aha. We do have some honest people and concerned guests," remarks Richard as he picks up the pay phone.

Over the scanner comes the news that a number of people are stranded at the Armory, which is only three blocks away. There's no food at the Armory and we're the closest restaurant. "I hope they like hamburger hot dish, 'cuz that's what's available right now."

The grateful elderly couple in room seven are a joy to be with. Richard has taken meals and coffee to their room. Here is a real gentleman. Stranded in a blizzard, in dire need of kidney dialysis, and still cheerful. We have found a bottle for him to measure his urine output. He will need that information if or when he gets to the hospital. The police officer stops in periodically to check on his condition and is informed of the situation. He agrees to have an escort ready for them as soon as the roads are passable. It looks like that will be tomorrow morning at the earliest. "Why can't more people be as appreciative as they are?" Richard remarks.

Suddenly the people in the lobby quiet down. They are listening intently to the scanner. One trucker, out on the freeway, did not heed the police warning about the freeway being closed and tried to make it through. He jackknifed his truck at mile marker 150 and is pinned in the cab. The police are trying to direct the snowmobile rescue workers to the trucker's location. Some of the rescue team have gotten lost in the blinding snow. They are now making a second attempt to find the trapped trucker. It gives our stranded guests something to think about. They are safe and warm and at this moment, hopefully thankful. Someone starts a spontaneous sing-a-long and everyone joins in.

Our guests have now been together for over twenty-four hours. The idea of the great blizzard is getting less and less glamorous. People are becoming more and more irritable. With no let-up in sight, *cabin fever* is settling in. Even the bar scene becomes boring when there is nothing else to do. Our staff is also becoming weary. There is no relief in sight for them; they are trapped at the hotel and the relief crew is trapped at home. Richard has been up over thirty-six hours at this point but he doesn't want to miss anything, so he keeps on going.

The latest weather forecast reports the winds should be dying down toward evening. If this happens, the snowplows will try to get at least an emergency route cleared to the freeway. The freeway will be opened by early morning. What good news! Some of the people start getting their suitcases and placing them near the door in anticipation of leaving early. However there have been times, here in the Midwest, when once the eye of the storm has passed over and all seems calm, the storm will suddenly intensify as the back side of the whirling cloud mass passes through.

Richard has gone into the kitchen. More of the bar crowd is returning and they are all hungry. I follow him, hoping to convince him to take a break upstairs. He is on his last leg. He has gone in one door and out the other, and when I finally catch up with him he is quietly talking with some of the hitchhikers. They are broke and getting very hungry. Could they please charge some food and send us the money when they get home? I know when he gets around to asking my opinion, I'll say yes. Remember, this was our first business and our first year in business, so we just naturally trusted everyone. How quickly one wakes up.

A happy thought passes through my brain: Wouldn't it be great to have the hotel full like this all the time? Then maybe we could afford to do some of the necessary room restoration. But that's after the new water heater, the new faucets, the new drains in the basement, and on and on and on.

I knew who it was when the phone started ringing. My sixth sense said it was Mathew, the night clerk, and he won't be able to make it to work on Sunday. How right I am. Richard always works the Friday and Saturday night shift but it will be impossible for him to keep going through Sunday. If he makes it through tonight's shift, he will be forty-eight hours without sleep. We just have to wait and see what tomorrow brings. Relief from the storm, I hope!

Our guests are now wearing on each others' nerves. However, for us the crowd does seem easier to handle on the second night of their captivity. They are cranky but tired and they just want to go to sleep, any place, any place at all. Many of them have now completed their phone calls and they know that they and their families are safe. The newness and the excitement has definitely worn off. Everyone, Richard and I included, just want it to be over.

Sure enough, by daylight the next morning, the storm has subsided. Now comes the task of burrowing out. Richard has tried to keep the steps shoveled during the night but it was impossible. Big drifts have packed hard and high across both doors. The guests are concerned about their cars: would they start after the bitter cold? The police call and inform us there is one lane cleared on the freeway and that the highway patrol is coming to escort our ailing gentleman and his wife to a hospital in the Twin Cities.

Several guests shovel out the couple's car, others get it running. And with a great deal of thanks to everyone, they are the first to leave. We all stand by wishing them well. It is quite a sight, as the flashing red light on the top of the patrol car, signaling its errand of mercy, heads south on Main Street followed by one lone car.

Everyone who can get into the lobby is waving good-bye and calling good luck. The understanding and patient endurance of the couple has impressed us all into a momentary silence. As the flashing red light fades, guests resume talking, already referring to the big blizzard in the past tense. The *Blizzard of the Century* has gone down in the annals of history, and the Palmer House has been freed to continue its' quest to re-capture the past.

"Listen, I Need A Job!"

(Part II)

O ne Saturday morning I received a very urgent phone call. "Hello, Al? This is Jeffery." His voice was all broken up and it sounded like he had been, or still was, crying.

"Yes, Jeffery, what is it? What's the matter?"

"Can I please come up and talk to you? It is very important."

"Well, certainly. Come right on over." Merlin had heard my end of the conversation.

"What's wrong?"

"I don't know, but he is sure upset about something. We'll see. He's coming right over." The phone rang again, which startled me since I was standing right beside it.

"Hello, Palmer House. May I help you?"

"Could you tell me the soup of the day?" There she was, the faceless soup lady, right on schedule.

"Bean with bacon," I announced. That voice was driving me crazy. What soup was she looking for? As I hung up the phone, Jeffery entered through the back door. I could see he had been crying, his eyes were all red and puffy. "Come with me, Jeffery. We can go into the Kennicott Room. Would you like some coffee?"

"No, that's all right."

As I grabbed my coffee and cigarettes, and headed through the door I almost ran over two ladies standing in the back hallway waiting to use the restroom. "Oh, excuse me," I apologized as I passed on by. I have always worried about that door and the small hall by the restrooms. Some day someone is going to get clobbered, but it hasn't happened to me yet, so I haven't fixed it.

I sat down in the Kennicott Room. Jeffery started pacing back and forth in front of me.

"My mother just called," he blurted. "Dad was severely injured in a fire he was fighting. He is in the hospital." He began to cry in earnest now, so I stood up and put my arm around him, trying in some way to comfort him. "She wants me to come home as soon as I can, but I told her I don't have the money."

"Well, don't let that bother you. I'm sure we can work something out."

He slowly began to regain his composure as he spoke, "All I need is fifty dollars for gas money. I can make it on that."

"You mean you plan on driving to Atlanta? Why, that will take three days and you might be too late if your dad is that badly hurt. Why don't you fly down? I'm sure your mother needs you today, not three days from now."

"But where would I get the money?"

"Richard and I can loan you enough to fly down. He is sleeping now, but I know he would vote in favor under these circumstances. Let me call the airlines and find out the cost to Atlanta."

"But Al, you two have been too good to me already. You don't have to do that much. All I need is fifty dollars and I can drive home."

I didn't listen to him. I went directly to the telephone. "Could you give me the number of Eastern Airlines, please?" "Yes, reservation desk? Could you tell me if you have any flights to Atlanta this afternoon or evening?" "5:15 p.m. Great! Would you have one seat available for that flight...? What is the fare one-way?... $125.00... Fine, would you reserve that space for Mr. Jeffery Murdock. He will pick up his ticket at the airport. Thank you. Good bye."

"Well, Jeffery," I said. "It's all set. You will be home this evening."

"But Al, I could just as well drive home."

"Nonsense. I'll run upstairs and get $150.00. That should be enough to cover the flight and expenses. You can pay us back later." I headed up to the apartment and very quietly got the money. I didn't want to disturb Richard, since he had worked all night. When I returned, Jeffery was in the restaurant talking quietly with Merlin.

"Here you go. Now get your things together and make sure you pick up your ticket thirty minutes before the 5:15 flight."

Jeffery took the money and firmly shook my hand. Merlin gave him an automatic handshake and he was out the back door. I stood by Merlin for a few moments contemplating what I had just done, and hoped that Richard would approve. I slowly spoke out loud, but actually I was only thinking to myself. "Golly, I hope I did the right thing and he doesn't run off with the money!"

Merlin looked up at me with a very compassionate smile and said, "Al, if we can't trust Jeffery, who can we trust?"

Obviously not Jeffery. He was never heard from again.

The Abortion.

It was late fall in 1975. I was given two ounces of real sourdough from a famous San Francisco restaurant. My friend commented that it was something I might enjoy working with since I was always looking for unique dishes to serve in the Minniemashie Room. The dough came complete with a set of "care and feeding instructions." It was the beginning of a Palmer House tradition which prevails to this day. The dishwashers were put in charge of the babies, our jars of sourdough. I say jars, because that two ounce sample has grown and multiplied to fill six wide-mouth half gallon jars, enough to make a batch of fifty biscuits.

We first began using sourdough at our gourmet dinners. Nancy, who was only a sophomore in high school when she started at the Palmer House, is in charge of making the biscuits. I remember one day of such preparation.

"I am sick and tired of making plain old sourdough biscuits." Nancy said. "Can't I try something new?"

"What would you do to make them different?"

"I was thinking, we could add frozen blueberries," she responded. It sounded like a good idea so I told her to go ahead.

Nancy is a natural born cook. She is tall and very thin, and goes about her work in the kitchen with enthusiastic speed. She talks very fast and is forever putting her foot in her mouth. Maybe that's why she is so thin. Her creativity, however, has led to some very exciting innovations not only at the Gourmets, but in the restaurant cooking too. Her blueberry sourdough biscuits were an immediate hit among our guests.

The first time they were served one of our guests was so impressed that she wanted to buy some starter to take home to make biscuits and pancakes for her family. I found a jar and proceeded to type out the instructions for the "care and feeding" of the baby. She was delighted and carefully carried her new-found treasure out to the car and back to Minneapolis.

Meanwhile, the Palmer House continued to move through a rather slow winter. Richard continued to strip the woodwork on the second floor, and I was busy picking out and hanging wallpaper for the various rooms which we were restoring. Richard worked eight to ten hours a day, in his grubby old clothes. He was surrounded by the smell of ZipStrip. Many times the fumes gave him a terrific headache, and I believe an occasional trip without leaving the Palmer House.

Winter is the only time we can accomplish what needs to be done to reach our goal of complete restoration. We have electricians, plumbers and carpenters running all over the place. It is a down time for them. We have to squeeze our work in before spring. Come spring, it is impossible to get anyone to work inside. Thus, the dust flies, the paint flies, and before we know it, winter flies. Spring is here and with it the welcome tourists start arriving.

One Saturday morning I entered the restaurant and, lo, who should I see but the Sourdough Lady from Minneapolis. "Al, Al," she cried out to me, "come over here. Have I got a sad tale to tell you." I poured myself a cup of coffee, and sat down to listen to her sad story.

She had left here last fall, all excited about her new-found kitchen delight.

"Right after I got home," she said, "I fed the babies, let them go for two days, and then fed them again until I had enough dough to make pancakes. They were a big hit, so I fed the babies again and let them set for another few days. When they grew enough, I put the dough in two jars and fed them some more. The next day we had sourdough biscuits. I even added blueberries according to your instructions. The feast of sourdough went on through most of the holiday season and I continued to feed the babies every other day. One time after Christmas I had to leave for a few days so I even made arrangements for my mother to come in and feed the babies. When I got back, we again feasted on all sorts of sourdough creations. During February, my dad was taken quite ill and I found myself running back and forth between the hospital and the house. Occasionally I would wake up in the middle of the night, wondering if the babies had been fed. I would get out of bed, put on my robe and plod down to the kitchen to see that they had been cared for. This went on for several months. Then, one night I woke up out of a sound sleep with sourdough on my mind. I had had it. I couldn't work, keep house, worry about Dad and the babies too. So in a fit of anger, I went downstairs, opened the refrigerator, took out the four jars of sourdough, and tossed them in the garbage." There was a long pause and the most saddened expression on her face. "Do you know what?" I waited for her answer. "I feel guilty. I feel as though I have aborted the babies."

Our babies at the Palmer House are alive and well. In ten years they have lived through the diabetes crisis, when one of our cooks fed them with one cup of sugar and one-quarter cup of flour, instead of the reverse. Another time a dishwasher spilled the entire tray of jars trying to carry all of them from the walk-in cooler to the baker's table. Five of the jars were destroyed, but one remained intact. From it we rebuilt our supply of sourdough. And to this day, we still feature blueberry sourdough biscuits.

Knockdown, Drag Out!

W hen the emergency buzzer screamed out in the middle of the night, we nearly hit the ceiling. It was the first time we heard it go off since we had purchased the hotel. Nothing is so earthshaking as the sound of that emergency bell. Every night when we retire we always tell the night clerk if anything should happen — fire, robbery, a recalitrant drunk, anything — do not hesitate to push the emergency button. All thoughts and fears rushed through our minds as we tried to get our pants on and get down the stairs to the lobby as quickly as possible. We stumbled around in the dark, looking for the light switch. The dog, who was also rudely awakened, began barking, a sharp, incessant bark which added even more to the confusion in the dark apartment.

Finally, half asleep and half naked, Richard and I stumbled into the hallway and down the stairs to the first landing. The noise was deafening. The shouting of obscenities, the high-pitched screaming of girls filled with fear, the loud thud of bodies being hurled against the floor, and the benches collapsing.

My first glimpse of the emergency was hindered for I had to duck as the old fashioned lamp which had been sitting on the front desk came whirling past my head and smashed against the wall beside me. There we were, Richard and I, standing at the top of the stairs overlooking our first knockdown, drag out fight right there before our eyes in living color in the lobby of our beloved Palmer House. I recall my very first thoughts, "My God, It looks like the first scene from a grade B western movie, and me without my camera."

The night clerk lay huddled in the corner behind the front desk. There were ten to fifteen people swinging and hitting one another, some on the floor, some being thrown against the desk. I could see one of our waitresses leaning over and shaking a young man on the floor. He had blood running from his nose and mouth. Her hair was scraggling all over her face and part of her skirt was torn. Three or four other women were screaming and yelling, trying to pull their men apart, or off one another. Suddenly, the east door burst open and in came the local police, which seemed only to agitate the melee. Their shouting added to the noise and as the police, two of them, drew their night sticks, they hollered for the fighters to stop. We did not dare to come down the stairs. The fighters were so crazed that they didn't seem to care who they were attacking. I recognized some of the combatants as part of the construction crew who were staying upstairs in room fifteen. Others I recognized as local men who frequented the Short Stop Bar. It seemed like an eternity before the officers got the fight calmed down. They ended it by dragging several of the local boys and the construction workers out the door. When the fracus finally subsided, Richard and I descended the stairs and tried to find out what happened.

Now, Matthew, our night clerk, is a very tiny man, a retired preacher. It took two cups of coffee and about five minutes of sitting him down before he was coherent. He was still visibly shaken as he began to tell us what happened. "The crew in room fifteen had come into the hotel after the bars had closed. Oh, I'd say about 1:15. They all said goodnight and went upstairs. None of them seemed drunk or out of line. In fact, this was one of the best crews I have ever seen in the hotel for a long time. As you know, I have been night clerk here for almost five years even before you boys ever bought the Palmer House. So, I went back to reading my Bible, I'm in my tenth reading. I was just beginning to read the second chapter of Ruth, or was it Samuel, no, I think it was Ruth. Oh, I really can't remember. I am so shaken up."

"What difference does it make?" Richard responded rather rudely, "Go on, tell us what happened!"

"Well," Matthew continued, "I heard some people enter from the Lewis Door, that's the south exit you know, so I glanced up to look into the mirror. Of course you know that's not there anymore either.

"Ah yes," I replied, remembering that there used to be a large three-foot mirror above the east exit, adjusted so that the person on the desk could identify anyone entering from the South. It was a good safety feature till we took it down one day for painting and it got broken. Hmmmmmmmm, seven years of bad luck, huh?"

"I didn't recognize any of them," Matthew said, "but I could tell they had been drinking. They came up to the front desk and demanded to know 'What rooms are those SOB's from the road gang in?' I told them they were all upstairs and asleep by now and I couldn't let them upstairs. 'We'll find the bastards ourselves,' they said and the three of them started up the stairs three at a time, making all sorts of noise."

"Why didn't you call us then?" I interrupted. "You knew there was going to be trouble."

"Well, I figured they wouldn't find the room they were in and would come back down. I suppose I should have called you. Then shortly after they ran upstairs, a bunch of girls came into the lobby hollering and screaming looking for the guys. I didn't know what to do. It all happened too fast. Then, before I knew it, some of the last guys to go upstairs came running down shouting, 'they're coming, they're coming! They're gonna meet us outside.' Just then, three of the construction guys started down the stairs with just their pants on, no shoes, no shirts, hollering, 'we'll show those locals a thing or two, we'll take 'em on outside and beat the shit out ov 'em.' Of course you know I don't swear. I'm just merely reporting. 'Like hell you will,' one of the guys at the bottom of the stairs shouted and he jumped right up the stairway and grabbed the first guy coming down. They rolled down the stairs the rest of the way and they were pounding each other like they was going to kill one another. That's when I pushed the buzzer and I called the police. It wasn't long before they were all at it and the girls were fighting and pulling hair, and the furniture started flying and I ducked behind the desk." He was clutching the Bible all the while he was recalling the incident and now he laid it down and took another sip of coffee.

The foreman of the construction crew, who was fully dressed and apparently had not been involved in the fight, had been standing near us throughout the whole story. "I feel really bad about this, but I am sure my boys didn't start it," he said. "They have been a real good bunch all summer."

We could see he was concerned. He appeared to be about twenty-seven, tall and ruggedly built from working outdoors most of his life. He was not your typical foreman.

"I heard some loud noise in the hall," he continued, "so I got up to see if my men were involved. All I saw was three guys headed down the hall and then they banged on the door. In fact, I thought they would break it down. Then one of them shouted, 'You sons of bitches been fooling around with our gals. Get your asses out here or we'll break the damn door down.' That's when I started to get dressed. As I closed my door and turned on the light, I heard John's voice, that's one of my men, say 'OK. We'll fight you guys but we didn't touch your damn women. We'll meet you outside.' Then a lot of angry voices rushed past my door and ran down the stairs. Before I could get dressed, I heard my men pass by too. I heard them say 'make sure you wait till you get outside. No messing around in the hotel.' So the locals must have jumped my men in the lobby."

As we reconstructed the story, a couple of the girls who had been involved, so to speak, were in the corner of the lobby. While we waited for the police to return one of the girls came over. "You know what started all this, don't you?"

"No, not really," I replied.

"Well, we girls were out on the town to celebrate Faye's getting married this week. We were all in the Sportsman Bar playing pool and having a good time kidding around with the construction crew. Nothing serious, just having a good time. After the bar closed, they went back to the hotel. Our guys had been out to New Munich and Greenwald and then they met us at the Hi-Ho. One of the girls was carrying on about the cute construction guys she had been 'fooling around with all evening.' She said it to tease her man, but he got furious and told the other guys he was going to get those 'pricks.' And before we knew it all the guys had piled into one car and were headed for the Palmer House. We girls knew they were all drunked-up and were just itching for a fight so we headed downtown also.

Well, we got here just as the guys from upstairs were coming down and wham, that's when it all started."

Just then the door opened and the police came in along with two of the construction crew. "The rest are cooling their heels in the slammer. They'll sleep it off and everything will be alright in the morning. How much damage was done?"

"Not too much physically," Richard replied. "Just the desk lamp, and some shattered nerves. I think things have calmed down now. Matthew, do you want to work the remainder of your shift tonight?"

"Yes, I think I will be alright now," he replied.

The hotel guests headed up the stairs. One of the men turned and said, "Real sorry about this. I assure you it won't happen again."

Richard looked up the stairs. "Don't feel too bad about it. We know the local hoods are hot heads. When they get to drinking, they are always looking for a fight. Good night now."

As the lobby cleared out and our nerves began to calm, Richard and I headed for bed. I can still hear that buzzer ringing in my ears. Even though we were not in the fight, we both felt knocked down and dragged out.

Got A Coupon, Smoke A Camel!

"When the hell did you start smoking Camel filters?" I asked Jim as I bummed a cigarette at the counter. Jim is one of our residents, a gentleman who moved in about five years ago. He is originally from Melrose, a town ten miles south of Sauk Centre. He had been a carpenter all his life, spending most of it in Kansas City. He retired here after being beaten up there.

He is a philosopher. He has an opinion on anything and everything. Sundays, when I am sitting alone and Merlin has gone for dinner, Jim would quietly come down the stairs carrying a glass of brandy. He and I would mix it with ice and Bubble Up and share.

"The King is still sleeping, I presume," he commented, referring to Richard, knowing full-well that Richard despises my drinking.

Our conversations would range from the latest battle to the time he and his buddies spent a night in a whorehouse in Kansas City. He was hard of hearing and talked very loud, which was disturbing to most people, but on Sundays when he and I would sit at the counter, I was never offended by the loudness of his voice.

I would tell Jim many of my frustrations during the week and he would listen and return with such wonderful answers like, "Piss on them, they are not worth losing sleep over."

"How come you are smoking Camel filters?" I asked once again.

"Got 'em with a coupon," was his reply.

I proceeded to show him a bunch of Xeroxed jokes one of the girls had brought in for the staff to look at Jim laughed at each one and then proceeded to tell me a portion of the many jokes he had heard during his past fifty years.

He had served in the second World War and although he appeared tough, and was occasionally crude, he was in fact an extremely sensitive person.

I remember a war story he told one Sunday afternoon. They had just liberated a town. And after the battle, they had parked their tank for a picnic lunch consisting of cold K-rations. One of the soldiers noted that it was Thanksgiving Day. They were joking about their plight, hiding their misery behind a mask of laughter, when there was a knock on the tank. A farmer spoke anxiously in his native tongue. He gestured frantically, trying to get his message through to the combat veterans. Eventually the soldiers realized that he was inviting them to a feast. They entered the village to join the farmer and his family in a bountiful dinner. Without the bond of a common language, the soldier and the family communicated with eyes and actions the feelings of a peaceful and united Thanksgiving.

Jim was full of stories and I was like a little child sitting at his feet. I will never forget the Jims who make up our society — never in the news, never on radio or television, but still a big part of our world. There is meaning to their life and a message in their words, if only we take the time to listen to them.

I am typing this while sitting in the lobby on a cold and snowy Sunday, listening to a Beethoven sonata broadcast by National Public Radio. It is my only alternative to the present BOOM-BOOM trend of music. Merlin is upstairs in bed, trying to get rid of a cold. He has taken all sorts of pills and over-the-counter cure-alls which I think finally have got the best of him.

"Thank you for the drink, Jim," I said as he ascended the stairs to room twenty-five. He nodded. "Catch you later," I called after him. "And thank you for the memories."

It's A Matter Of Public Safety!

SIXTEEN DIE IN BRECKENRIDGE HOTEL FIRE!!! Screamed the headlines in the local newspaper. It was not only a tragedy for the hotel and the families involved, but a horrible thought for any owner of any hotel. "I stayed in that hotel years ago," Richard remarked as he read the copy.

"So have I," I answered. "Back in the '60's."

The headline really struck home because we in fact live in an old hotel. We are concerned about the possibilities of fire. We have installed a fire safety system in the kitchen and placed emergency lights strategically throughout the hotel.

"There must be something more we can do to protect our building and the occupants," Richard remarked.

"We could install a sprinkler system like they did at the Anderson

House a couple of years ago," I offered.

"Why don't you call John in Wabasha and ask him who he had install his system?" I could tell Richard was very serious.

"But Richard," I interjected, "it will cost a mint. Where will we find the money? We're living hand-to-mouth right now." It was strange because normally it is Richard who is concerned about balancing the checkbook.

"Well, it doesn't cost anything to make some inquiries," he answered.

One week later, a representative from Valley Builders and Piping Corporation arrived at our front desk. He was a very tall and assertive person with a wide smile and easy manner. We both felt very much at ease with him.

"John from the Anderson House mentioned that you might be considering a sprinkler system," he stated.

"Well," Richard said, "we are concerned about safety, and we haven't got much money — but I bet you hear that all the time."

He smiled. "Well, for what it is worth," he began as he looked around the lobby, " you can usually pay for it by your savings in insurance premiums. Gee, but you have a lovely old building here. They don't make them like this anymore."

"I understand that you specialize in putting sprinkler systems in older buildings so that they blend into the character of the structure itself," I stated.

"Well," he answered, "if you ever get down to the Anderson House you can see for yourself how well it fits in with their decor."

"When do we ever get away?" Richard snorted, then asked, "Would you like a tour?"

"Sure," he replied.

He spent most of the day talking and taking notes and making little drawings on a note pad. "Let me take this back to the office and discuss it with my partner. I will get back to you with some ballpark figures within the next week." He was finished with his coffee but his pen was still working.

"Can you give us some idea so we can lose some sleep over it this weekend?" Richard chuckled.

"Oh, I'd say you'd be talking in the neighborhood of forty to fifty thousand for the system. Plus a new water main from the street. That might run you another five or six thousand. Plus the electrical hookup to the control system for another four or five thousand. I'd say roughly sixty to seventy thousand, give or take a thousand or so." We both gasped. We had no idea from where the money would come. "But don't worry," he concluded. "I'll get back with some meaningful figures by next week."

"Real glad you could come up," I said, extending my hand to shake his.

"Why not? Why should you pay the bank thirteen or fourteen per-cent interest? I don't need the money and I will split the interest payments with your sister." He was now talking directly to Richard.

"I can see you are," he smiled, knowing full well he had hit us over the head with a financial bombshell.

"Yeah, nice meeting you," Richard added as we walked him to the door.

We watched him leave and as we walked back to the desk, Richard said. "It isn't a matter of the money. It's a matter of safety."

But I was thinking. "Seventy thousand dollars!" My god, that seemed like an insurmountable amount of money to me. Especially after all the money we had been spending just to repair the old building. All capital funds were spent. "We could go to the bank," I offered, but I knew that they would want us to refinance the entire mortgage, and we'd have to give up our seven percent interest. We were both sort of commiserating out loud.

The next day when the **Daily Times** arrived I received another shock. Our favorite get-a-way, The Hotel St. Germain, was being closed. It was just another in the latest list of the classic old hotels to be condemned, closed, or destroyed by someone or something. This one was condemned by the state fire marshall. It was hard for us to imagine, for we had just spent New Year's Eve at the St. Germain.

We noticed it had more safety features than most of the large high-rise hotels in the Twin Cities. But, there it was on the front page with a large picture of the fire marshall doing his duty.

"Richard, the fire marshall is closing the Germain," I reported shoving the evening paper in front of his nose.

"What next?" he said. "There won't be a moderate-priced place to stay anymore."

"Yeah," I interjected, "what will the typical family do when they visit a city where they don't have relatives? How many people can afford fifty to sixty-five dollars a night just to sleep? Besides I wouldn't be caught dead in some of those new plywood and plastic jobs. There is no charm or elegance or history in them."

Richard and I had always been lovers of the old mansions, old hotels and ancient movie palaces. There was the Hotel Duluth with its ornate lobby, or even the Hotel Powers in Fargo, a simple but homey hotel where one could stay at a reasonable rate.

Richard's father tuned in to our turmoil during the following week. He had grown to love the Palmer House as much as we did. The hours he'd spent working here made it imperative to him also that it not be condemned or destroyed.

"I've been thinking," he began.

"Yes, Fred, what have you been thinking?" My remark was prompted by the fact that whenever he began a sentence with 'I've been thinking it meant that a new idea to promote the hotel was to be soon forthcoming.

"You guys need a sprinkler system, right?"

"Wrong," Richard said. "It isn't even required by the state."

"Wait and listen to what I have to say," he interrupted. "I had a talk with Terry last week when he was here and I think you should install the system."

"But think of the money," Richard interrupted.

"I am," Fred answered, raising his voice. "Look, I've got enough money from the farm tied up in C.D.'s that would pay for it. You could pay me back later and you wouldn't have to pay a ridiculous rate of interest."

"NO," I interjected. "We will do it on our own."

"NOW DON'T BE FOOLISH!"

Here we go again. We can never have a conversation with Fred without somebody blowing up, usually me.

"LISTEN TO ME A MINUTE," he demanded. We both shut up and listened.

"Install the system, I will pay for it with a loan to you and you can pay me off over the next few years. It's as simple as that."

"But that's not simple, Fred," I said. "Why should you take your money and invest it in the Palmer House?"

"Why not? Why should you pay the bank thirteen or fourteen percent interest? I don't need the money and I will split the interest payments with your sister." He was now talking directly to Richard.

The next week the contract for the sprinkler system was signed. And the following weeks marked the most hectic we have seen in the Palmer House. Pipes here, pipes there. Saws here, saws there. Grease here, grease there. Workers here, workers there. Beer bottles here, beer bottles there. Noise, pounding, sawing, hammering. We thought the system would never get installed. Outside, Main Street was blocked off for the digging of the water main. Holes were drilled. Walls were bored. Mud was tramped in and out, up and down. Grease, mud, noise, hammers, saws and sprinklers.

One could not walk through the lobby without stepping over pipes or gear. "What are you doing here?" was the question of the day. Thank heaven much of the work was done at night after the restaurant was closed. But still neither of us had any idea of the size of the project we had undertaken.

The telephone was ringing as I came down the stairs. "Good morning, Palmer House. May I help you?"

"Yes, I would like to speak with the owner or manager please." The voice was calm and very resonant.

"This is one of the owners," I answered.

"My name is Torbert Bybolte and I represent the State Fire Marshalls office."

"Yes," I answered, "I recognize your name. You were recently on the front page of the **Daily Times**, condemning the St. Germain Hotel."

"I see my fame has preceded me," he laughed. I did not laugh, I could not see anything funny.

"What can I do for you?" I asked matter-of-factly.

"I would like to make an appointment to inspect the Palmer House next Wednesday, if that would be convenient for you?"

"Well, let me check the book." I grabbed the appointment book to see if we had any parties or luncheons scheduled.

"The calendar looks okay at the present time," I replied.

"Good, then I will see you next Wednesday. Let's say about one-thirty?"

"I guess it will have to be," I replied. "Thank you very much. Good bye." CLICK.

I held the receiver in my hand for quite a while trying to recall the entire conversation. Why, I thought to myself, after seventeen years, would the fire marshall decide to inspect this hotel. We had to ask for an inspection before we bought the place and we have a written letter stating there were no violations against the building as of the day we purchased the property. Why now, with the sprinkler system almost installed, would someone suddenly decide to inspect? I hung up the telephone. I couldn't wait for Richard to get up.

"Richard, Richard, wake up. You'll never guess who was just on the telephone."

"What...who... What time is it?"

"A little after nine. Are you awake? The fire marshall just called. You know, the one who was just in the **Times**. The one who closed down the St. Germain."

"Yeah," he answered sleepily.

"He's coming here next week for an inspection."

"A what?"

"An inspection."

Richard jumped out of bed. "Why next week? Why all of a sudden does he want us?"

"I don't know, but I just talked to him and he is coming next Wednesday."

"Did you tell Terry?"

"Terry who?" I stupidly asked.

"Terry, the guy who's installing the sprinkler system."

"No, how could I? I just got the call. You are the first one I've told."

"Why, after all these years with no inspections, would he be coming now?" Richard was mumbling out loud the same thoughts I had earlier.

"Well, at least the sprinkler is almost completed. That should make a big difference," I said as he washed his face.

"Well, (blub, blub) I think, (glub, glub) we should make sure Terry is here on Wednesday. He could be a big help to us I am sure (blug, glub)."

"I'll take the dog downstairs. You take your time," I answered.

Chris was jumping up and down. He was whining to go out, wildly anticipating his morning smells. As I opened the door to the hallway one of the workmen nearly stepped on the dog. He yelped, and then, the dog tried to bite him on the leg. "Is Terry going to be around today?" I asked the workman as he tried to maneuver a twelve-foot piece of pipe up the stairway and fight off a twelve inch dog all at the same time.

"I donno," he barked back as he disappeared up the stairs.

The next week seemed to fly by. The workers were frantically trying to complete the system. Terry had promised to be present on the day of inspection to give us moral support. We felt good about the whole inspection.

According to national statistics there has never been a multiple death recorded in the United States where a fire had occurred in a building protected by a working sprinkler system. Even though we knew this, the tension mounted as the days passed. I guess I was internally angry because it seemed we were under constant surveillance by all sorts of government agencies: Health inspectors. OSHA inspectors. Internal Revenue inspectors — city inspections, electrical inspections, wage inspections — pest control, water control, yard control, show control, out of control. Just think, it wasn't even 1984 and "big brother" was everywhere.

The fateful Wednesday arrived. Terry and Richard and I waited for the moment when we would come face to face with Mr. Bybolte. "There he is, just getting out of that car over there. I'd know him anywhere," Richard snarled as he stood by the door.

"I bet he will be impressed with the sprinkler system and the emergency lights we have already installed," I muttered out loud. Richard opened the door.

"Hi, my name is Torbert Bybolte." He extended his hand.

"I recognize you from your picture in the *Times*," Richard stated shaking his hand.

"Al Tingley," I said. "And this is Terry Schwick from Valley Building and Pipe Company." They shook hands.

"Terry, nice meeting you. Here is my card." The marshall handed each of us a card officially designating him as being from the State Department of Public Safety, Fire Marshall Division.

"Well, I see you are way ahead of me, you have a sprinkler system." He was looking up at the ceiling. "Great idea. Of course, it is not required under the code in Minnesota."

"Yes," I interrupted, "but it is the *cadillac* of safety."

"Let me explain my job," he began. "I am here to inspect and to call attention to the Uniform Fire Safety Code as set down by the Department of Public Safety in the state of Minnesota. A few years ago the state legislature empowered the Fire Marshall's Division of Public Safety to develop a life safety code as it should be applied to hotels and resorts in the state. That is my division. I inspect only hotels and resorts. We chose to begin with the older outlying hotels and then work toward the central cities."

"What was wrong with St. Germain?" Richard interrupted. "We stayed there this past year and there was a sprinkler system in that building."

"Well, er..." he was searching for a name.

"Richard," I interjected.

"Well, Richard, as I said, sprinklers are not a requirement in Minnesota. However, there are trade-offs which are allowed." None of us understood "trade-offs" at the time, but we would soon find out.

"Well, we might as well get started with the inspection," Mr. Bybolte said as he started up the stairs. Terry, Richard and I followed. He stopped at the first landing and looked at the domestic standpipe which was installed in 1901 when the building was constructed. A standpipe is a series of pipes connected to the water system of the building, with a folded fire hose in a rack and a valve located near the hose. In case of fire, any person could take the hose from the rack and turn the valve and head down the hallway with a ready supply of water. A very forward looking invention for the period in which it was used.

"Well, this is what I mean by trade-offs. This domestic standpipe system is not up to code and therefore would have to be replaced, but since you have a sprinkler system you may keep this as it is, as long as the hose extends the length of the hallway," Bybolte explained.

So this was a trade-off and a better part of the afternoon was spent looking for "trade-offs" from the roof to the basement as the inspection continued.

"I will be writing up my orders and recommendations during the next couple of weeks. You should have them soon after." A few hand shakes, a couple of good-byes and it was over.

Richard, Terry and I sat down over a cup of coffee. "Well, how do you think we did?" Richard asked Terry.

"I will say I think he was surprised that you were already installing a sprinkler system. I think it will help some."

"Yeah, but he wanted a sprinkler head in the laundry chute and we'll have to change the door so it is self-closing." I interjected.

"Big deal," Richard answered. I wasn't sure if he was referring to my comment or Bybolte's.

The work on the sprinkler system progressed and was finally completed and hooked up by mid-July. Just three days before we received the report from the fire marshall: Complete with all TWEN-TY—TWO VIOLATIONS.

We were shocked. Oh, there were some very minor things, such as fire retardant doors and the self-closing laundry chute. But the major ones amounted to thousands and thousands of remodeling dollars — such as completely enclosing the fire escape to the north of the building.

"Why build another smoke tower like they had in the MGM fire?" was the comment by our local editor. "If I were escaping from a building, I would much rather smell fresh air upon leaving the building than face three flights of enclosed stairs."

"Break an exit door through the north end of the restaurant," I summarized. "Build an entirely new exit at the south end of the hotel, thereby eliminating a sixty-two foot dead-end corridor. 'Dead end corridor,' what the hell does that mean?" I asked aloud.

The report also called for all kitchen exhaust fans to be vented at roof level. Our roof is seventy-five feet above the exhaust vent in the kitchen. "Can you imagine a suction fan strong enough to pull air seventy-five feet up and out a vent. And what about the grease buildup?" I questioned. Our present fan only had to draw air three feet to the outside. "Can you imagine the Curtis Hotel venting their kitchen twelve stories up?"

By the time we had calculated the cost of correcting all the code violations, both large and small, which came to an additional mere fifty thousand dollars, we were shattered. This cost on top of the already installed sprinkler system would be enough to bankrupt us. And guess what? Good news comes in bunches.

"Good morning, Palmer House. May I help you?"

"Yes, this is the **Daily Times** calling. Is it true the fire marshall is going to close the Palmer House?" I was stunned by the frankness of the caller's statement.

"Certainly not," I answered.

"Well, I understand that you have only ninety days to correct the code violations. I assume if they can't be completed you will have to close."

"You are assuming altogether too much," I responded.

"Well," she continued, "assuming you did complete all the requirements, would that not financially break you and therefore you would have to close the doors?" It was clear to me that she was bound and determined to get a screaming headline: *"Famous Old Palmer House to Close."*

"I am sorry to disappoint you, ma'am," I began slowly raising my voice, "but the Palmer House is not about to close its doors. You have us confused with the St. Germain." And I hung up. It was a first for me to hang up on a reporter, but all she wanted was negative news.

"How are we going to be able to do all this?" Richard said as we again read through the violations.

"Let's take a few of them at a time," I suggested as I began to read some of the minor violations:

• *Install lighted exit signs throughout the various hallways and meeting rooms;*

• *Install fire retardant doors leading to the various floors on the back staircase;*

• *Install fire retardant curtains and drapes in the restaurant and Minniemashie Room.*

The list went on and on. "To think we installed an automatic sprinkler system. What good did it do us?" Richard lamented, lighting up a cigarette.

"What makes me angry," I countered, "is that he told us the domestic standpipe system could remain intact and now in the orders he says, 'Standpipe system in the stairwell must be replaced with an approved standpipe system.' I remember, it was the first of his famous trade-offs." And as our anger mounted, the lines of battle were drawn.

The only way to get any relief from the inspector's report was to seek variances and alternatives. We chose to hire an attorney to help us sort out the various rules and regulations and to see if certain variances could be obtained. Had we had the money, I doubt that Richard or I would have raised an objection about complying fully, but the money was not there and it was a matter of survival.

"Well, according to law you must first ask the governing body of the city to recommend variances to the state office," our attorney began. "You have to appear before the City Council and ask that they grant you variances which would then be requested of the state." It seemed like a long uphill battle, but we were ready for it. They talked about a uniform fire code, but the only uniform on this code was ours. There were a number of hotels similar to the Palmer House that Richard and I had recently visited that didn't have half the safety features we already had, even excluding the sprinkler system.

How vivid that first council meeting stands out in my mind. We had asked a number of our friends who patronized the hotel and restaurant to be at that meeting. Four other business people were present as our attorney presented our case:

"It isn't as if we are asking the council to recommend the variances because the building is unsafe. We believe the sprinkler system which is proven to be one of the greatest lifesavers alone make it safe. But if that isn't enough, then consider this fact: The boys at the Palmer House just do not have the funds to complete these requirements within the alloted time frame. It is simply a matter of economics."

The City Council decided to take the case under advisement and check with the city attorney. The matter was tabled until the next meeting.

At the next meeting the city attorney, who was unable to attend, submitted a prepared statement to the council, citing "the responsibility of granting the variances lay with the state fire marshall." He went on to recommend that "the application not be granted and not be denied."

The attorney for the Palmer House strongly disagreed with the city attorney's opinion. "Not granting and not denying the variances would be action by inaction on the part of the council," he argued.

This headline appeared in our friendly local paper:
FIRE RULES WAIVER SOUGHT FOR PALMER HOUSE

And this excerpt came from our pushy reporter, fifty miles away: *The owners plan to ask the City Council here for a variance. If the council approves their request, the State Fire Marshall's office in St. Paul must review the case. If the fire marshall rejects the variances and the violations are not corrected, **the hotel could be closed.***

For a period of three months the council and we worked back and forth to come to some conclusion. Finally, on Wednesday, September 26, 1979, the City Council moved to support our request for variances. The resolution was drawn up, signed, and sent to the State Fire Marshall's Office.

The waiting was intermitable. First, the Fire Advisory Panel had to meet and inspect the building again. Then they had to go into session over the requested variances and make some kind of recommendation.

It was mid-January before we heard any word from the office in St. Paul. When the letter did arrive, it brought with it another shock wave.

"We are sorry to inform you that all five of the variances which were requested by the Palmer House have been denied by the Advisory Board. However, you will find listed alternative solutions to the variances which, if completed according to the enclosed time frame, will meet the requirements of the State Fire Marshall's office."

Moneywise, the alternatives were not quite as expensive as the original requests, but with our tight budget the letter was of very little consolation.

"Well, we don't have to enclose the fire escape, but we do have to lower it to the ground," Richard said reading one of our alternatives.

"Just what we need," he continued sarcastically. "If we lower the fire escape to the ground every kid in town will be climbing up to the roof."

"Yes," I interjected, "and knowing Sauk Centre, we will probably be cited for having an attractive nuisance which may cause a tragedy."

There was some good news with the bad news. We didn't have to vent the kitchen exhaust up to the roof. But we did have to replace the fan and cover the top of it. If we made some changes in the kitchen, we could use it as an exit from the dining room, thereby not having to cut through a north door. "It does seem rather inconsistent," I mentioned to Richard. "Before, we couldn't use the kitchen as an exit because it was a hazardous area, and now if we move the steam table and change the door egress, it can be used."

"Hmmm," he replied "must be one of their famous trade-offs."

So, after all was said and done, all the variances were denied. The panel saved face, and the alternatives were such that we could save face. The City Council was vindicated and everyone was happy, except our poor checkbook.

Five years have passed, the Palmer House is still open, and the sprinkler system has yet to sprinkle. We have completed all but one of the original orders. We have until January of 1985 to complete this portion.

One man did die in a fire, but it was across the street. The building was not a hotel and therefore it did not come under the jurisdiction of Mr. Bybolte. The Hilton, the MGM, the Stoffers Inn, and hotels in Benson and Austin — just to name a few — have all had fires. But with the double fail system at the Palmer House now complete, with radio controlled smoke detectors, and a direct hookup to the fire station one-and-a-half blocks away; we have perhaps the safest building in Minnesota. And we have a hundred thousand dollars debt, after being in the business ten years, to prove it.

The Black Box!

It was exactly twelve o'clock and the restaurant was again filling up with hungry people when the telephone rang. "Good noon, Palmer House. May I help you?"

"Al, this is Billie Jo."

"Who?" I hastily asked.

"Billie Jo. You know, the guy opening the refinishing place on the hill?"

"Oh, yes," I recalled. I was not used to hearing a southern drawl in Sauk Centre.

"Well, Al, we're all gonna have a grand openin' here at the refinishing business and I was a-wondering if you-all would mind if I placed a box in your lobby for a drawing. You-all get a lot of traffic there and I sure would appreciate it."

"Sure, Billie," I quickly answered. "Sure, put it in, but I gotta go now, I'm busy." And I hung up. I was cooking that day and behind as usual.

That evening Richard was patroling the lobby when Billie Jo came in with his big box. When I say big, I mean BIG! About three feet high and three feet wide.

"What in hell is that for, Billie?" Richard exclaimed, staring at the box covered with solid black paper.

Running out into the lobby I called to Richard, "It's O.K. Richard, he called earlier and asked if he could put a box in the lobby so people could sign up for a drawing for his grand opening."

"Well, my god, does it have to be so damn big? Where are we going to put it?"

"Oh, put it on the showcase, it's only for a week," I answered.

"Well, that's ridiculous. A box that big for a drawing. Well O.K.," he capitulated. " Put it there, but it's still too damn big."

Billie, a little reluctant, set the box on the showcase and started to leave.

"Oh, Billie," Richard called out to him, "what prizes are you giving away?"

"Oh," said Billie, "three free dinners at Willie's Cafe." A pause, then Richard hit the ceiling.

"You expect me to have a box in my lobby for my restaurant customers to win three free dinners to Willie's Cafe? You've got to be crazy. Take that damn monstrosity out of here. I have never heard of anything so idiotic."

I turned toward Richard — "Honest I didn't know, when I gave him permission to bring in the box. I had no idea he was giving away dinners to Willie's Cafe. I never thought to ask..."

Richard was still shaking his head as he muttered, "Of all the stupid asinine schemes!" I swear sometimes I think I have a *lunch box* for a partner!

Pauline

(Part 1)

One early spring a car pulled up in front of the hotel, three people got out and changed our lives! After what seemed like hours of standing on the sidewalk looking up at the hotel and talking among themselves they decided to enter the east door. Both Richard and I were behind the desk as a very lovely and gracious lady stepped forward and asked if we had a single with bath available. Richard answered in the affirmative.

"Well, my name is Pauline Wilcox and I am from New York and am here to represent Columbia Artists Management Corporation. I have been invited here by a Mrs. Peter Prim to speak to a committee of the Alliance for the Arts here in Sauk Centre this evening at the elementary school. Is that within walking distance?"

"The elementary school?" Richard replied. "Sure, it's just about two blocks from here. Mrs. Prim...We know her. Welcome to Sauk Centre and the Palmer House."

"This is my sister and her husband from Minneapolis. They were kind enough to drive me up here but they have to return soon. I wanted to stay downtown, so Mrs. Prim suggested I take a room here."

Her manner was that befitting royalty. Tall, with an exquisite figure, and a voice and smile which made you think of a warm, sunny day. She signed the guest register and Richard immediately went around the desk and picked up her luggage. "Here, let me show you to your room. I will put you in room number eight. I know you will enjoy it. Our restaurant will be open until 8:00 this evening. Would you like a pot of coffee in your room?"

"No, I'm fine," she replied with a smile. She then turned and kissed her sister good-bye and shook hands with her brother-in-law. "Thank you for driving me up. I really do appreciate it, I will take the bus back tomorrow. Bye now. See you later." She watched as they left the hotel and started driving away, then proceeded to follow Richard upstairs.

I was familiar with the Columbia Artists Corporation. They were very active on the east coast and specialized in bringing professional artists to the small towns throughout the United States. They presented a large selection of famous artists under a pre-sold ticket plan that guaranteed three or four concerts in a local community which would otherwise be unable to afford such famous names.

While Richard was upstairs seeing to Mrs. Wilcox, I grabbed the telephone and called Pat Prim. "Hi, Pat. This is Al Tingley at the Palmer House. Your speaker has just arrived and what a charming lady she is."

"Oh, Pauline is there? Great, are you coming to the meeting tonight.?"

"What meeting?"

"You know, we are going to contract with Allied out of Minneapolis or with Community Concerts out of New York. Since I worked with Pauline and Community Concerts, when I was in Ortonville, I think we should go Community. But part of the group favor Allied. Why don't you come and listen to Pauline's presentation?"

"Well, I wasn't planning on going tonight, but I am really intrigued by this lady. We'll see. Bye."

"Bye now, hope you make it."

Richard was standing beside me as I hung up the phone. "Who were you talking to?"

"Pat Prim." I answered. " I called her and told her Mrs. Wilcox has arrived. She wants me to go to that meeting tonight when they vote to choose a concert series."

"Why don't you? She was telling me a little bit about it upstairs. Boy, is she lovely. Something different from the usual check-ins we have here. Go to the meeting tonight," Richard suggested as he lighted up a cigarette. "I'll cover."

It was about an hour later when Mrs. Wilcox descended the staircase, looking like a queen. She was dressed in a flattering calf-length gown with a smattering of gold sequins, a short fur cape of pure mink, and a gold clutch bag. She carried herself with an air of grandeur, attracting the attention of the people standing in the lobby. Spotting her descent, Richard met her at the foot of the stairs and gave her his arm. "Shall I escort you to a table in the dining room?" he asked with a very warm voice.

"Why, thank you, Sir. I would be delighted."

They entered the restaurant more like king and queen than innkeeper and guest. He escorted her to the corner window table and held her chair as she was seated. "Our special this evening is Beef Burgundy on rice and your waitress will be here shortly. What time is your meeting?"

"I believe eight o'clock, but I had better check."

"I think Allan already has; he called Pat right after you arrived."

"Oh, how thoughtful. I wonder if she and Peter will be joining me for dinner?"

"He didn't say anything, but I will go and ask him." The waitress appeared with water for the table. "This is Pauline Wilcox from New York. She is here to see if we can get a Community Concert association started. Now take good care of her." And to Pauline he said, "This is our head waitress and she will get anything you want. I'll see you later. Have a good dinner."

As the restaurant filled up with the early dinner crowd, I helped the cook put the last batch of sourdough biscuits in the oven. We already had five steak orders up and more were coming. The Beef Burgundy looked delicious, bubbling in the pan, and the aroma was like the nectar of the gods. Our evening business had been increasing rapidly over the past year and we were very proud of the food for which we were becoming noted. I was enjoying the atmosphere when Richard entered to ask me if Pat Prim would be joining Mrs. Wilcox for dinner.

"I really don't know. She didn't mention it when I spoke to her this afternoon, but I'm sure they will be here to take her to the meeting."

"Boy," Richard said again, "isn't she a lovely lady? Why don't you go out and sit with her and make her feel welcome until they arrive."

"I might just do that," I said as I finished putting some *pretties* on four plates. Pretties at the Palmer House are the same as garnish in other places. This evening we happened to have some fresh parsley and cherry tomatoes. As soon as we had caught up with all the present orders, I left the kitchen and went over to the corner window table and introduced myself to Mrs. Wilcox.

"Please sit down, I hate eating by myself. I do it all the time. You see, I travel six months out of the year and generally eat alone. I enjoy company; and besides, I am thrilled with your hotel. It is so warm and friendly." She went on to relate that she was sick and tired of all the fancy hotels she had to stay in. And rarely did she have a chance to talk with the owners "such as you and ah, ah, Richard." She loved what we were doing here. And her room, "It's so homey," she said. She was such an easy person to talk to. It was like sitting with someone I had known all my life. Dinner arrived and with it coffee.

"Do you mind if I smoke?"

"Certainly not," she smiled. I put my cigarette back in the pack. It seemed impolite to smoke while she was eating.

"Please go right ahead. It doesn't bother me at all," she insisted.

"No," I replied, "I don't need one anyway. Besides I smoke too much as it is." She started to nibble on her chicken salad sandwich. "Is that all you are going to eat? A sandwich?" I asked.

"Oh, I always eat light before a meeting. I get so nervous before a group of people."

"How long have you been with Community Concerts?"

"A long, long time," she remarked matter-of-factly.

"And you're still nervous?"

"I guess I will never get over it," she answered, changing the subject. "Now tell me about Sauk Centre and the Allied Arts Council. When I talked to Pat on the phone, all she said was that she felt Community Concerts should have a series in this town."

"Well, all I know is that the council wanted to get a concert series started and the only one they knew about was the series out of Minneapolis. Then Pat mentioned you and that you might be willing to present your story. I am familiar with Community because we used to have it back in Maine years ago when I was a kid."

"Oh wonderful, then you know we can bring you everything from the Boston Pops to a single like Max Morath, the jazz pianist," she commented proudly. Her eyes glittered with excitement whenever she mentioned Community. "You know," she continued, "we are a division of Columbia Artists Management Company and have been using the guarenteed audience plan for fifty years. Rarely does a community drop the audience plan once it becomes a member of our series."

"Would you care for some more coffee, ma'am?" the waitress asked as she refilled my cup.

"No, not right now, thank you," she said, looking up with a smile. "What do you have for dessert?"

"Dessert," I interrupted, "you haven't even finished your sandwich."

"I have to save room for dessert."

"For pie we have banana cream, coconut cream, graham cracker cream, apple, cherry, blueberry, sour cream raisin, pecan..."

"Hold it, that's enough. Do you have your own baker here?"

"We sure do," I stated proudly. "Wait till you meet her."

"Yea," answered our waitress, "but don't ever tell her you don't like her rolls."

"Why, does she bite?" Mrs. Wilcox, responded.

"No," I interrupted. "But, I remember one morning there was a guy at the counter. He was complaining to the waitress about his caramel roll. Well, it wasn't long before the baker was standing in front of him with both hands on her hips, asking in a very menacing voice, 'Is there something wrong with my rolls?' "

" 'No, ma'am,' the customer rebutted meekly, "they're very good,' as he swallowed the last bite." We laughed together.

Pauline finished her coconut cream pie just as Mr. and Mrs. Prim entered the dining room. Upon seeing Pauline, there was much hugging and kissing, like a family that hasn't seen each other for years. I immediately acknowledged their entrance and removed my coffee cup and myself to the kitchen.

* * * * *

"Are you coming to the meeting tonight?" Pat Prim called to me as she helped Pauline with her coat.

"I don't know. Why, do you need me?" I answered.

"Of course we need you, we want Community Concerts, don't we?"

Pauline laughed and responded in a very pleasant voice, "You want me, don't you Al?" The tone of her voice and the expression on her face caused me to blush slightly.

"We'll see." I answered coyly. " I'll wait till the restaurant closes. Then I can walk over. I'd like to hear your speech." I winked and the threesome headed for the south door. "Bye," I waved.

* * * * *

I was sitting in the lobby looking at the evening paper.

Richard had just closed the restaurant and was standing behind the front desk. "Aren't you going to the meeting, Allan?" he asked.

"I don't know. I suppose I could sit in for a while."

"Well," Richard remarked, "if we get Community, Pauline would be staying here a lot. I like her, she is so elegant. Do you know what I did while you were sitting with her in the restaurant?"

"No, what?" I asked, putting the paper down and walking over to the desk.

"I ran down to the florist and bought a long stemmed rose and put it in her room."

"That was a great idea," I replied. And typical of Richard, I might add, ever the compassionate one. With a heart of gold, he always thinks of extra touches which make people feel so welcome. "You had better get over to the school if you're going to that meeting. It's after eight," Richard commanded.

"Yes, I suppose," I replied. I put on my coat. "But I'll be back soon."

"O.K. I'll be here." He put on his glasses and began studying the daily receipts.

I was surprised by the large turnout at the school. There must have been fifty people present. The chairman was just thanking the first speaker from Minneapolis. There was great applause.

"Now, ladies and gentlemen, I would like to present our second speaker, who comes to us all the way from New York to explain the Columbia Artists' program of Community Concerts, Mrs. Pauline Wilcox." With a flourish and a bow, the emcee greeted Pauline as she stood before the audience who soundly welcomed her.

"Thank you. Thank you very much for that warm welcome on such a cold night." As Pauline spoke she commanded such attention by both her soft, pleasant voice and her knowledge of her subject. I felt certain, then and there, without having heard the previous speaker, that the group would elect to invite Community to organize Sauk Centre...

Pauline held my arm very firmly as we left the meeting and headed back to the Palmer House.

"You had them eating out of your hand, Pauline. You presented your program with such finesse. And now people are dreaming of meeting your celebrities. It was marvelous," I announced.

"Why, thank you Mr. Tingley," she curtsied and tugged at my arm with approval.

Richard was standing looking out through the door when we arrived at the hotel. He opened the door and asked, just like a little kid inquiring about a ball game, "Did you win, Pauline?"

"We sure did," she smiled.

"She knocked them dead with her presentation," I quickly added with enthusiasm.

"Well keep your coat on Pauline," he replied taking her hand. "We're going to the bar to celebrate."

* * * * *

"I haven't had this much fun in years!" Pauline commented as Richard and I escorted her, one on each arm, up the oak staircase from the lobby to her room. Richard unlocked her door and flicked on the light. "Thank you both so very much for a wonderful evening. I am so glad I will be coming back for the organizational meeting this fall. Good night again." She leaned over and gave us each a peck on the cheek.

"Good night," said Richard.

"Good night, sleep well. And welcome to the Palmer House," I called back as we headed down the stairs.

"Isn't she just about the most terrific person we've ever had staying here?" I remarked to Richard. But he was already talking with the night clerk.He was explaining to him, over and over, as Mathew is hard of hearing, just whom we had escorted through the lobby and up the stairs.

"You hoo, you hoo!" It was Pauline calling from the top of the stairs.

"What is it, Pauline?" Richard asked.

"Who should I thank for my lovely rose. It's just beautiful!"

"A woman as lovely as you deserves a beautiful rose," he answered.

"Well, it's just perfect and I love roses. Good night again." She turned and left.

"That was just a perfect touch, Richard," I complimented as I headed upstairs. It had been a long day, as usual.

* * * * *

From that day forward, like the seasons, spring and fall we look forward to Pauline's visits. And always, the long stemmed rose stands waiting. Because of her efforts the Palmer House has been graced by the likes of Paul Lavall and the Band of America, the New Christy Minstrels, and the famous pianists, Veri and Jermanus, to name a few. Their pictures now hang in our hallway gallery. For whenever an artist is staying at the Palmer House, we always make sure to obtain a signed, glossy photograph.

"I sure like your hotel. It really intrigues me," Max Morath said to Richard one night as he sat by a window table in the restaurant. "It's got a personality all its own. You don't find many of these places left today." He devoured a plate of old-fashioned meat loaf, requesting four extra blueberry sourdough biscuits in the process.

On another occasion, Les Brown and His Band of Renown put on such an exciting show that Richard and I decided to drive all the way to South Dakota to watch them perform the next evening. Stopping to eat before the show, who should we meet but Les.Recognizing us, Les shook our hands and with great excitement said, "It's been years since I've had fans follow me from gig to gig. Come on boss, let me buy you a drink."

And yet another time, the entire cast of Camelot was staying at the hotel. Their cast party lasted until the bus left the next afternoon. We felt sorry for the audience at their next engagement, knowing full well there had been very little sleep among the cast members. But we loved it.

* * * * *

CLICK, CLICK CLICK CLICK, CLICK CLICK CLICK CLICK. RING —— RING —— "Hello," the cheery voice on the other end said.

"Guess what?" I replied very matter of factly. " You've finally been screwed into the wall."

"I beg your pardon?" Pauline stated in amazement.

"Pauline, this is Al. I said you have finally been screwed into the wall. Remember? The portrait we had taken of you. We hung it to-day."

"Oh Al, it's you, darling," she began to laugh. "I just couldn't figure out what you were saying. How are you? My, but it's good to hear your voice."

"Yours too," I answered. "Well, we've been busy as bees this past month, over eighteen Christmas parties in just four weeks but we have been enjoying it. How was your Christmas?"

"Just wonderful. The children joined me and we had a great visit before they left for Florida. I'm going to Florida myself for a couple of weeks to visit some friends." She was as pleasant as ever.

"I despise you," I said angrily. "You have it made. Travel everywhere and doing what you want when all I do is stay here at the Palmer House."

"Oh, you poor baby," she replied in her wonderful playful manner.

"I miss you, I haven't been dancing since you were here two months ago," I chided.

"We'll make up for it when I get there in the spring."

"When are you scheduled?" I asked.

"Around the last week in March," she said.

"Great, you can help me celebrate the big five 0."

"That's right, your birthday is the twenty-ninth. Yes, I'll be there." Her voice rang like a clear sounding bell.

"This is one birthday I really don't want to celebrate. I remember when my dad turned fifty I thought he was about the oldest man alive." Pauline began to laugh. "I suppose it won't be so bad if you're here, but it still seems pretty old," I continued. "Just thought I'd call and let you know that you are now a permanent fixture at the Palmer House."

She laughed again. "I guess I'm permanent if I have been screwed into the wall. I do appreciate the phone call, Al."

"I told you I would call once in awhile. I miss you very much and look forward to your next visit." I started to talk softer as Merlin appeared behind the front desk.

"Well, I will see you in a few months, darling. I miss you."

"Same here."

"Bye."

*   *   *   *   *

March 29th came all too fast that year. I had received birthday cards from people I thought had forgotten I existed. I told Richard I didn't want any kind of celebration, except maybe he and I and Pauline could go out for dinner. The day passed very quietly, as the restaurant is closed on Sundays during the winter months. It was 4:00 and Pauline and I were softly talking in the lobby when the east door burst open and a loud female voice cried out, "Happy Birthday, Al. We're here!"

I was startled to say the least. I did not recognize the voice or the face. She came into the lobby extending her hand, "You remember me, don't you? Patsy, Patsy and Bill, the entertainers. Dah Dah." And she started to do the can can, "Dah dah dah dah da dah da da."

Unfortunately, I remembered. How could I forget?

On her last visit she kept everyone up all night with her raunchy jokes. We were bored to tears. "Oh, yes, hi Patsy. Nice to see you." I stood up to shake her hand and she about pulled it from its socket. "I want you to meet a friend of mine from New York Pauline. This is Patsy." Pauline remained seated and nodded but Patsy grabbed her hand and began pumping as though she expected water at any moment.

"Where's Bill?" I inquired.

"Oh, bringing in the stuff from the car. We're here to help you celebrate your birthday. Remember, I told you we would."

"How thoughtful," I remarked. "And I suppose you would like room three again?"

"Yea," she answered as she snapped her gum loud enough to wake the dead. I moved toward the desk just as Bill entered. He dropped a heavy suitcase, just missing my toe, and slapped me on the back so hard I went spinning. They registered and went upstairs to get settled.

"They're not going with us, Al, for your birthday supper are they?" Pauline asked, quite concerned.

"I don't know, but I can't very well ignore them. They did drive all the way up here to help celebrate."

"But she's so..." Pauline stopped abruptly.

I have never known Pauline to say a bad word about anyone so I finished her sentence for her.

"...'Crude' were you going to say?" I smiled and held her for a moment. "Oh, we'll work something out."

"Hi, Pauline." It was Richard on the stair landing.

"Well, hello dear, you're up," Pauline replied cheerfully. "Did you sleep well?"

"O.K., except the dog kept jumping up and down." Chris was already ahead of Richard and whining at the door. I stepped over and opened the door and he leapt out and headed for the parking lot. Richard descended the stairs in his stocking feet, carrying his shoes as usual.

"You will never guess who just checked in, Richard," I said.

"How could I? I just got up, and what's more I couldn't care less."

"Patsy and Bill," I said.

"Who?" He sounded like an echoing owl. "Who?" he repeated again.

"Patsy and Bill, you know, the entertainers from the night club." Still he carried a blank look on his face. "You know the ones that sat up all night with you last year telling raunchy jokes."

"Oh, not them. My god, what are they doing back here?"

"They came to help Al celebrate his birthday," Pauline interjected.

"Well who invited them?" Richard asked, trying to squelch a big yawn.

"I don't know, but they just arrived and announced they were here to help celebrate my birthday," I answered. I entered the restaurant to fetch Richard a badly needed cup of coffee, then returned.

"Would you like a cup, Pauline?"

"No, thank you dear. I've had my quota for the day, especially if we are going out this evening."

"What are we going to do with Patsy and Bill? We can't ignore them."

"How about you celebrating with them, and Pauline and I will go out," Richard reported entirely too exuberantly.

"No, I want to spend my birthday with you two," I demanded.

"Maybe, we should go in separate cars so we can leave if we get bored," Pauline offered diplomatically.

"That's a possibility, but I'd rather not have them along at all," Richard stated.

"Why does everything at the Palmer House have to get so complicated," I said as I headed back to the door to let the Chris in.

"O.K. So what time will we be leaving and where are we going now that we have a new wrinkle?" Richard asked, now slowly coming back to life.

"I thought we talked about the Minnewaska House in Glenwood last night?" I replied.

"Are we going to have to pay for their supper, too?" Richard wondered glancing upstairs.

"I doubt it," I interjected, really not knowing what I was talking about.

"Well," Pauline began, "why don't we all relax for a while. We won't be leaving for a couple of hours and maybe by then something will work out."

"O.K." I said, "I'm going upstairs to take a shower and rest a bit. We'll see what happens." I gave Pauline a little kiss and headed upstairs.

It was 6:30 when I headed back down the stairs, which I hated to descend because I could hear the loud voices of Patsy and Bill. Poor Richard, I thought to myself, trapped in the lobby and not able to get away. How true it is: We are hostages in our own home. I decided to go back into the apartment and call him on the telephone. It is a ploy we use quite frequently to save one another from ear banging experiences.

CLICK, CLICK CLICK CLICK CLICK, RING —— RING ——
"Richard, this is Al."

"Yeah, what do you want?"

"Well, I was on my way downstairs when I heard Patsy and Bill banging your ears,"

"Yeah, so what?" he sounded a little perturbed.

"I thought I would call so that you would have an excuse to get away."

"Yeah, yeah, so what am I supposed to do, just walk away?"

"No, tell them you have to call someone on the phone and I will come downstairs and take over."

"O.K. O.K. I'll be right up." Click.

When Richard entered the apartment I could tell he was upset. "Don't tell me we are going to have to put up with them all evening. She sure thinks she is funny. And that voice, God she is so crass."

"Maybe, if they do go, we can take separate cars," I said.

"But won't that look funny?" Richard replied. "You'd better get on down there and entertain them."

In the hallway I ran into Pauline. "Hi, dear." I startled her.

"Well what's the verdict," she asked. "Are they joining us for dinner?"

"I don't know what to do. After all they did drive all the way up here just to help me celebrate. So what can I do?"

She put her arm around me as she said, "I understand." "Why don't we invite them along and we'll make the best of it."

"HERE COMES THE BIRTHDAY BOY!" came the loud voice from the lobby. "We thought you had fallen in and disappeared for good. Ha ha ha ha." Patsy cracked up at her latest *funny*.

"We were just talking," I said as we reached the lobby.

"Well?" Patsy asked "When are we leaving and where are we going?" This phrase must have reminded her of an old song, for she started to sing. "Where we going? When are we going? What are we gonna do? We're on our way to somewhere, the three of us and you. Ha ha ha." She was now dancing around the lobby, fortunately, all by herself. I glanced at Pauline who registered a very bored and blank look.

Richard stood on the stair landing watching and when he spoke the entire dilemma was solved. "Well, get your coats on if we're going out for dinner. I'll go out and bring the van around." He descended the stairs, grabbed his coat and headed out the door.

"Well," Pauline uttered, "that solves that. I'll go up and get my coat."

Patsy and Bill already had their coats on. "You mean we're gonna get to ride in that luxurious van? Wow, wow, wow!" She stated while waltzing with herself again.

"Come off it, Patsy. You don't have to make a fool of yourself all the time," her husband scolded. This was the first time I had heard Bill speak. And from the looks of things maybe it was a first for Patsy too. She began to pout and said, "All right, I'll behave myself. I'll be the model of good behavior."

"That I'll have to see to believe," Bill mumbled as he opened the door and escorted her out.

I watched them climb into the back of the van as Pauline descended the stairs. She looked lovely as she slowly extended her hand to me. "How do I look?" she asked.

"Ravishing," I remarked as I put my arms around her and swung her around off her feet. In the midst of this twirl she whispered in my ear, "Happy Birthday," and out the door we swept.

*   *   *   *   *

The supper club was crowded with early diners, mostly older couples. The hostess greeted us as we entered the dining area.

"How many in your party?"

"Five," Richard said as he glanced back and counted.

Patsy was standing beside me snapping her gum in my ear and talking between snaps. "Boy, this sure is a swanky place. Are my diamonds on straight? Hee, hee, hee."

The dining room was beautifully appointed. The walls were deep red velvet draped lavishly with gold cording. In the middle of the dining room there was a huge, ornate fountain surrounded by an oppulent salad bar. As we passed the fountain, Patsy said, "I hope we don't sit too close to the fountain. They always make me want to pee."

Upon hearing that remark Richard coughed, or did he gag, I'm not sure. We reached our table and I immediately stood behind Patsy's chair waiting for her to be seated, while Richard held Pauline's chair. As Patsy sat down she looked up at me and cracked, "You're the one who is fifty. I should be holding the chair for you."

"You're welcome," I replied.

I bowed and seated myself across from Patsy and Pauline and beside Bill. Richard sat at the end of the table.

"Why can't you ever do something like that, Bill?" Patsy chided.

"You never stand still long enough," he answered.

"O.K. O.K. Knock off the cat-calling," Richard commanded.

The waitress appeared and began taking bar orders. Gin and tonic for Richard. Brandy Manhattan on the rocks for Al. Martini for Bill. And a whiskey sour cocktail for Pauline.

"My such fancy drinks, too much for me, gimmie a beer," said Patsy.

"Thank you," said the waitress as she passed the menus.

"Betcha the prices are steep here," Patsy interjected! "Especially if you go by the size of the menu." Bill kicked her under the table. "Ouch," she cried out loud.

After the drinks arrived Richard lifted his glass. "I propose a toast." All raised their drinks except Patsy. She raised the bottle of beer in one hand and a beer mug in the other. "To Allan and a half a century, Happy Birthday."

"Happy Birthday," the others repeated in unison. The response was loud enough for other diners to hear. Many of them turned, smiled, raised their glasses and nodded to me. I acknowledged their good wishes by slightly standing and bowing while holding my drink in the air. The crowded room was filled with a rousing, spontaneous applause, which I again acknowledged.

"Fifty years old," Patsy repeated very slowly. "God, that's old."

"Thanks," I said sarcastically, flashing an obscene gesture.

"Be careful," Bill whispered to me. "She can be unpredictable."

"You're telling me?" I whispered back.

"Are you ready to order?" the waitress asked. But no one had even looked at the menu.

"No, why don't you bring us another round of drinks first," Richard replied politely. He lighted a cigarette, which in turn caused me to light one, which in turn caused Patsy to light one, which in turn caused Bill to speak.

"I thought you were going to quit?"

"That was this morning," she muttered.

"I think I will have the filet mignon, medium rare," Pauline suggested to Richard.

"Pauline," I interrupted, "you'll never be able to eat all of that."

"Of course not, but you can finish it for me, if you like." Everyone laughed.

"I don't see any hot dogs on the menu," Patsy said.

"Oh, really?" I replied. "There's one at this table." More laughter. She lowered her menu and stuck out her tongue at me.

Bill gave me a little tap. "Watch it," he cautioned.

* * * * *

I felt sorry for the waitress. Our party was doing some of the very things customers do to our waitresses. We were all giving orders at once and speaking out of turn, making it very difficult for her to keep her tickets straight. We didn't tell her if we wanted separate checks or not, and made her repeat the choice of potato each time for each person. Two of our party asked her to repeat the evening specials at least three times. I was embarassed to death. To add to the this, I found out later, it was her first night on the floor.

After we had our turn at the salad bar, I knew I would never finish the meal I ordered. I do that every time I eat out. I fill up on the salad bar because I am so hungry, then Richard bawls me out for not finishing my meal.

"Ketchup on steak?" I called out to Patsy.

"What are you doing, eating raw meat? she retorted.

"You might just as well have had a hamburger. With all that ket-chup, you can't even taste the meat," I laughed.

Conversation was very sparse for the next few moments as everyone felt uncomfortable. The Muzak played softly in the background. Suddenly all diners seemed to stop talking. Patsy chose this moment to jump up from her chair and in her loudest, most emphatic voice, blared at me, "SEX! SEX! SEX! THAT'S ALL YOU EVER WANT. THAT'S ALL YOU EVER HAVE ON YOUR MIND. SEX! SEX! SEX! AND I'M TIRED OF IT!!!!!!!!!!"

One hundred heads turned simultaneously. Two hundred eyes burned through me. Here I sat with no hole to crawl into.

"I told you to take it easy," Bill said into my very hot, red, perspiring ear.

As I slowly tried to regain my composure, I felt my heart to see if it was still beating. Patsy leaned over the table and with a beautiful smile, and a very soft and sincere voice said, "Happy Birthday, Al. I'll bet you won't forget your fiftieth, will you?"

TANSTAAFL!

The telephone rang around ten in the morning. It was the President of the newly established United Federal Savings and Loan in Sauk Centre. "This is Bud Tessler from the United Federal. Is this Al?"

"Yes. What can I do for you?"

"We are planning a grand opening of our bank here next week and are wondering if you would be willing to serve lunch to anyone who comes to our grand opening. We just don't have the space."

After pausing a moment I replied, "Fine, but how do you plan to accomplish this?"

"Well, we planned on handing out tickets good for redemption at the restaurants. Then you could send the bill to us and we would take care of it."

"Sounds like a good idea to me. Would this include all the restaurants in town?"

"Yes, the Palmer House, the Red Carpet, the Ding Dong, and the Hi Ho.

"I like the idea. All your customers would have to do is present the ticket to our waitress and order from the menu or our noon special. When are you planning the grand opening?"

"Next Tuesday from nine to nine. Would that be alright?"

"Sounds good to me. I had better stock up on specials and lots of hamburgers."

"Thank you very much. And, remember, send the bill to me."

"Thank you for thinking of us. Good bye." I hung up the telephone. "Boy, that will make for a busy day." But I had no idea what was in store for the Palmer House, even though I suspected that a free offer of anything would excite the locals.

*   *   *   *   *

I ran downstairs early that Tuesday morning, figuring I would get ahead of the game. By 9:00 the orders in the kitchen were so backed up that I decide to call in another cook. Already we had six orders for filet mignon, and rib-eye steaks, plus many other large entrees which I felt exceeded the expectations of the bank. Walking over to the telephone, I dialed the bank, "Hello, Bud. This is Al at the Palmer House. I believe several of your customers are going overboard. We are getting orders for steak dinners, shrimp dinners, you name it. Some of these dinners cost close to eight dollars. Shouldn't you put a limit on your *free* lunch?"

"How much would you suggest?" Bud asked.

"Well, our noon special runs about two-fifty. I would guess that's probably what you had in mind."

"I agree. I didn't figure anyone would be ordering filet mignon for breakfast. In fact, we had thought maybe a roll and coffee would suffice."

"Well, Bud, you won't believe what people will do when something is free."

"How true. Let's limit it to two-fifty per ticket. Thank you and I will call the other restaurants."

By 10:00 the restaurant was jammed. Richard came in the kitchen and announced, "They are lined up in the lobby." One hour later the kitchen had reached its capacity and beyond. One of our freezers was not operating and the other was located in adjacent room. The cooks had to leave the kitchen, run to the next room, open the freezer, find the item, close the freezer, run back to the kitchen and place the item on the grill or in the deep fryer. One small deep fryer and a two foot by two foot grill was all that was available for cooking. Certainly this was not the best arrangement for traffic like this.

My daughter, who was with us for the summer, was helping out. The orders came in so fast that we finally gave up trying to hurry. After all, there was no way of hurrying food being prepared in a deep fryer or on a grill. So each of us in the kitchen decided to take a pack of orders and fill them as best we could.

Suddenly, my daughter came into the kitchen, her eyes filled with huge crocodile tears. "Daddy, Daddy, I dropped all my tickets in the freezer." She pointed to the other room. Her dilemma, together with four waitresses calling in additional orders, simply added to the confusion already reigning over the kitchen. In the middle of all this, Richard entered the kitchen again. "They are filling up the lobby and there isn't a seat anywhere. What's taking so long?"

"My god, Richard, we are overwhelmed. And we can't get enough food on this teen-weeny grill."

"Well, you should see the line at the bank across the street. It's almost a block long. Boy, what people won't do for a free lunch. The word sure has spread fast."

"We're out of hamburger buns," someone screamed.

"Send Merlin to the store," I barked. "No. You better send him to the bakery and tell him to get ten dozen. We've got the whole day to go."

The lobby was teaming with people. There were faces that I had never seen in the restaurant before, and for that matter, I will probably never see again. The crowd wouldn't move when someone wanted to leave the dining room — no doubt they were afraid they would to lose their place. Oh, I wondered, what happened to the time when people believed something for nothing was a handout and it was a disgrace to accept it.

"When can we get in? We've been here for half an hour already," came the cry from someone in the crowd.

"We have to cook the food you know!!" I shouted as I fled back into the kitchen through the back door.

Utter chaos was the only way to describe the kitchen, the cooks were approaching apoplexy, and the waitresses were practically pulling their hair out. The customers were taking it out on the waitresses, and the waitresses in turn were barking back at the cooks. The buns from the bakery had arrived, and since the burgers were already fried, it was now just a matter of getting them put together. Richard burst through the doors and stated. "Will there ever be an end to people? I can't believe it? I told one person there was a two-fifty limit. His bill came to two-dollars-ten cents and he had the gaul to ask for forty cents change. How cheap can some people get? I even noticed some of them are getting in line again at the bank to get more tickets. Jesus!"

"I know, I know," I answered, stopping long enough to wipe the sweat from my eyes. "We are still backed up about an hour." I stirred up a Denver but had no room for it on the grill. Running into the back shed, I grabbed a large cast iron fry pan and put in on the stove. At least I could start the Denvers now.

"Where the hell are the potatoes? I'm all out of hash browns!"

"In the walk-in!" I yelled.

"I can't find them."

"They are in the sack hanging in the back."

She slammed the walk-in door, "I found them she hollered. But since when did we start hanging anything up in the walk-in? I'm not used to things being put away." Just then there was a earsplitting crash over by the dishwasher.

"Oh no!!" I cried. "There go the profits." Even I utter that nonsensical line in times of crisis. In her haste, the dishwasher had dropped an entire tray of cups, twenty-four to be exact, at the cost of a dollar-sixty-five each. Since it's no longer legal to take breakage out of paychecks, we just picked up the pieces and got on with trying to cope with our *free lunch* day.

This pace continued throughout the day without letup. We were all tired and irritated to the point where we were arguing with one another over the silliest of things. Richard kept coming in with the latest report on how full the lobby was and how people were complaining about how long they had to wait for their free food. "Some people have been served twice today," he reported.

"We're out of buns again," I hollered. So start serving our hamburgers on bread,"

"Don't worry, they'll complain about it," Richard commented as he left the kitchen.

By 9:00 that evening, the lobby was still loaded with people. Richard cornered one couple returning for their third meal, and closed the doors. "I'm sorry. It has been a long day and we are out of food," he announced.

"But what about our free lunch tickets?" they queried.

"Take 'em to the Hi Ho," he replied, retreating to the kitchen.

It was another two hours before we got things cleaned up. Every dish and pot and pan was dirty. No one had time to wash them. In fact, we hardly had time to eat. When the receipts were totaled, we realized just how busy we had been. We had tripled our previous high. Three days in one, and brother we felt it. The receipts and my aching feet acknowledged the fact that TANSTAAFL is for real: There Ain't No Such Thing As A Free Lunch.

"They're Here, They're Here!"

" They're here again, they're here again," the waitress semi-whispered as she burst through the swinging doors and into the kitchen.

"Who's here?" the cook asked as he looked up from the grill.

"The lovers, the lovers," she answered shortly.

Almost everyone who has worked at the Palmer House Hotel during the past eight years knows who the lovers are. Or, to put it more correctly, nobody knows who they are. At least not their names, nor where they come from, nor even their license numbers. Still, we all recognize the lovers.

For the past eight years, sometimes once a month, often twice a month, they arrive at the Palmer House for breakfast, usually about 10:00 or 10:15. They take the corner table by the window, and move a chair so they can sit side by side at a table which will not normally seat two people comfortably on the same side. They don't mind. They sit as close to one another as possible. "I'll have two eggs over medium, bacon, hash browns, toast, and coffee. She'll have two poached eggs on toast and coffee." The waitress pours coffee and leaves them staring silently into each other's eyes in silence.

Their mysteriousness has perked the curiosity of everyone at the Palmer House. One waitress reports she has it all figured out. "They are both married and have separate lives. He is a truck driver with a regular route to this area and arranges to meet her whenever he is in town. They both arrive and leave in separate vehicles.

No one has ever seen them embrace, although they do a lot of hand-holding under the table. Only once in eight years have they ever added more than a simple hello or even given a knowing smile, that was about four years ago. I was standing in the lobby and he was waiting for her to return from the restroom when he spoke, "How much for a room?"

"With bath — fifteen dollars for two people. Ten dollars for a room without bath. However there is a sink in every room," I answered.

"Thanks," he replied. She had returned now and they headed into the restaurant for their favorite table.

Some forty-five minutes later I was cleaning up the banquet room when a waitress came to get me. "They are at the front desk Al," she reported.

"Thanks," I replied and hurried to the lobby. He was standing at the desk holding out a ten dollar bill.

"We'll take a room without bath please." I handed him the registration card; and he signed in a handwriting that was undecipherable. I gave him the key and they disappeared upstairs. I don't know when they checked out, but the key was laying on the desk later that afternoon.

To my knowledge, this is the one and only time they have ever spoken, except to make an order. But you can count on their arrival for breakfast every other week or so. It remains as one of the great romantic mysteries of the Palmer House.

Paranoia And Spinach.

I never thought the day would come when I would get paranoid about spinach. Now you see, I happen to like spinach. Years ago Mother used to serve any greens that could be found — dandelion, turnip, Swiss chard — you name it, we ate it. Sometimes reluctantly, but you can bet we ate it, even if it took a lot of vinegar to kill the taste. Yet, how much taste is there to spinach? Not much, huh? Maybe it was the Popeye cartoons, the movies, or the commercials on the radio that made me want to eat spinach, I don't know. But now that I'm serving others, I think differently.

Every so often I get a craving for spinach, so I serve it at the restaurant. That's when my paranoia begins. Just today a young man ordered our special, which consisted of stuffed pepper, cole-slaw and the vegetable of the day, spinach. Already I have had so many people send back their spinach that I feel guilty about scooping a portion on this guy's plate. So I found myself holding off on the vegetable and giving him french fries. When the waiter came to pick up the order he asked, "Where's the vegetable?"

"He doesn't like spinach," I replied.

"Did you ask him?"

"No," I said, "I just know he doesn't like spinach."

Soon the waiter returned, "Guess what! He wants a side dish of spinach."

"Well, blow me down."

Good Bye F. Scott, Hello Sinclair.

I t was a bitter cold night in St. Paul, Minnesota. I had been working overtime at the office. There was a blizzard outside and the
city had pulled the busses off the streets. At 9:30 I walked out of the
office and found no transportation home. I decided to stop at a local
bar for a drink before trying to find a way back to Minneapolis. The
name of the bar was Hello Dolly's, it was located in the lobby of the
old Capri Hotel. Golly, it was cold outside. It must have been twenty
degrees below zero and the snow was still falling. It is unusual for it to
snow when the temperature is this cold, but I guess anything can
happen in Minnesota, and usually does. That's probably why they
call it the winter wonderland.

As I entered the bar I could see the weather had taken its toll on
the customers. There was one bartender, one patron, and a piano
player. I ordered my usual drink, then walked over to the piano bar
and sat down.

The blonde girl tinkling the keys was very pretty, slim with deep set
blue eyes, lovely figure, but lacking musical talent. I fondly
remembered my young daughter playing her first piano recital. She
was quite accomplished in comparison to this lady. After a couple of
unrecognizable numbers it was time, for a "potty break," hers not
mine. The "music" ceased and the jukebox began to play. Frank
Sinatra was crooning an old tune as I sipped on my drink, and began

wondering how I was going to get back to Minneapolis. My reverie was interrupted by a voice speaking directly to me. "Didn't you come through North Central Publishing Company a short time ago?"

Hardly cognizant of the question, I looked over toward the voice and said, "I bet your pardon?"

"Didn't you go through North Central Publishing Company a few days ago on a tour?"

"Ah...er...yes," I suddenly responded. "I went there with a salesman. He was bidding a handbook the Medical Association is going to publish."

"I thought that was you. My name is Dick Schwartz and I am a compositor for North Central."

"Gee, you have a good memory." I was truly amazed and impressed. "Do you come to this bar often?" I asked.

"Once in awhile. I came down tonight to buy some spray paint for my radiator.

"In a bar?" I inquired smilingly.

"I didn't realize it was such a bad storm," he answered.

"Yeah, it is really bad," I agreed. "They have pulled the busses and I don't know how I'm going to get back to Minneapolis. I will probably have to spend the night in my office." There was a long pause as the jukebox changed tunes. "Do you like piano bars?" I asked.

"Yeah, sometimes," Richard answered, "but this gal can't play for shit."

"I'm sure she was hired for her looks. If you really like piano bars, you should visit the Rainbow Bowl and Lounge on Broadway in Minneapolis," I said taking a sip from my drink.

"Broadway,..Broadway?" He took a long drag on his cigarette.

"Just take Washington Avenue from downtown and go north to Broadway."

"Oh, I know where it is," he replied.

"Well, they have a piano player there that is out of this world. There isn't a thing he can't play. You name it, and if he doesn't know it, he'll learn it. A bunch of us go there nearly every Friday and Saturday night."

A man came staggering into the bar from outside. "Is it still snowing out there?" Richard asked.

"Can't see across the street. It's a bad one," he answered as he sat down at the bar.

The piano player had returned and was beginning to "play" again. Richard quickly finished his drink and picked up his package. "Well, I had better see if I can plow my way back up the hill. Hope you get back to Minneapolis okay."

"I doubt if I will try. I'll probably sleep in the office tonight, so I won't be late for work in the morning."

"Nice meeting you. I might see you at the ah...ah..."

"Rainbow," I replied, finishing the sentence for him. "Nice meeting you, too." I still had half a drink to finish and I probably would have a couple more if I was going to stay at the office all night.

"Bye now," he called as he opened the door. The snow came swirling in.

"Brrrrr." All of us shivered as the cold night air swept through the bar.

The winter passed with lots of snow and cold weather, and socializing. Richard showed up quite frequently at the Rainbow and joined the gang at the piano, even though he was not much for singing. He did request a favorite song one evening: "Poinciana." From that night forward everyone knew when he entered, for the piano player would break immediately into a jolly refrain of "Poinciana."

Living in Minneapolis and working in St. Paul was tedious. One evening Richard and I were talking about our jobs and living conditions. "I have been thinking about getting a bigger place up on the Hill," he said.

"The Hill?" I questioned.

"You know, Summit Hill in St. Paul. It's the most beautiful tree lined street in the world. Some of the most beautiful estates you have ever seen are on Summit Avenue. You should drive over there and see it someday." I could see Richard was in love with St. Paul and its environs.

Within the year Richard had purchased a large older home on Holly Avenue. He asked me one evening if I would be interested in renting some space in his eighteen-room mansion. I was delighted. First, to get closer to work, and secondly, because we had become good friends. However, there was fear and trepidation about the move on both our parts. He had never shared a house before and I had had lousy luck with roommates since my divorce.

The house which sat on the Corner of Kent and Holly, was coincidentally originally owned by Doctor Ogdin — the physician who delivered F. Scott Fitzgerald. We roomed together there for seven years until we formed the Dauntless Corporation and moved to the corner of Main Street and Sinclair Lewis Avenue in Sauk Centre.

It was Good-Bye F. Scott, and Hello Sinclair Lewis.

Lewis' Birthday Party.

The phone was ringing as I bustled in from the frigid weather. It was only fourteen degrees below zero this morning, with a wind chill of thirty-two below. I had just finished running down to **The Herald** office to proofread our latest ad, and I speculated that the kitchen workers had the radio turned up so loud they couldn't hear the phone; an inevitable occurance. I pulled off my stocking cap and I grabbed the desk phone. "Good morning, Palmer House. May I help you?"

"Yes, this is the bakery calling. We are wondering what color flowers you would like on your Sinclair Lewis birthday cake for tomorrow. And incidentally what year was he born?"

"1885," I replied and added. "I really don't think Sinclair would mind which color scheme you choose. Why don't you use your own discretion?"

"O.K. Thank you."

That's right, tomorrow is the Sinclair Lewis Foundation's annual meeting. They hold it every year on his birthday, February 7, in the Minniemashie Room. They have a big cake each year and the color doesn't matter. Many times, however, I have thought that it would be more than fitting to serve Devil's food cake rather than Angel's. I am sure *Red* would get a kick out of it...

You Got A What?

I guess I am secure enough to share with you one event which happened nearly ten years ago and has continued throughout the course of our ownership of the Palmer House. Recently this ongoing event has played a much more active role than ever before. Ladies and Gentlemen, We have a ghost! A what? That's right, a ghost! An honest to goodness, ectoplasmic spirit! This fleeting and fickle spirit was first discovered by Richard on one of the many lonely and quiet night shifts he has endured throughout the years.

We soon found out, after running the Palmer House for only a few short weeks, that it was necessary to have an alert, authoritative night clerk on duty both Friday and Saturday nights. That's when the drunks, the crackpots, the weirdos of all sorts arrive at all hours of the night and morning looking for a place to crash. Richard has had many an experience with inebriated persons. Once a drunk stumbled up to the desk and slurred out at him, "How mush er yer rooms?"

"Eight-fifty," Richard answered.

"I'll give ya five, O.K.?"

"I said the rooms are eight-fifty, and that's it."

The drunk fumbled around with the crumpled bills stashed in his many pockets. "Goddamn it, I thought I had more money than this," he mumbled to himself, tipping and swaying first on one foot and then the other. He dropped a greenback and in his drunken state of wobbling around looking for it, he blurted, "Goddamn it, I heard it drop, didn't you?"

Richard watched with a determined stare. He had seen this performance many times, performed equally well by both men and women. "Do you want the room or not?" he challenged.

"I guess I'll just sit in your lobby for awhile."

"Oh, no you won't. If you don't take a room you will have to leave or I will call the police."

"I'll give you six bucks and that's all," the drunk snarled.

"Then get outside," Richard said raising his voice and reaching for the phone.

"O.K. Don't get your water hot. I'll take the goddamn room."

Trying desperately to assume an injured and righteous attitude, the drunk threw down a wad of crumpled bills and reached for the registration card. It was a mere formality, as seldom can we read the information scribbled upon it. Taking the key and turning around, the drunk bumped into the showcase. A standard trick. The items in the case bounced and the vase of flowers we have on top started to fall to the floor. Richard reached out and snagged it in midair. He's getting very proficient in saving the flowers.

"Whasa num ba o' the room?"

"Number ten," Richard said shaking his head as he watched the drunk grab the stair railing and haltingly pull himself up the stairs. "Yup," Richard mused "the bars get all their money, then toss them out and I'm supposed to feel sorry for them. Horseshit."

The phone rang, chasing the drunk upstairs. "This is the Hillcrest Motel calling. Do you have any rooms available?"

"No rooms with bath left, but I do have some nice rooms with the bath down the hall."

"Just a minute." Richard listened to the ensuing discussion about the room with no bath. "We'll send the couple down anyway. They can look for themselves."

"O.K." Richard replied, then mumbled, "People, are so fussy these days. They have to have a room with bath. They are willing to pay fifteen to twenty dollars more a night just to have the privilege of sitting on the pot in their very own room. Disgusting."

At 2:00 a.m., the stream of hot rods and motorcycles finally begins to die down as the last of the weekend revelers head for their homes, nests, pads and burroughs. The quiet of the night has begun to descend in the lobby and throughout the hotel. Richard is able to sit down with a newspaper for a few minutes of relaxation. It has been a long night. Along with registering a number of guests he has cleaned the restrooms, cleaned the Kennicott Room, swept and dusted the lobby. Maybe he can get a few minutes of rest before the local police officers drop in for coffee and a discussion of the latest shenanigans.

It is a late-summer night, warm enough so the furnace would not kick on. There was the inevitable creaks and groans of an old building which night clerks get used to and eventually identify and ignore. Richard cocked his head toward the ceiling when he heard footsteps along the upstairs hallway. Probably the drunk heading for the bathroom, he thought. He cracked the newspaper to another page. Again he heard footsteps in the upstairs hallway. He put down the paper, and trudged upstairs. Once in the hallway, he looked both fore and aft, no one was in sight. He could hear the drunk snoring in room ten. Everything was quiet by room seven and eight. He recognized the wheezing in room four. Room five was gone for the weekend. He went down the hall to the bath and shower rooms. They too were empty. Figuring it was someone on the third floor, he climbed the next flight and gazed up and down the hallway. No sign of anyone or anything. Shaking his head he returned to the lobby and the newspaper.

A few minutes had passed when again he cocked his head at the same sound in the hallway upstairs. Not waiting to listen any longer, he immediately dashed upstairs. There were still no signs. He stood for a moment and strained his ears, listening for the footsteps which were not forthcoming. Sitting down on the top step of the stairwell he lighted a cigarette, ears perked with curiosity. There were no footsteps, only the occasional snoring of the drunk in room ten.

Richard slowly descended the stairs back to the lobby, wondering momentarily if he was hearing things. Then he dismissed the incident from his conscious mind. As he reached the lobby the local on-duty officer entered. "Got the coffee pot on?" he cheerfully asked.

"Of course, it's always on."

Richard escorted him into the darkened restaurant, lighted only by the florescence of the soda fountain. "Well, the town seems pretty quiet tonight," Richard said as he poured a hot cup of coffee.

"Oh, there was the usual noise and scuffles at the Zoo, but not as bad as some nights," the officer stated. "Gosh, that coffee's hot," he added as he tore the cup from his mouth and reached for a napkin.

"Of course," Richard replied with a chuckle, "I just poured it." Richard scrunched out his cigarette and reached for another. As he was fumbling for some matches the officer flipped out his lighter and placed a flame in front of him.

"Checked in some drunk tonight. Tried to beat me down on the rates as usual. I get so sick and tired of those bastards who can go out and drink all night, then stagger in here and want me to give them a rate break. It happens every weekend. I think I will just put up the 'No Vacancy' sign when I see them coming. Drives me batty," Richard ranted as he blew smoke up toward the ceiling.

"Yeah, I know what you mean. They got plenty of money for booze, but the next thing you know they go out and apply for fuel assistance. Do you know I have a neighbor who is drawing food stamps, general assistance money and unemployment, and he drives a better car than me. Not only that but he bought his family a color T.V.! Goddamn. Look at the hours I put in and I can't even afford a color T.V. This town needs a union or something." He took another sip of his now cooled coffee.

"Yeah, I suppose so," Richard replied in his usual non-committed way. Then working to change the subject he asked, "What about that accident that happened out by the narrows. Was the kid drinking?"

"Of course, aren't they all?" the officer replied. "I have yet to see an area where so much drinking goes on among teenagers. I know this is Stearns County, but good god, there's a lot of kids drunk on the weekends."

The officer gulped his coffee and headed out of the restaurant. "Catch you later," he called back.

"Thanks for stopping," Richard answered as he crushed his cigarette. He poured himself another cup and slowly walked into the lobby. Retrieving his heavy corduroy jacket from the coat rack he settled into a comfortable position on the bench by the window. The thought of the footsteps crossed his mind for a split second just before he rested his eyes.

I was not aware that Richard had been hearing strange noises. When he first broached the subject with me, he had been hearing footsteps for some time. One evening we were sitting in the apartment when he said to me, "I think there is a ghost in the building."

"What!" I exclaimed.

The very thought that Richard would mention ghost was strictly out of character for him. I had known Richard for nearly eight years and never once had he given me the slightest idea that he was predisposed to believe in the supernatural. Had it been the reverse, that is, me telling Richard there was a ghost in the Palmer House, it would be true to form, because I am somewhat of a free spirit anyway. Richard is the practical one and he certainly isn't an advocate of occult. "A ghost!" I exclaimed again. "What makes you say that?"

"Because I've heard something many times in the past few months when I am working nights. I hear footsteps coming down the hall from room twelve or thirteen, when I know there is no one in those rooms. I run upstairs and there is no one there. Even up to third floor. Still no one there. I know there is something up there but I can't explain it." He paused then continued.

"I am not one to believe in ghosts. But did you know that someone once committed suicide upstairs years ago? I heard the Quinns talking about it back in the '50's. Also a man hanged himself in the Palmer House bar by jumping off the pool table. They found him dead in the morning. In fact, I think it was Jack Norgrin who found him."

I shivered a little as Richard was talking because this was so unlike him and rarely had I seen him so serious. He wasn't pulling my leg. Naturally inquisitive, I was fascinated by his discourse and now I was really starting to get into the idea of having our own private spirit.

We occasionally discussed the ghost over the next few years, but were not willing to share our knowledge with anyone else. It was difficult enough to get the locals to support us without having the word get around town that the Palmer House was not only historical but it was also hysterical and haunted. But every so often Richard would mention that he had heard the footsteps again during the night.

* * * * *

One day a chambermaid was furious because someone locked her in room thirteen. One of the guests heard her pounding and shouting and unlocked the door. This was truly spooky. First of all, room thirteen is locked with an old fashioned skeleton key. It does not have a spring lock which could mistakenly trip when jarred. In this case, someone had to deliberately turn the key to lock the door. When the guest heard the pounding and went to the door, the key was in the keyhole on the outside. All he had to do was turn it to unlock the door.

The maid accused the guest of playing a prank on her and came downstairs to vent her anger. When she told me about it, I figured it was one of the staff playing a joke on her. The thought of a ghost had long vanished and had not been mentioned by Richard or myself for a long time. We all laughed about it and soon it was a forgotten matter.

That is, until it happened a second time. This brought Richard and I head-on with the situation. Richard was the first one to bring up the idea of the ghostly intervention. "Do you think he locked her in room thirteen?"

"I don't know," I said. "I really hadn't thought that much about it. But I suppose, it could have been. However, you haven't mentioned hearing anything lately, so I thought the case was closed. How could *he*, (which is the encoded pronoun Richard and I use for discussing our ghost in front of others), suddenly become active after remaining dormant for so long?"

"Oh, he's out and moving about," Richard said. "I just haven't told you about it. I figured it wasn't that big of a deal."

I was serving on the Sinclair Lewis Foundation Board of Directors, an organization which sounds very intellectual but in truth is more of a housekeeping overseer. If you don't mind spending one night a month listening to the president read the bills and deciding if they should be paid or not — and naturally they are going to pay them because they owe them — then this is the organization for you. They have managed to keep up Sinclair's boyhood home and they periodically apply for a federal grant, and complain when they don't get it. Now, however the Board of the Foundation has decided to raise some money on their own to help with the upkeep. The idea of having a fund-drive called the "Friends of the Lewis Home" was presented to the board and accepted by it. And further, it was decided that a good kick-off for this fund-raiser would be to have an open house at the home. I wonder how many Sauk Centrites even know where it is, let alone have ever visited it.

The event was held on the second Sunday in May. The weather was perfect, not a cloud in the sky, not a single breeze blowing. The sun was getting higher in the sky and its warmth added to the pleasantness of the day.

The Board of Directors had gathered early to set the tables for the refreshments. When all was ready the Board sat down to await the appointed time for the guests to arrive. Suddenly, out of nowhere, came a whirlwind. It passed through the yard, scattering cups and napkins hither and yon. It was over in an instant and suddenly it was dead calm again. The astonished Board members busily scurried around picking up the scattered napkins and cups. I turned to the president and with a knowing smile said to the blue sky, "Thank you, Sinclair." He looked at me as though I had lost my mind. I had the strangest feeling at that moment that it was a courtesy call from Red Lewis himself. I recalled that it was a cold day in January, when Dr. Claude Lewis emptied the ashes of Sinclair from the urn in which they had been transported from Italy to America. A sudden gust of wind, then too, swept out of nowhere and scattered some of the ashes. I thought to myself as we were resetting the cups and napkins, "Wouldn't it be marvelous if the footsteps that Richard was hearing in the hotel and the spirit of Lewis had something in common."

But enough of this nonsense. I will drive myself buggy if I keep up this train of thought. That was six years ago and all thoughts of ghosts were laid aside as work on restoring the Palmer House proceeded. Yet every once in a great while Richard would mention, in passing, that he had heard the footsteps again.

But the spirit would not rest. One of our guests, who was staying in room two, came downstairs complaining that she had been kept awake all night by a dripping sound in her room. During the night she finally got up to investigate and found that the clothing in one of her suitcases was very damp. I asked her if her suitcase was in the bathroom. "No, it was sitting right next to the T.V. Which is where I heard the dripping sound. And besides, I got up twice in the night to see if a faucet was dripping and it wasn't!"

"O.K." I said, "show me the suitcase and where it was setting." We headed upstairs to room two. The thought of the ghost had not yet entered my mind.

Once inside, I saw the suitcase in the middle of the room, fifteen feet away from the bathroom. The ceiling was not wet or even damp. I went up to the third floor and entered room twenty-one, which was directly above room two. There were no pipes in the vicinity, nor water spots on the floor nor dripping from above.

I started back downstairs and the thought of the spirit entered my mind. As I returned to room two I was startled to hear the guest blurt out, "You don't have a poltergeist in the hotel, do you? I definitely heard water dripping. My clothes are all wet and I'm going to make you pay for the dry cleaning!" Then she stomped out of the room.

I sat on the bed, looking at the wet suitcase and then up at the ceiling. There must be a logical explanation. It was snowing a little when she took the suitcase out of the car. Perhaps some snow settled in the cracks of the case and had melted. That was it.

I ran downstairs and found her in the restaurant. "I've got it. There must have been some snow on your suitcase and when it warmed up it melted and dripped inside."

"It doesn't snow in my trunk," she said, "the suitcase was in the trunk of my car and it was completely dry when I carried it in. No, it's that prankster ghost that did it."

"No," I retorted, "I've been here for seven years and this is the first prank, as you call it, that has ever occurred." I turned and walked out into the lobby. My mind was spinning now. The maid was locked up in room thirteen not once but twice. Richard still hears footsteps. I wondered if it all could be true...

Nearly a year-and-a-half passed with little or no mention of the spirit. No pranks, no tricks no whirlwinds. Then one evening a guest who had rented a room on the third floor by the month, came over to me as I was sitting in the lobby. He sat down across from me and very quietly and calmly asked, "Is there a ghost in the hotel?"

I looked up from my newspaper, "Is there a what in where?"

"A ghost, you know, a spirit?" he said.

"Why would you ask that question? Have you heard something?" I asked, trying to feel him out.

"Well, I heard something outside my door last night, two or three times. Finally I opened the door. There was no one in the hallway and all the doors were shut, so it wasn't someone going down the hall to the bathroom."

"What did it sound like? I mean, how would you describe it? The sound, I mean."

"Well," he looked up at the ceiling and placed his hand on his chin contemplating his answer. "It was like footsteps. Like someone walking down the hall past my door. I checked the radiator to see if it was coming from there. Then I looked out the window to see if it was coming from outside. But no, it was definitely footsteps outside in the hallway."

"I wouldn't worry about it," I said. "It was probably birds on the roof."

"At three o'clock in the morning in the middle of the winter?" he commented with disbelief.

I got up and slowly walked away. I wasn't going to tell him any more. At least not at this time. I'd wait and see if he brought up the subject again.

The phone rang and I answered, "Palmer House, may I help you?"

"Could you tell me the soup of the day?"

"Split pea with ham."

"Thank you." CLICK. The soup lady again. I wonder who she is.

As I hung up the phone I heard the click of the dog's feet coming down the stairs. Richard's up. I went to the door and let the dog out. As Richard surfaced behind the desk he said, "Get me a cup of coffee, please."

As I brought his coffee to him I said, "Guess what?"

"Now what?" he growled.

"Arvid just asked me if we had a ghost upstairs."

"When?"

"Just a few minutes ago. He said he heard footsteps in the hall last night. He looked out but there was no one there," I said excitedly.

"Oh, don't get started on that ghost thing again. Any checks come in today? Land O' Lakes or anything?"

"No," I answered. "Just a couple of bills and a card from Tootsie."

"Are you still writing to her? I don't see what you have to write about all the time," he said as he lighted a cigarette. "Did Joe call?"

"Not yet," I replied. "Who's Joe?"

"Oh, never mind."

I could see that Richard was in no mood to discuss the ghost, at least not at that time. But I was most anxious to continue my discussion with Arv.

It was not until about 2:30 that afternoon that I saw Arv again. He was sitting in the T.V. lounge. "Hi Arv," I said as I entered the lounge. I found myself an ash tray and asked, "Are you involved?" refering to the program that was on the television set.

"No, not really," he answered and he reached over and turned off the set. "What's on your mind?" he asked with a knowing grin.

"Tell me exactly what you heard and what makes you think it was a ghost." I lighted up a cigarette and offered another to Arv.

"Thanks," he said. Then with a bemused expression he began to tell of his experience the previous night.

"I don't know quite how to explain it. At first it sounded like little children talking fast and giggling. Naturally I was awakened from a sound sleep. I thought the noise was coming from outside. I went to the window to look out, even though I knew it was too late for children to be out. When I looked at the clock it was three in the morning. Maybe it's the radiator, I thought. I put my ear to the radiator. No, the heat was not even on. I sat on my bed awhile then I heard footsteps in the hall by my door. I quickly ran and opened it. Nothing. I looked up and down the hallway and all was quiet. I could hear the guy in room twenty-eight snoring up a storm. I closed the door and returned to bed. I was just about asleep when I heard a thud next to the wall by my headboard. I panicked this time, wondering where in the hell the noise was coming from. Opening the door quickly, I again encountered nothing. I must have stayed awake another hour or so but there were no further noises. Then I fell asleep, mainly out of exhaustion. Is that what you wanted to hear?" he asked as he finally lighted the cigarette I had given him.

"Yes, but only if you're not making it up."

"I'm not, I swear to God, that's what I heard last night."

Arv was getting a little uptight. I suppose because I had implied that he was lying. Arvid was not your typical twenty-four-year-old kid who drinks, smokes pot and raises hell all night. He was raised on a small farm north of Alexandria. He was in the service, where he did a tour of duty in Vietnam. While there he got turned on to drugs and alcohol. After a few years of drifting, he decided to enter a treatment center where he joined AA. He is still an active member of AA. He enrolled in technical school to study welding and after graduation he got a job in Sauk Centre at a manufacturing plant and took a room at the Palmer House. Subsequently, it was hard to believe that he had any reason to make up the story of the noises he heard. And it was all the more meaningful to my inquiry since the ghost had never been discussed in his presence.

"Well," I said, "I think you are right. There is a ghost in the Palmer House. We have known it for years. Richard has heard it often but we've never told anyone about it. Local business is tough enough to come by without adding a ghost." I continued to fill him in on all the experiences we had had with the spirit. The chambermaid, the dripping water, the irate guest, the works.

As I was telling this, I noticed Richard standing by the door listening. "Hey Richard, come on in. I was just telling..."

"I heard, I heard," he said as he came in and flicked his ashes in my ash tray.

"Did you tell him about the guy who visited Sauk Centre this summer and what he said?"

"No, I don't remember you telling me that."

"Oh, you do too. I told you," he said in a disgusted manner.

"What was it?" Arv broke in, "something about the ghost?"

Richard took a long drag on his cigarette, looked up toward the ceiling and slowly exhaled. "I used to go to school with this guy's brother. He was back in town this summer for a visit. He was much younger than I so I didn't remember him. We were chatting at the counter about Sauk Centre when he asked me if I had seen the ghost at the Palmer House. I played stupid because I was curious as to what he knew about it. If you have owned the Palmer House for ten years you must have heard or seen the ghost. I did, he said. I not only heard him, I saw him one night.' "

Then, Richard retold the man's story:

"Me and the Amos boy were best of pals in high school. His folks owned the Palmer House at that time, so we spent a lot of time there. One night he invited me to stay overnight. We were staying in room fifteen and telling stories and jokes and giggling like kids do. Suddenly, we heard a thump...thump...thump...in the hallway outside the door."

"That's the hallway that goes by my headboard," Arv piped up excitedly.

"Shhh!" I said, "let him continue."

"Well, the Amos boy said it was the ghost, but let me tell you, I thought he was pulling my leg. Then he told me how the ghost had chased him down the hall one night as he was going to the bathroom. You can imagine two kids in a hotel room at three in the morning talking about ghosts. I thought I'd wet my pants right there. Now I had to go to the bathroom. But I was not about to go alone. I convinced my friend to go with me. We got out of bed and put on our bathrobes. We unlocked the door and peeked out into the dark hallway. There wasn't any lights in that part of the hallway. He walked out first and I held on to his bathrobe. The dark hall seemed to go on forever. We made it to the bathroom and locked the door. When I finished we again peeked out. There was no in sight, so we started back to the room. It was then we saw it. Like a mist or a heavy fog hovering in the hallway between the door to room twelve on the east side and room thirteen on the west side, almost at the entrance to the dark hall. I know my heart stopped right there. I was never so scared in my life.

'Come on, it won't hurt you,' the Amos boy said. 'I've lived here a couple of years now and I've seen it several times.'

"We drew closer to the fog as we inched our way down the hallway. It seemed to be moving toward us. Then it started to rise and floated over our heads. When I looked up and down the hall toward the bathroom it was gone. It didn't take us long to get to our room and lock the door. I never did stay overnight with him again..."

The T.V. lounge was silent, except for the sound of breathing. "Wow," Arv exclaimed. "And he told you that story on his own? You didn't even have to ask him?"

"Are you afraid?" I asked.

"No, I'm intrigued, fascinated, and curious as hell as to what it is." We sat and discussed the suicides that had happened in the hotel and became convinced that the spirit was obviously trapped in the hotel for eternity.

The phone rang and I ran to answer it. "Hello, Palmer House. Yes, just a minute," I said. "Richard, it's for you. It's your mother."

Arv walked by the desk and glanced up at the clock. "My god, it's late. I better get to work."

It was nearly a week before we had the opportunity to sit down again and explore further the events which were taking place, now basically confined to the third floor. "I've decided," Arvid began the conversation very thoughtfully, "to see if I can't find an opportunity to confront the spirit or whatever you call it. Last night I was again awakened by this strange thumping noise." He looked upward as he was trying to find the right word for the sound he had heard. "Like a... like a... like a distant thumping on the pavement. Not so loud as to feel the building move, but if it were close that would be the sound. Then I heard a faint swishing sound. I ran to the door and quickly opened it. Nothing! I glanced at the clock. It was 3:30. I returned to bed. Then I felt the presence again. This time I spoke to it quite loudly and dinstictly; 'What's the matter? Don't you believe in God?' I asked. There was utter silence for about five seconds and then all of a sudden in the next room I heard a loud crash. It sounded as though furniture was being dropped to the floor. I jumped out of bed and ran into the hallway. Nothing, just the ordinary sounds of the night, deep breathing and quiet. I entered the bathroom which is directly behind my bedroom."

He stopped his train of thought, jumped up and said to me, "Al, come upstairs with me. I want you to see and hear this."

Leaving the lobby we bounded up to the third floor, taking two steps at a time. We arrived at the bathroom, a large open room fifteen feet square, which contains a shower stall, a stool, a small vanity table and a heavy chair. "Here, you take this chair," Arvid said excitedly, "and when I get into my room, let it drop to the floor."

He left the bathroom and there I was, feeling like a fool, holding this chair about two feet in the air. "O.K.," came the voice from behind the wall, "let it drop." With a crash, the chair fell to the floor. "That's it! That's it!" came the excited muffled voice through the wall. In a matter of seconds he was back in the bathroom. "That's it! That's exactly the noise I heard when I said, 'What? Don't you believe in God?' It must have picked up the chair and let it drop."

"Let's not get carried away with this thing," I said. "I certainly believe there is something unusual going on in the hotel, after hearing reports for ten years, but a furniture-throwing spirit is carrying it a little too far."

"Do you think I am making this up?" he asked, rather hurt that I would cast doubts on his story.

"No, Arvid, I just think you have been trying too hard to find out what this is all about."

"Al, Al," someone had climbed all the way to the third floor to find me.

"Yes, what is it?" I called down the corridor.

"Telephone!"

I turned to Arvid trying to reassure him. "Hey, I don't doubt you. I'd give anything to get an answer to this thing. I'll be right back. Got to get the telephone."

"Don't bother to come back up now. I gotta leave. But I would like to talk about it again." He stood there looking like a little boy who had just had the air taken out of his balloon.

"We sure will. You are the first person who has been willing to pursue this whole mystery."

I ran down the hall and down the stairs. Taking the telephone behind the desk I said, "Hello, this is Al. May I help you?"

"Yes, could you tell me the soup of the day?"

* * * * *

It was one of my blessed, restful Sunday mornings. I relish winter because the restaurant is closed and I can have a little time to myself. There were a few guests staying that weekend but most were friends who were not demanding. I could relate to them in a laid-back manner. Siegfried and Tillie were two. They often stay here because he's an entertainer and frequently he performs at a roadhouse nearby. He is a rugged, masculine, German patriarch type and Tillie is a butterball of creativity, full of fun and a joy to be around.

I was sitting at the counter, holding a cup of coffee in my hands, when the door to the lobby burst open. "Do you have a ghost or something in this place?" It was Tillie, and she came on like Attila the Hun. She headed behind the counter and poured herself a cup of coffee.

"What do you mean, a ghost?" I said very innocently.

"You know damn well what I am talking about. That thing that kept me awake all night. It even entered my room!"

"Who," I said, "Siegfried?"

"Huh, I should be so lucky."

"Well, sit down here and tell me about it. It can't be that bad." I was very quiet and noncommital. Even though I was bursting to find out if she could shed new light on the spirit. She sipped then stated her story.

"Sigie and I didn't get home till after two in the morning. You know, after-hours parties. We visited with Richard for a few minutes and then headed upstairs. Sigie immediately found the T.V. lounge across the hall and I, as usual, trundled off to bed. I could hear the T.V. softly across the hall. I was not quite asleep yet when I heard the prattling of little voices outside my door. I thought it was the T.V. so I didn't pay that much attention to it, at first. But then the babbling kept getting louder and louder, so I got up and opened the door. I tiptoed across the hall and there was Siegfried, sound asleep in the chair. The T.V. was hissing and covered with black spots, so I turned it off and let him sleep.

"I had just gotten comfortably settled in bed again when I heard the prattling of children's voices again. I got up to look out the window to see if some children might be out on the street. But there was nothing moving out there, either. I glanced at the clock and saw that it was 3:15.

"Just knowing it was after three and I hadn't had any sleep yet made me very tired. I closed my eyes but I'm sure I wasn't asleep, in an instant the room suddenly became very cold, as though all the heat had been drained out of it. I was afraid to open my eyes, not knowing what was in the room. It was an eerie sensation. Then something brushed my face. I thought it was Siegfried playing a joke on me, but the feeling was soon all around me. I didn't want to open my eyes. The presence moved across the room toward the window. Suddenly the room warmed up again and everything was back to normal.

"I opened my eyes, jumped out of bed and hurried to open the door. All was quiet. I crossed the hall to the T.V. lounge and there was Siegfried still asleep in the chair. I know damn well there was a ghost or a spirit in my room."

Tillie was pale as she finished relating her encounter. I just knew she could not have been making this up. I had goose bumps. Combining this experience with the past ten years of different, yet interrelated stories by various individuals, none knowing the other, certainly gave credence to the presence of our ghost.

I felt so frustrated and left out. After all these years, after having slept in practically every room in this hotel, I have still not encountered the spirit. I envied Richard, at least he had heard footsteps.

It was a little after ten-thirty one evening as Richard and I entered the Tic Toc Bar for what I thought was to be a relaxing drink. No sooner had the bartender served us our drinks, when he called down the bar, "Hey, Dick or Al, telephone."

"Who would be calling at this hour?" Richard asked, looking at me. "You take it," he said. "It must be the night clerk."

Heading back through the entire length of the building, I picked up the phone. "Hello, this is Al."

"Oh, Al, you know those two guys that rented room two this evening?"

"No, I don't know them, but I know the room is rented."

"Well one of them, the smaller one, just came down to tell me that one of the twin beds is soaking wet, right in the middle. And it's wet all the way through to the box spring."

I was taken back for a moment. Then I answered, "How could that be? That room wasn't rented last night. In fact, I was watching T.V. in that room last night."

"Well," he answered, "I just went up there to look at it and sure enough, the bed is soaking wet."

"Hold on, I'll be right over." I hung up the telephone.

Walking back to where Richard was sitting I tried to figure out how the bed could be wet. "What was that all about?" Richard inquired.

"It was the night clerk. One of the guys in room two says his bed is soaked clean through to the box springs."

"How could that be? That room hasn't been rented for a couple of days," Richard said, looking puzzled.

"I don't know but I'm going over to take a look. You wait here. I'll be right back."

I was trying to picture the location of the water pipes above the room as I ran across the street and into the lobby. When I was passed the front desk the night clerk reported, "He doesn't seem terribly upset."

Thank God for small favors, I thought as I climbed the stairs and went down the corridor to room two.

"Come on in, the door is open," came the reply to my knock on the door. The room was larger than most of our rooms. The brown plywood walls were beginning to show wear. They had been installed in 1963. Actor Lorne Greene, had spent several days in Sauk Centre and had stayed at the Palmer House. The room had been refurbished just for him. A large window looking north was shuttered with a replica of stained glass. Straight ahead was one of the original armoires which we had restored to its original beauty. On the south wall were twin beds with brass headboards and a nightstand was tucked between them.

As I entered the room I noticed the older man was seated on one bed, his eyes glued to the blaring television set. The smaller man greeted me with "Here is the wet spot." He led me directly to the bed near the bathroom door and began his narrative.

"I was just going to pull back the covers and get ready for bed when I touched what I thought was a stain. I discovered that it was a very wet spot," he stated, looking up at the ceiling where there was a dark spot.

"That stain has been there for years," I commented.

I had seen that dark spot many times and it never seemed to change. But his assumption was correct; it was directly above the wet spot on the bed. Pulling a chest away from the west wall and moving it closer to the bed, I climbed up and felt the ceiling. Dry as a bone. Not even a feeling of dampness. It certainly would have been soaking wet or at least damp had that much water penetrated.

After jumping off the chest, I moved it back in place. I then began feeling the floor. It too was dry. Only the mattress was soaking wet, as though someone or something had deliberately dumped a pail of water directly on it.

"You certainly can't sleep in here tonight. Let me get you a key. You can stay in the room across the hall."

"Fine," he smiled, "but let's set up the mattress and box spring beside the bed so that it will dry out."

Very thoughtful, I thought to myself, for a guest to be concerned about the beds. I got the key for his new room and settled him in across the hall. His roommate remained in room two for the night.

"Well, what was it?" Richard asked as I re-entered the bar and sat down.

"Beats me. The bed was soaking wet for about two feet in circumference. I mean soaking, right through to the box spring."

"The plumber was working in the shower room on the third floor yesterday. Maybe it leaked through the ceiling," Richard said as he took a sip of his beer.

"Couldn't have, I checked the ceiling, first thing. It was bone dry. I even poked my finger in the little hole that was already there and it wasn't even damp behind the plaster."

"It had to come from some place," Richard said.

"Richard," I mused, "remember the girl in room two about two years ago who insisted her suitcase was wet? She said she heard dripping water all night."

"Oh, Allan, you're not going to suggest the ghost again?"

"Why not? Wait till you see that bed. There is no way it could have gotten that wet by a simple drip and besides, where did the water come from?"

"What did you do with the guy that was supposed to sleep there?"

"I gave him room number four. He took it very calmly, even suggested we set the mattress and box spring on the side to dry."

"Well, there has got to be some logical explanation."

"After they leave tomorrow we will tear that room apart. There has to be an explanation!" Richard stood up and looked back at me. "Don't get another beer, he said. We can have one in the apartment."

"Good night," the bartender called to us as we went out the door.

* * * * *

The gentleman in room two checked out about 9:00 a.m. I wasted no time in getting a key and going into the room. As usual, the television was left blaring, and the lights were on.

I started by moving the box spring and mattress out of the way, no easy job for a skinny thing like me. I again pulled the chest over to the bed and felt the ceiling. Then I ran up to the third floor and measured the distance from the shower room to the spot on the ceiling below. Almost twelve feet. There was no water or noticeable dampness in the shower room. Downstairs, back in room two, I examined the now nearly dry mattress.

"I just heard about your visitor." The voice startled me and I let out a slight scream.

"Sorry, didn't mean to frighten you."

"My god, but you did, Arvid. How'd you hear about this?" I asked.

"Are you kidding? Nothing is secret in the Palmer House, Merlin told me. Think it was the ghost?" he bubbled, as he looked up at the spot on the ceiling.

"I can't explain it," I said. "Even last night, after they discovered the wet bed. I checked the spot and it was completely dry."

Arvid scrutinized the headboard now. "Al, look at this!" He was slowly moving his hands over the brass. "Notice all the splash marks here." Then turning to the other bed, "Notice there are no marks on this one."

"Yes," I said becoming interested. "It looks at though every time a drop of water fell on the bed, it splashed up on the brass."

"But wait a minute," he continued, "you are not going to get a splash when water hits a soft surface like a bed spread."

Arvid ran to the bathroom and reappeared with a glass of water. "I'm going to drop some water on the mattress from up here." He stood on the chest. I knelt down so I could see the impact of the water on the soft surface.

"It looks to me like a considerable amount of water was deliberately sloshed directly onto the bed at an angle to the headboard with a velocity strong enough to cause the splash marks," he said, after still studying the situation.

"Let's put this room back together," I replied. "The maid will be in shortly to make it up. And I don't want to arouse anymore suspicions."

Later that day, Merlin stopped me on my way through the restaurant and asked, "Do you know what I just saw, Al?"

"No, what?" I questioned.

"I just went up to room two to look at the headboard. As I got to the doorway I saw the maid sprinkling the room with Holy Water. But don't worry, she didn't see me."

* * * * *

Weeks passed without a sign or sound from our elusive friend, when again a new wrinkle was added to the perplexing mystery. This time it was Merlin's story. Now mind you, he has been a resident of the hotel for more than ten years. He has heard stories and tales of the ghost but has always remained skeptical. In all his years of living in various rooms and on different floors, he has never reported a sight or sound that might be considered an unexplained experience.

"Al, Al!" Merlin rushed up, his face flushed and his voice strained to a slightly higher pitch.

"What is it, what's the matter?" I asked, trying to stay calm.

"Last night I had a visit from the ghost!"

"Come on, Merlin, it's your imagination. You've been hearing us talk about it too much lately."

"No, I swear it was the ghost," he said excitedly. "I thought it was hogwash for ten years but last night it knocked on my door."

"It what?" I exclaimed.

He was serious, I could tell by his voice when he told his story:

"Last night I was sound asleep when I heard two loud knocks at my door. I woke up and glanced at my digital clock. 'Who,' I wondered. 'would be knocking at 3:30 in the morning?' I jumped out of bed with just my shorts on, that's the way I sleep, and fumbled with the dead bolt on my door. After opening it, I called out, 'Who is it?' There was total silence, no one at the door, no one in the corridor, just quiet. I know I heard a knock, I wasn't dreaming."

"Why, after ten years, should the ghost suddenly decide to bother you? I am sure you were having a bad nightmare," I said, trying to calm him down. I started to walk away but he grabbed my shoulder. "It was no nightmare! I definitely heard a loud knock! It's never happened before."

Our conversation was interrupted by Arvid coming down the stairs. His room is directly across the hall from Merlin's. "Arvid," I called to him, "did you hear any loud knocking on Merlin's door last night?"

"I was going to tell you about it," he said as we walked back toward Merlin. "I woke up last night when I heard Merlin fumbling with his dead bolt on the door. I glanced at the clock and it was 3:30. I didn't hear a knock or anything, just his fumbling with his door. I thought that was an odd time for him to be getting up."

"Well," I explained, "he said he heard a loud knock on his door and it awakened him out of a sound sleep."

"I know I wasn't dreaming," Merlin insisted.

"If Arvid heard you unbolt the door, you must have done it," I said agreeably.

The telephone rang and I quickly ran to answer it. "Good morning, Palmer House. May I help you?"

"Could I get an order of fries to go, please?"

"Sure could. To pick up or to be delivered?"

"Oh, I'll pick them up in about ten minutes."

"O.K., bye."

Arvid was standing by the front desk with a wondering, pondering expression. "I would love to spend a night in the Sinclair Lewis boyhood home."

"Why the home?" I asked. "What's that got to do with what we've been talking about?"

"Nobody has ever stayed all night there since it has been restored and declared a national landmark. Who knows what could be learned by spending a night there?"

"I follow your train of thought," I said smiling. "But I think you're reading too much into this whole business."

His proposal was an unusual idea. And to my knowledge no one has ever spent a night in the Sinclair home.

No one at the Palmer House has ever been hurt or confronted by the spirit. Nothing has been resolved as to its existence or conversely to its non-existence. To this day, I have never heard, seen, nor witnessed any of the exciting ectoplasmic events personally. Hopefully, my day will come.

The Clubhouse.

"Good morning, Palmer House. May I help you?"

The lady's voice on the other end was a little hesitant as she introduced herself. "I am calling on behalf of my club. We are mostly business women and we have a monthly dinner meeting and we are wondering if the Palmer House would like to serve us."

"What day of the month do you meet?" I asked, not realizing at the time that we were maneuvering ourselves into another trap.

"Monday evening," she answered.

"And approximately how many members do you have?"

"Thirteen to fifteen usually attend, but we are trying to increase attendance."

"Certainly, we will be glad to have you meet at the Palmer House."

Initially Richard and I were thrilled. We set aside the Minniemashie Room the first Monday of every month to host the group. We set the table in white linen and orange napkins with full place settings. They would choose which meal was to be served.

At the time of their arrival, Richard and I would position ourselves at the door, remove their coats and wraps and direct them to the private dining room. Candles were on the tables and marvelous home-cooked food waited to be served. Some of the members were getting up in years and had to be helped to the table with walkers. There were also some younger members. All in all they appeared very appreciative of our efforts. We weren't sure what they discussed at their meetings, but hopefully it was how wonderful we were treating them.

Soon we began hearing complaints. Two dollars was too much money. The food was too hot. Our choice of food was limited and so on and so on. Of course none of these comments were made directly to us. We would hear them only via the grapevine. So and so said the food at the Palmer House was cold, or there was not enough food on the plate. Obviously, this irritated us, but we continued to host the club for another two years and we continued to hear constant negative comments over the back fence. It got to the point where we hated the first Monday of the month.

We tried everything possible to please them. I remember one evening in particular when I even heated the plates before putting on the food. All I got was a nasty note in the suggestion box which said, "I burned myself on your plate, Al Tingley. You'll hear from my lawyer in the morning."

"What was her tongue doing on the plate, anyway," I wondered.

One day a contingent of women finally came to see me about the cost of the monthly meal. "Why can't we get something like the Rotary gets every week at a reasonable price, like one dollar-fifty a plate?" they inquired.

I informed them that Rotary doesn't get table cloths or candles or special service. They said that was fine. So we started to serve them under the new slimmed down contract. And sure enough the comments about town changed. "Guess what? At the Palmer House you don't even get table cloths. The food is good but there's not enough of it."

One evening about 5:30, just before the meeting, Richard and I stood in the lobby and watched as a few of the ladies headed into the bar next door for a couple of cocktails, at the cost of one dollar per shot. The next thing we knew, they were in the lobby complaining about the cost of the meal. We had had it. Finally, we told one of the officers that they might take their meeting somewhere else where they would be happier. And lo and behold, they did. They went to a little local cafe down the street and we heard nothing more from them for over a year. Then one day the new president called and asked if one of their special functions could be hosted at the Palmer House. I was reluctant, but decided that they could if they wouldn't make a habit of it. Guess what? They made a habit of it.

They are here again tonight, sixteen women. A few of the names have changed and some of the faces, but nothing much else has changed.

Now I ask you: "Who needs their collective heads examined?"

Free Wheeling!

It was a sultry late night in July when they began to arrive. Richard was working his usual all-night vigil. He was walking from window to window, inspecting the trees we had so lovingly planted in front of the old building. Six of them had been broken down by the hoods and vandals leaving the bars late at night. Of course, they are bigger now, the trees I mean, and can withstand more of the blows than they used to.

As he patrolled, he saw three powerful and noisy motorcycles pull up outside. The riders were of the typical ilk, ugly and unshaven. And you should have seen the men. Richard got behind the desk quickly as they entered the east door of the hotel. "We need three rooms, for the six of us."

"All I have left are rooms on the top floor, and they are without bath, or air-conditioning."

"Fine. How much?"

Richard told them the price and they paid without so much as a grumble, which is rare. As they loudly tramped upstairs with their luggage and ladies, Richard sighed, relieved that he was not hassled.

It was not long before more motorcycles pulled up in front and more gang members entered. "Our buddies have rooms here, don't they?"

"Yes, but it is very late and they are probably sleeping. I don't think you should go up and wake them."

Imagine, about twenty-five gang members dressed in their traditional colors, confronting one rather short and nervous desk clerk in a small town hotel lobby at 2:30 in the morning. What could he say? So they all took off upstairs, packed with six packs for an all-night stay at the Palmer House.

Mind you, I was sleeping through most of this, but about 6:00 in the morning I was awakened by a thunderous assult. It sounded like a thousand motorcycles all throttling for a tumulteous exit. I dressed immediately and came running downstairs just in time to see one gang member blast off in a blaze of noise.

I took a quick run upstairs . There I found the doors of three rooms open, perhaps because of the heat of the night, and there, draped in every fashion, were sleeping bodies — on the beds, on the floor, and even on the dresser. The smell of booze and smoke was overwhelming. The faint odor of burned rope hovered in the air. Thirty cyclists were jammed into the three small rooms, normally rented for six.

We didn't roust them. We didn't have to. They rousted themselves, roared off, ripping us off in the process.

"What could I do?" Richard lamented.

Later his frazzled nerves slowly mended enabling him to be in shape for the next unknown encounter. Needless to say, we didn't hang their pictures in our gallery of distinguished visitors.

A Town Divided.

It was the coldest day of January, with a wind chill of nearly fifty degrees below zero. Approximately fifteen teachers had taken to the streets, passing out leaflets to tell their side of the story. The restaurant was closed and, as I was turning off the outdoor restaurant sign, I waved to the group as they passed the hotel. "When you are through, why don't you come in for a cup of hot chocolate?" I called to them.

"Sounds like a winner to us," one called back.

I went back into the restaurant to make sure the hot chocolate machine was still on. It wasn't long before they filed into the lobby, chilled to the bone. "You sure picked a great night to walk the streets," I greeted them as they entered. Richard was already pouring cups of chocolate.

"Brrrr, my feet are frozen stiff," one of the teachers said as she stamped her feet back into circulation.

"Bet you will think twice before you set another strike date," I replied. I could've bitten my tongue. I had promised Richard I would not get involved. The town was already in a schism due to the strike. But offering coffee and hot chocolate seemed the humane thing to do on such a cold and bitter evening, and we would have done it for anyone, no matter what their cause, with the exception of maybe our motorcycle friends.

There was good-hearted bantering around the table as the group warmed up. We have always enjoyed a good relationship with the teachers and they, in turn, have shown great support for the restaurant over the years. But the strike tension was ever-present. However, since we are in business, we are compelled to keep our politics to ourselves. Politics and business are inseparable, yet incompatible, in small town life.

Years before we moved to Sauk Centre, as the story is told, a businessman ran for mayor and won. During his term of office the city was deliberating whether to install, downtown parking meters. The issue became intensely heated and divided the farmers from the townspeople. Soon after the decision was made to install the meters, the mayor resigned. It is told he succumbed to the tremendous pressure of an economic boycott by the farmers against his agricultural-related business.

I thought nothing about it as I entered the restaurant the next morning. A waitress approached asking, "Where is all the coffee trade this morning? We haven't had a customer."

"Oh, it's probably too cold for anyone to venture out today." I had passed it off without reflection.

By the third day it was obvious that the coffee crowd was boycotting our establishment. Richard and I began to wonder what we had done wrong. We had the same waitresses, the same coffee, and the same location. We did not realize our transgression until later that morning when the telephone rang: "Good morning, Palmer House. May I help you?"

"Teacher lover!!!" CLICK.

"What was that all about?" Richard asked as he came from behind the front desk.

Stunned and silent, I stood holding the receiver at bay with only the dial tone wasting away. Finally I said, "I'm not sure, but it sounded like a hate call. They just screamed 'teacher lover' and hung up."

"Have you been in an argument in one of the bars again?" Richard accused.

"No, not since last year. You were with me, remember?" I hung up the receiver, the voice still echoed in my ear.

"I heard you had a party the other night here after the restaurant closed," a local businessman said as he passed by the front desk. His tone was solicitous and catty.

"Party?" Richard asked. "What party? Where?" He lighted a cigarette.

"In the restaurant on a very cold January night," was the response. "Free coffee and hot chocolate."

"What did he mean by that remark?" Richard asked as he took a drag on his cigarette. The telephone rang.

I did not answer him. I answered the telephone instead.

"God, I hope it's not another one of those calls," I said picking up the telephone. "Good morning, Palmer House. May I help you?"

"Yes, could you tell me the soup of the day?"

"Boston Clam Chowder." CLICK.

"Soup lady?" Richard asked.

"Who else, it's eleven o'clock isn't it?"

I looked out the window and noticed Ben from the **Sauk Centre Herald** crossing the street. "I know," I said to Richard as I headed for the door, "I'll ask Ben what's going on. He knows everything."

"You better put on a coat," Richard called after me. "It's cold out there." I went out anyway and it sure *was* cold.

"Ben! Ben! Got a minute?" I was holding the door open and my damp fingers were freezing to the metal frame.

"What is it?" was his curt reply as he moved quickly past the south door.

"Could I talk to you a minute?" I continued, ripping my fingers from the door and placing them in my mouth. I had pulled off some of the outer skin. Stepping toward me with some hesitation, Ben acknowledged my presence.

"Golly, it's a cold one," Ben conceded as he shivered and pulled his storm coat around him. "You'll get the death of cold standing out here like this." I was still sucking my skinless fingertip. "What is it you want?" he asked.

Richard joined me and answered with a question, "Why would we be getting hate calls?"

The question caught Ben off guard. After a moment of stuttering, he finally blurted, "Well, I don't know how much truth there is to it, but I've been hearing different people say how you and Al gave the teachers free coffee one night after the restaurant was closed."

"Oh, my god," Richard uttered. "All we did was have them come in that night for something hot to drink. It was a wicked cold evening and we would have done it for anybody."

"Besides, they even paid for it," I chimed, "Is that why everyone is so uptight?" Richard asked.

Ben nodded.

"Of all the petty, stupid, ridiculous notions," Richard expounded as he flicked his cigarette.

"Well," Ben said, "you know a small town. Anyway, that's why some of them aren't coming in for coffee. They think you are supporting the teachers."

"Oh, for god's sake, how childish of them." I stamped my feet and wanted to cry as I walked back into the lobby.

"Well, you asked me," Ben called back. "So don't blame me."

"We're not blaming you, Ben, but it does seem pretty petty," Richard replied. "We'll get over it, but I think anyone would have shown the same courtesy under similar circumstances."

"I suppose so," Ben said as he started down the street.

Richard entered the Minniemashie Room with a pot full of coffee as I sat in the dark smoking a cigarette. "Allan, are you in here?"

"Yes." I replied. "Doesn't that take the cake? We try to be good samaritans and we get kicked in the ass." He poured the coffee.

"Oh, we'll get through it, but now do you see why I didn't want you to run for City Council or any other public office?"

"No. Why not?" I challenged, playing the devils' advocate.

"Because," he replied. "We can't afford it if you get elected."

Pauline.
(Part II)

I t was spring again. Most people judge the coming of spring by the robins returning. At the Palmer House spring arrives when Pauline checks in.

Today was hectic, as we began the membership drive for next year's concert. The Kennicott Room was filled with people coming and going. The phones were constantly ringing, but by contrast the restaurant was dead.

"Why don't you and Pauline go up to the apartment and watch television till the night clerk arrives. Then we'll all go out for a drink," Richard suggested as he peered over the top of his reading glasses from the front desk.

"Great idea," I conceded. "I'll show you the video tape of **"Same Time Next Year."** She was sitting in the lobby looking a little tired. Yet still attractive.

"Oh great, I'd love to see that dinner theatre," she answered. I gave her my arm and we ascended the stairs.

"Behave yourselves up there," Richard smiled as he looked up at us.

The apartment was a little chilly, as always, so I seated Pauline in the over-stuffed rocking chair and threw a snug-sack around her. "It's not that cold. And I'm not an old lady yet." She laughed and I laughed and Chris clawed at the sack.

"Get down, Chris," I yelled at the dog. "He gets nervous everytime we bring someone into the apartment. It's like it's his private domain and he's very protective of his territory."

"I'm dying to see the video tape," Pauline said as she tucked the sides of the snug-sack into the chair. " You told me so much about the performance on the telephone."

"You'll love it." I smiled as I pushed the play button.

Good Evening and Welcome to
The Palmer House Dinner Theatre
This evening's performance is being presented by:
"The Dauntless Players"

I reached over to turn the volume up just as the door to the apartment burst open. Richard came running in so fast that the dog began to growl. "Allan, Allan, come downstairs. Hurry, the whole ceiling in the restaurant is falling down. Hurry!" He was still yelling as he bounded back down the stairs.

Startled and excited, I dashed out of the apartment, forgetting Pauline. I tripped on the rug in the hallway, losing my balance and fell against the wall. I had been meaning to fix that rug for about three months. Ignoring it, I raced down the stairs, two at a time, until I reached the restaurant door. Three of the large acoustical tiles had come loose from the metal track which holds them in place. Richard was frantically trying to hold some of the metal tracks which were now loosening up all over the ceiling. I immediately jumped up on the counter to hold a track that was ready to pull loose. If it fell it would smash our glass-globed chandeliers.

"My heavens! What's happening?" Pauline remarked as she entered the restaurant.

"Watch out, Pauline," Richard yelled from above. She ducked but not soon enough. She was hit by tile cascading down from the southeast corner. She held her hands over her head and backed out into the lobby.

"Thank heavens it isn't concrete," she laughed.

The sight of Richard and I holding the ceiling up, above the chandeliers, with pieces of tile skittering all over, was simultaneously both tragic and funny to me.

"The sky is falling. The sky is falling," said Henney Penney to Ducky Lucky," I shouted.

"It isn't funny, Allan," Richard snapped back. He looked like a middle-aged Atlas holding up the world. "We just spent two weeks cleaning all these damn tiles and now look at it."

"We won't have a dropped ceiling any more," I called back.

"That's right," Pauline said matter-of-factly. "It's already dropped."

"Maybe you should say, it is still in the process," I responded as another metal track came clanging down from the ceiling, knocking over a lantern and displacing the silverware setting on the tables.

"Well, we can't hold this damn thing up all night," Richard growled.

"Pauline," I called, "get me the wire clippers in the tool box under the counter."

"Well do something pretty soon, my arms are tired," Richard echoed.

Richard's brother-in-law just happened to stop by. Seeing the plight Richard and I were in, he immediately got a ladder from the closet and grabbed the wire cutters from Pauline.

"Hi Pauline," he acknowledged as he set up the ladder near the first chandelier. "Hey, didn't you guys just finish cleaning these tiles?"

"Yes, damn it. It was my Christmas present," Richard replied. "Why couldn't it have fallen before we cleaned it?"

"Watch out, Pauline," I hollered as another ten-foot section of track came loose on the east side. Pauline was trying to help hold the ladder which was so rickety I don't even know why we keep it. "Hold it, here comes one down around the lights." I grabbed the fragile globe just as it teetered off its precarious perch.

"Don't break a globe, we haven't got any more!" Richard cried.

"I'm not trying to break anything," I yelled back. "I'm only trying to catch things in midair."

"O.K. Take it easy," Richard hollered.

"I'm going to cut the last hanger and we will lower the whole track down around the light," his brother-in-law answered.

"Easy, easy."

"Watch it!"

"There goes another tile." We were all talking at once and the mass confusion was suddenly captured for posterity as Merlin, standing in the doorway, snapped a picture with his trusty camera. The flash took me by surprise. I thought for sure one of the dining room lights had shorted out.

For the next hour we must have looked like the Three Stooges as we continued to drop the remainder of the ceiling. Then we tackled the clean up. Dust, plaster and nails, and who knows what else. It took us until eleven-thirty.

"It was a good thing the restaurant was closed when it happened," said Pauline as she carried out the last of the tiles.

"Yeah, the last three people left just after you two went upstairs." Richard replied, now beginning to regain his composure.

"Golly, when you came into the apartment, I thought the building was on fire, or God knows what," I said, taking a drag off his cigarette.

"Now what are we going to do?" Richard wondered.

"Well," I pointed to the east windows, "we can finally open up the original stained glass windows."

Four beautiful stained ripple-glass windows had for some unknown reason been covered over by a former owner. You could see them from the outside, but inside they were covered with plaster. Actually, that was one of our first priorities when we started remodeling, but we were so inundated by more pressing repairs that we never got around to it.

When the restaurant was finally cleaned and presentable, Richard took Pauline's arm. "You run upstairs and get your mink, darling. We're all going for a drink." He escorted her to the stairway.

"Just think if that had happened fifteen minutes earlier," Richard stammered as he searched for a cigarette.

*   *   *   *   *

We startled the night clerk when we returned. We were laughing so hard he could not understand it. But he should have expected it by now, for we always have a great time when Pauline comes to town.

"You take Pauline upstairs. I'll be up in a few minutes," Richard said, moving behind the desk. As we started up the stairs I heard, "Oh, so you rented a couple of rooms, good." Richard never quits worrying. I looked back as he removed the registration cards from the rack and studied them.

Pauline gave me her key as we approached her room. "Shhh," I cautioned. "There are people sleeping." I unlocked the door and bowed deeply with a wave of my hand. As she entered, I followed, leaving the door wide open behind me. I helped remove her coat.

"Didn't we have a good time this evening in spite of everything?" she said, smiling as I hung her coat on a hanger.

"Indeed we did," I replied. I leaned forward to give her a good night embrace and we both lost our balance and landed laughing in the middle of the bed. A guest who was obviously quite drunk wandered by and stuck his head in the open door.

"Oops, sorry 'bout dat." Then scratching his head he turned and said, "Don't let me interrupt anything. Nite." And he was gone. Our laughter grew to hysterical proportions as I helped her up.

"Thank you, for the lovely rose," she said as we kissed good night.

"See you in the morning," I said, glancing back just before I closed the door. And again we both broke out in gales of laughter.

Red's Heritage.

Have you ever stopped to think how difficult it is to get every stray hair out of a room? And imagine, the many awkward positions one must assume to insure cleanliness. I have just finished such a cleaning project, and to my knowledge the room is immaculate. It would pass the most meticulous inspection. But I can't help but imagine what might happen sometime:

A guest has just checked into the hotel with his wife for a romantic weekend. He enters the room and jumps on the bed, but she looks behind the doors, in the drawers, and under the bed. Then she steps into the spotless bathroom. The glittering mirrors reflect her image and the clean smell of deodorant fills her nostrils when suddenly she looks down into the bathtub and "EEERRRHHHWWWOOOKKK." She has spotted one lonely pubic hair. Now it isn't very long before he is at the front desk demanding his money back and we never see him again, and we will never know why. I am amazed at the perfection the public demands from the food and lodging industry. I truly believe that very few homes are kept as neat and clean as our rental rooms. It is an endless effort for us to keep a building that is over eighty-years-old in an immaculate condition. However, we are blessed with very good help.

When we first moved into the Palmer House we inherited two chambermaids, Hessie and Tessie. Now these two old gals are of German extraction, from the neighboring ethnic town of Elrosa. I often listen to Hessie and Tessie babbling about, in their own mix-mucks of languages, as they make the beds and clean the rooms. They converse a mile a minute, independent of each other, each one carrying on as if she were the only one talking.

One day I sent them off to purchase some paint for a particularly dreary room. They trotted off to the local hardware store, walked in and asked which paint was on sale.

It so happened that this day the store had mixed some purple passion for a customer and the color did not match his newly installed carpet. "I'll give you a good deal on five gallons," the storekeeper said. "One dollar per gallon."

"Alright then," Hessie said with a gleam in her eye, certain that I would be pleased with the deal she had struck.

"We'll paint on de turd floor tomorrow," Tessie announced as she opened the door to the Palmer House. Then, looking up at the old building, she noticed a light burning in the room upstairs. "Didn't you make out da light in room turteen when you cleaned it today?" she asked Hessie accusingly.

"Of course I made out da light. I remember I did because I was carrying da linen down da hallway when I dropped da key. So I dumped da linen down da chute and went backa to pick up da key and rechecked the room."

Together they fastidiously cleaned the rooms, putting to use their inherited Germanic work ethics. We still retain them for their chambermaid services, but have forever taken away their interior decorating duties.

The German heritage in this part of Stearns County is very strong, even though Sauk Centre was initially settled by English folks relocating from the east coast. When the railroads came through, the Germans, the Poles, and the Slavics followed. And the names of the towns tell the story of traveling immigrants — Avon, Albany, Freeport; all named for towns back east. While the Catholic and German influence can be seen in St. Michael, New Munich, St. Anthony, Meire Grove, Elrosa.

There is still a saying in this area that if one wants to go drinking, they take the Hindenburg route, which consists of approximately five little German towns noted for their beer drinking facilities. Many a night Red Lewis recalled traveling the Hindenburg route. And even Richard talks of the times the boys made the trip. It is a tradition cut from the mold of John's place.

Elrosa is a typical little German farming community. It is located eleven miles south of Sauk Centre on the Hindenburg route. The most conspicuous building is the grain elevator, seen just as you enter the community after slowing down for the railroad tracks. It is a neat little community of one and two story houses, a grocery store, a little cafe, and two very large and gauche buildings. One of them is a Butler Building made of corrugated steel.

My first remembrance of driving through the village was seeing old bathtubs set upright in the front lawn with the inside painted a brilliant blue. A pretentious statue of the Virgin Mary was placed lovingly inside each tub and hordes of artificial flowers surrounded the shrine.

We stopped for a drink and as Richard and I entered the door, every eyeball in the place simultaneously turned and stared in our direction.

"Where's youse guys from?" the friendly bartender asked.

A Horse On Us!

Here I am in the middle of the Minniemashie Room listening to a recording of the St. Paul Chamber Orchestra, under the direction of James Russel Davies. What a day it has been! I have been bored to death today. Same people in the restaurant — same old coffee group. Richard counted twenty-five coffee drinkers and only one ordered any food, and that was a cookie. One of the waitresses began chiding the customers, "What would you do," she asked, "if we took away the dice boxes?"

Dice boxes are illegal in the state of Minnesota. However, from the very first day we took over the restaurant, we allowed them to remain. They had become a tradition. First they shake to qualify, then they shake for the coffee, then they all put a quarter on top of the napkin holder and shake for the quarters. I am willing to bet that the winner of that quarter-shake pockets more money than the restaurant.

Today, they were so noisy shaking dice that two tourists, both of whom had ordered large expensive breakfasts, walked out without eating. What to do? It is illegal, yet not enforced. Even the local gendarmes occasionaly shake dice at the Palmer House. Sure, we could stop it. We could take away the dice boxes and have them go elsewhere. But it is a *Catch 22* situation. If we removed the dice boxes, we would be considered S.O.B.'s of the lowest order. It's six of one and a half dozen of the other. We're damned if we do and damned if we don't. It's another example of how we do not run the business, it runs us. In this case, it's a horse on us.

Broadway West!

It is Sunday. The one day that I especially love in the winter and early spring for the restaurant is closed. I usually arrive downstairs around 9:15 in the morning and just putter around all day. Oh, there are Sundays in the past where I have cleaned carpets, scrubbed walls, hung wallpaper, or even rearranged the Minniemashie Room. But this is one of those lazy, warm, spring Sundays. Richard is still sleeping and I am reading the paper.

Around 2:30 or 3:00 Richard comes downstairs and we decide if we are going to get out of town for a little while. Usually it's Richard who suggests where we should go.

"St. Cloud? Osakis? Alex?" he mumbled. Or how about driving to Wadena this afternoon and having dinner at the Pine Cove?" he questioned, carrying a shoe in each hand.

I opened the door for Chris and he made a beeline for his familiar haunts or his latest girlfriend's house. Who could blame him on a day like today.

"O.K." I replied as I closed the screen door. I had already tied the big wooden door back. It was so nice out, about sixty degrees already.

"We could have dinner at the Pine Cove, then stop downtown at those two scuzzy 3.2 bars before we come home," he continued.

Now 3.2 stands for the maximum percentage of alcohol allowed in beer. No hard liquor is sold on Sundays, so these 3.2 bars do a booming business on the Sabbath. They are hangouts for young people and those into pool or pinball or, lest I date myself, video games.

We hadn't been to Wadena for almost a year. The Pine Cove was built as the club house for the golf course nestled in a secluded grove of pine trees just off the highway. It had just recently become privately owned. We had driven by it many times but had never stopped. We were duffers but not golfers.

We began to make final preparations to leave, which is no easy matter at the Palmer House. We checked with Merlin to make sure he would be standing guard. We checked the dog for water, food, and shagged him back into the apartment. We checked all the lights. We contacted the night man to make sure he would be on time, as Merlin completely caves in at the stroke of ten. We left a note for the morning cook detailing the soup and the special for the day. We made sure the room reservations were in order, and everytime we headed out the door we thought of something else. Many times I have thought it much easier to stay home than to take a few hours off work. We finally got in the van, and checking to make sure we had enough cigarettes and at least four cups of coffee, we departed.

Wadena is fifty miles north on Highway 71, which winds through some of the most scenic territory in central Minnesota. Here flowing prairie is occasionally blocked suddenly by huge stands of pine. The fields that day rolled to the horizon and looked like a Grant Wood painting with Grandma Moses characters scattered about. We were both enjoying the scenery so much, hardly a word was spoken. The van radio was playing *oldies but goodies* from the Wadena radio station and all in all it was very relaxing, when:

"TONIGHT LIVE! WADENA'S VERY OWN MADHATTERS ARE PERFORMING 'EVENING ON BROADWAY' ON STAGE, AT THE PINE COVE. COME AND ENJOY A DELICIOUS MEAL AND AN EVENING OF SONG AND DANCE AT THE PINE COVE. DON'T FORGET, SHOW STARTS AT EIGHT O'CLOCK."

"Hey, that sounds great!" Richard remarked. "You love live shows. Imagine holding something like that in Wadena."

"Why not?" I answered. "It's nice to see somebody has imagination." Little did I know that this Sunday afternoon excursion would launch a whole new venture at the Palmer House.

The excitement was already in the air when we arrived at the Pine Cove. The parking lot was so full that we had trouble finding a spot. We always do when Richard is driving the van. He hates to park it. I have yet to see him attempt a parallel park. We found a spot within walking distance of the town and we hurried into the restaurant. People were standing in line and I couldn't believe this was all happening in Central Minnesota.

We were finally greeted by the hostess, "I believe I have a table very close to the stage, but it has a poor view and there will be other people joining you."

"Beggars can't be choosers," I said tritely as we were escorted to our table for our first dinner theatre since leaving Minneapolis-St. Paul.

We watched as the crew prepared the lights and props. It all had an air of immediacy which added to the excitement. A couple joined us at the table. They had probably reserved it a long time ago. With a little wine, their tension eased and we began an enjoyable conversation. At last, the lights began to dim. The orchestra started the overture and both Richard and I were transported to another time, another world, far away from the down to earth everyday life in provincial Central Minnesota. And as the characters began their dancing and singing, I mentally visualized all this activity in the Palmer House. Imagine "the arts" in the Prairie? What audacity! But it was all there before me. We could rent a portable stage and place it in the Minniemashie Room. We could re-block the sequences to fit the available space.

During the second act I could no longer withstand my enthusiasm. I blurted out to Richard, "Why don't we invite them to come to the Palmer House. It would be like taking the show on the road."

He gave me his most incredulous look, which made it clear that I was to shut up. I, however, was so ecstatic about my idea that I had great difficulty watching the rest of the performance. I knew I could do it. I just had to bring dinner theatre to the Palmer House.

After the standing ovation, I rushed to meet someone from the cast; the director, or anyone to talk to about my plan, a Palmer House production. When most of the crowd had left and the others had congregated around the bar, I found my way to the basement. There, all the actors and actresses were kissing and hugging, still hyped up after a successful performance.

"Hi. My name is Al Tingley from the Palmer House Hotel in Sauk Centre," I said to one of the actors. He was half-dressed and his make-up was smeared as he was trying to remove it.

"Hi," he said, hardly looking up.

"How would you like to perform this show in Sauk Centre?" I blurted.

"Yeah, sure. But you better talk to Belinda, she's the director," he quickly said while silently scrubbing.

"Excuse me, sir, which one is Belinda?"

"She's around somewhere."

Confusion and excitement reigned both inside me and inside the room. I had no idea which person was Belinda.

"Pardon me, sir," I interrupted as a young man was busy twirling a young girl around in an ecstatic pirouette. "Do you know where I can find the director?"

"Sure," he grinned, "as soon as I stop twirling her, I'll let her talk to you." He stopped. "This is our director," he proudly announced bowing deeply.

"Hi Belinda," I said, extending my hand. "A great performance. And so well put together. My partner and I just got back from New York where we saw Chorus Line, but I enjoyed your show much better." Without even a formal introduction, she grabbed me, hugged me, and kissed my cheek. I must have said the right thing for she immediately grasped my hand and began to point out the various cast members, who were also in various stages of ecstacy. And then I saw him — Richard — slowly making his way down the stairs towards me.

"Over here, Richard!" I hollered over the din of the excitement. "Over here, come meet the director, Belinda, uh, uh..."

"Bestrum," she whispered in my ear. That was our introduction.

"Belinda Bestrum," I called out as Richard fought his way through the crowded room.

"That was a terrific performance," Richard said as he drew closer. "It reminded me of *Chorus Line* which we saw last year in New York."

"Do you think you could come to Sauk Centre and put it on?" I asked excitedly. "We don't have anywhere near this size stage or seating, but I'm sure it could be done." Richard was quite silent as I presented my idea.

"We'll have to discuss it with the Madhatters Board to see what they think," she said rather matter-of-factly. It was obvious she just wanted to join the cast in their revelry. She wanted to celebrate this successful performance before contemplating another.

"Here," said Richard as he handed her a Palmer House book of matches. "This is our hotel and our telephone number. I'm Richard and he's Al. You can talk it over and let us know what you come up with."

"O.K." she said as she took the match book and disappeared into the cheering crowd.

"Let's get out of here and let them enjoy their success," Richard remarked as he started for the stairs. I agreed. It was a poor time to approach them, but, my mind was whirling with ideas. The thought of having a live musical review at the Palmer House was all-consuming. Patrons were still chatting and exclaiming about the evening's performance as we headed through the parking lot in search of the van.

"Well you have lost your mind this time for sure," he stated.

"But I think we could hold a dinner theatre right here at the Palmer House," I countered.

"Come on, Al. We couldn't seat enough to make it pay." He had lost his excitement. "Besides what would you serve them? And who is going to attend? You don't really believe Sauk Centre will support it, do you? And remember how angry you get when you try something new and different, and then they don't show up. You get grumpy and then you mope around for a whole week."

"But Richard, I think it is something that will work. You saw what they did in Wadena. Besides, don't you want the third floor hallway and the stairs carpeted, now that the walls and ceilings are finished?"

"Sure, but you know there's no money for that now."

"How about letting me try a dinner theatre and all the money we make will go into carpeting?"

* * * * *

One week later, I was in the apartment when Richard entered and announced, "There's someone to see you downstairs. He looks familiar but I can't place him." Most unlikely, I thought to myself.

As I rounded the second landing, I immediately recognized him as the half-made-up man from Wadena.

"Hi, I am with the Madhatters in Wadena," he said shaking my hand firmly. "Belinda asked me to stop in and see you, since I was on my way to the Twin Cities."

"How about some coffee?" Richard offered.

"No, no thank you. I really can't stop that long. Belinda said you might be interested in production *Evening On Broadway* here at the Palmer House."

"Definitely, if it's at all possible," I exclaimed.

"Well, we discussed it at our board meeting the other night and we would like to do it."

"Great! Here, let's go in the Minniemashie Room. You can get a better idea how I think it can be done." We started for the room, Richard had already gone on ahead to turn on the lights.

"Well, it certainly isn't the Pine Cove," the actor said as he stood in the doorway, "It's rather small, isn't it?"

The Minniemashie Room is twenty-five feet wide and forty-five feet long, with a high, tin ceiling painted black. The south walls are painted yellow with some sort of sparkling effect left over from the days when it was the Palmer House Bar. The north wall now contains my old, large reed organ and an upright piano. "Ah, but the room has no fixed seating so it is possible to make the best use of table and seating arrangements," I responded quickly. As he walked into the room further, he noticed the sketch of the Minniemashie Lady as created by Richard's niece.

"Nice drawing," he commented.

"That's our logo for this room. I like to think of her as Carol Kennicott, the heroine of **Main Street**."

"That's right," he said, "this is Sinclair Lewis' home town, isn't it?"

"It sure is," Richard chimed. "He even worked here as a desk clerk and a bellhop."

"Didn't he win a prize for literature?"

"The Nobel Prize," Richard answered.

We presented *Evening On Broadway*. They came. They saw. Richard carpeted.

"Oh, What A Beautiful Morning!"

" Take all the keys to the third floor and pick your own rooms," Richard shouted to the manager of the tour group. The suitcases, the props, the make-up kits, the lighting men, the actors and the actresses, the stage crew came pouring into the lobby, talking excitedly about opening night. In the Minniemashie Room the waitresses scurried around with the last minute preparations. The huge orange drapes glistened under the bright spotlights. The tables decked out in white linen with sparkling glassware and china were further accented by soft candlelight. The entire east wall was transformed into a mural of waving prairie grass with a life-size windmill silhouetted by a bright florescent orange sunset deep in the blue Oklahoma sky. We had expanded our horizon in order to fit the musical *Oklahoma* into the Minniemashie Room.

The staff was singing bits and pieces of the score. Even the cooks in the kitchen, busy preparing poached walley pike and filet mignon, were humming. *"Oh, What A Beautiful Morning."* It was like a dream come true. Each time we geared up for Dinner Theatre or Gourmet or any function in the Minniemashie Room, I often had to pinch myself to be sure it was really happening, for this is my plaroom. It's everything I've wanted the hotel to be, and for a few short hours, it did not seem like an old hotel with more restoring to be done and hundreds of bills to pay. It was the Sheraton Ritz and the Waldorf Astoria and the Helen Hayes Theatre all rolled into one.

"I'll get it," Richard calls out as the phone rings. It is hard for him to hear with so much confusion in the lobby. "Palmer House. What? Tonight? No, I am sorry. We are completely sold out but I do have a couple of openings for tomorrow evening's performance. No, I don't have any cancellations for tonight...I don't expect any at this late date. Just a moment. Yes, can I help you?" Richard covers the receiver with his hand as he tries to help the two young men leaning over the front desk.

"Could we get some change for the Coke machine?"

"Why don't you get it at the cash register in the restaurant, please," and he points to the restaurant.

"There's no one at the register."

"Just a minute," Richard lays down the phone, unlocks the gate behind the desk, and heads for the restaurant with the two men in close pursuit. One nearly trips over the three large suitcases in the middle of the floor.

"Watch out!" someone else hollers. When Richard gets into the restaurant a line of customers approach the till.

"Just a minute." One could see that Richard is feeling harrassed.

"Could I get five ones for this five?"

"Are you sure, you only want five?" Richard says as he counts out the ones.

"Sir," a young Levi-clad student queries Richard, "do you take personal checks? I must have left my wallet at home."

"Where are you from?"

"Minneapolis. But the check is good. It won't bounce." Richard hands him a pen. People are still in line to pay their bills and they are becoming more irritated at this delay.

"Could I get my change please?" one of the men standing in the doorway calls out to Richard.

"Yes, yes," Richard replies in a rush. "Just a minute."

Richard takes the check from the young man and glances at the check number, number 108. He knows from experience that the check will probably bounce. But what can he do, in the confusion of the moment. So he turns it over, stamps it, and places it in the till. Quickly he hands change to the man in the doorway and continues helping people. Only I know how uptight he really is.

"Get the phone at the desk, Allan. It's about tickets for tonight."

Trying to get through the crowd in the lobby is like trying to cross the street at rush hour, but I survive and finally reach the phone, "Yes, may I help you?"

"I was just talking to someone about tickets for tonight. Do you think you could possibly squeeze in four more? I didn't know we were going to be in town, so I didn't make reservations. And we want so much to see *Oklahoma*." I recognize the voice. It is a local who has attended a few of our special functions in the past but to my knowledge has never patronized the restaurant for as long as we have been here. I decide to make a concession.

"I haven't had any cancellations yet, but I guess we could squeeze in another table. It's going to be crowded, O.K.? But I will find some place for you. Dinner is served between 6:15 and 7:30, so we can can clear the tables before the show starts at 8:00."

"Oh. thank you very much. See you tonight." Click.

"Yes. may I help you?"

A rather short, stalky woman was standing at the desk holding a large paper sack.

"Would you mind terribly if I left this bag of groceries behind your desk until I come back? I have a few more errands to run and I hate to carry this around. I won't be too long."

"Sure," I say as I reach for the bag. I set it on the floor, not realizing Chris is sleeping under the chair. I startle the hell out of him. Imagine that poor dog spending every day since we purchased the hotel, behind the desk sleeping or should I say, *trying* to sleep with everything that goes on. He is a lot like me. We both can't wait for the restaurant to close each night, so we can relax in the lobby.

"Thank you so much," the lady says as she heads out the door.

Almost as quickly as the confusion and hustle and bustle in the lobby begins, it ends. Richard comes out of the restaurant with a cup of coffee and cigarette and moves in behind the desk.

"Jesus, I wish everyone wouldn't come to the till at once. And with everybody standing around waiting, this kid wants to cash a check, and the people are hollering for everything under the sun. God, it makes me nervous. What's this bag of groceries doing on the floor?"

"Oh, some lady came in and asked me to hold it for her while she does some errands. I've never seen her before."

"Oh swell. Leave it at the Palmer House. Pick it up at the Palmer House. Use the toilet at the Palmer House. They can sure find the Palmer House when they want to, but they can't seem to find it when it's time to eat. I get so tired of all the potty trade and the favors we are asked to do. I wonder if other businesses in town put up with it."

As I head upstairs for a quick rest, I hear the various soloists and choruses for *Oklahoma* warming up in the hallways and it sounds more like McFail's school of music than a hotel.

Trying to relax an hour before dinner theatre is pointless, but, I open myself a bottle of beer and sit down. The dog is in a mood to play, but I do not share the same idea. I throw him some dog biscuits and command him to lie down. It's hopeless, as usual.

After a refreshing shower, I don my dark brown suit. I bought this suit on sale in 1968 and I'm still wearing it. Richard and I are forever wearing jeans and work clothes around the hotel and I know the minute I go downstairs, I will get, "Oh, look at the dude. Where are we preaching tonight? Going to a wedding?" It never fails. The same comments every time for the past umpteen years. One more beer and I'll be ready to face the world. I can see Dorita bowing with a sweep of her hand. I know it's getting close to "Showtime."

As I descend the stairs and ignore the few whistles from some of the residents, Richard chimes from behind the desk. "When are you going to start seating them?"

"Let me check with the kitchen." There is already a lineup at the ladies restroom, a sure sign that it's time. I disappeared through the kitchen door.

"We can't find the walleye, and it's supposed to thaw out first," the cook yells in my ear, as I notice one of the dishwashers up to her elbows in blueberries.

"You are supposed to use the blueberries while they are frozen," I chastise. "Now all the biscuits will turn blue. Use some frozen ones and we will re-freeze these."

And then *Murphy's Law* takes over. The restaurant fills with customers. Any other Saturday night, the restaurant would be dead, but it never fails, when there is a function in the Minniemashie Room, people seem to come out of the woodwork.

"I can't cook dinner for the theatre and the restaurant both," the cook balks back to a demanding waitress. "Where is Jane? She was supposed to be here."

"You know she is always late," the waitress answers.

"Don't worry, she will be here," I say confidently, glancing at the ticket board. "Two eight-ounce ribeye steaks, medium, two pork chop dinners, both with hash browns. Have you got the hash browns on yet?" I ask the cook.

"No, I haven't even got the potatoes peeled yet," comes her curt reply.

"I'll get the potatoes peeled, you continue with dinner theatre." I spout, entering the walk-in cooler, tripping over a beer case that someone had left right in front of the door. I find the potatoes on the top shelf. I am surprised that there are some even boiled. I close the cooler and begin my search for the paring knife.

"You had better put an apron on, Al. You will ruin your good suit," one of the waitresses yells as she throws an apron at me, hitting me in mid-stride, covering my eyes.

"I haven't time. I have got to start seating people soon," I reply blindly.

After peeling about a dozen potatoes and grating them on the grill, I am relieved in more ways than one, when Jane opens the door. "You take over," I command, throwing the apron at her in turn.

In the lobby, Richard is besieged by people standing at the desk holding out their money and their checkbooks. "When are you going to start seating people?" he asks just as I emerge from the restaurant.

"In just a minute," I call back.

In the Minniemashie Room everything is just about ready. However, this show has such a huge stage that it takes up one half of the entire room. The lighting men are removing the ladders and the pianists are warming up with practice scales. I turn toward the door and fifteen people are standing there, tickets in hand, waiting to be seated. "I'll be with you in a moment," I say. "Please move away from the door. The staff can't get through."

There is a shuffling of bodies and finally a waitress makes it through with a tray loaded down with lettuce salads. I have a mental picture of where I am going to seat everyone. I hope I've counted the seats right this time. It would surely be a hassle if I've oversold.

Jane appears in the doorway. "The kitchen is ready to go when you are, Al," she announces.

For the next thirty minutes, between the waiter and waitresses bustling back and forth with wine and beer and salads and coffee and seating people and changing tables and an occasional cast member rushing in to check on something, order finally emerges out of the chaos. When the last dirty dishes are cleared, the two pianos begin sounding the overture. Excitement mounts in the audience. The score of *Oklahoma* is so familiar that I can nearly hear the guests mentally singing the words.

The lights dim, the mood is set. Aunt Ella steps into the spotlight and begins pushing the handle of the old butter churn up and down. From stage left the magnificent baritone voice of *Curly* fills the Minniemashie Room. "There's a bright golden haze on the meadow," he sings, working his way between the tables nodding to various audience members. "There's a bright golden haze on the meadow." The crowd immediately answers with applause. "The corn is as high as an elephant's eye, and it looks like it's climbing clear up to the sky." The show is on. A full scale production of this great Broadway musical comes alive in the Palmer House.

The audience is spellbound as the show continues. Laurie sings her dream song as she moves to stage left and sits in the shadows. Here she is to fall asleep as the dream wedding and fight take place. As she settles in the chair which is arranged for her singing of *Out of My Dreams and Into My Arms*, it slips off the back of the stage and she collapses right along with it. The audience gasps and holds it collective breath. The director who is standing stage right exits stage right. The pianos however, continue to play and softly from beneath the back of the stage the beautiful words float upward and into the ears of startled on-lookers, *Out of My Dreams and Into My Arms*. True to the great Broadway tradition, the show goes on. Even at the Palmer House.

Leader Of The Pack.

" I want my toast toasted," she barked at the waitress.

"The lady said she wanted her toast toasted," the waitress repeated to me as I continued scrubbing the potatoes.

"It is toasted," I said, doing a slow burn. "I just took it out of the toaster." I was approaching upset.

Since the bottom dropped out of the economy, both Richard and I were putting in way too many hours. "I'll toast it for her again," I mumbled as I removed the filling and threw the previously toasted bread in the garbage can. "And I'll make sure she knows it's toasted this time." I continued to prepare the evening meal, at the same time checking periodically to see that the toast was dark but yet not charred. "Here," I finally said to the waitress, "see if this meets with her approval." She smiled as she carried the toast back into the restaurant.

Often I wonder why customers can't understand that service people have bad days too. We try to smile and treat everyone with kid gloves and we do our best to fulfill the old adage — *the customer is always right*. However, customers having a bad day feel justified in taking out their frustrations on waiters and waitresses, cooks and cashiers. If we are frank with them, they snap and reply, "Well, I don't have to eat here anymore." And they are right. But it seems to me people could react to one another with a little more courtesy than I seem to be witnessing in this present day and age.

"Merlin, come here," she commanded as he walked through the restaurant. "Look at this sandwich! Don't you think this toast is burnt?"

Why Merlin, I wondered? Why put him on the spot?

I would say it was a little dark," he responded politely, "but I happen to like dark toast."

"My stars," she retorted. "If this is the way I am going to be treated, then I'm never coming in here to eat again."

"Lady," he replied, to my astonishment, "You have been coming here every day for ten years. Is that all it takes for you to take your business elsewhere?" He moved slowly away from the table and into the lobby.

"She's still sputtering out there," the waitress stated as she entered the kitchen.

"Well, it makes me mad. The toast was toasted the way we always do it. I am sick and tired of people who want their eggs up and down, their toast dark, their toast light, their milk hot, their coffee weak, their coffee strong...Dammit all" I said, throwing a tin pan across the kitchen trying to vent my frustrations. The waitress quietly left, leaving me to my own derisiveness.

The next afternoon one of our waitresses remarked, "Hmmm. Wonder what happened to the coffee ladies today? They weren't in this morning and I haven't seen them this afternoon. It sure seems strange not running for this and that."

"Do you miss them?" I asked firmly.

"Well, no, not exactly. In fact, it has been rather a calm day."

"Do you know that one of them complained yesterday and told Merlin she was never eating here again?"

"You mean just one woman can control that whole group of ladies?"

"Apparently," I replied, "She's the *leader of the pack.*" I frowned as I thought to myself.

Ten years we have cooled them in the summer and warmed them in the winter. Usually for the privilege of serving them hot water. We catered to their whims, their birthdays, baked rolls on their special occasions, attended their funerals and weddings, worried about them when they were in the hospital, sent cards or flowers befitting each occasion. We have been an integral part of their lives almost every day. If I had known that all it would have taken is a piece of dark, but not burnt, toast, I very well might have scorched it sooner.

The "Stars" Of The
Lawrence Welk Show.

The return address on the envelope read: Columbia Artists Management Corp., 52nd Street, New York, New York. I was excited as I tore open the letter. I hoped it was an inquiry about reservations for the 'Stars of the Lawrence Welk Show.' Their concert was scheduled for Sauk Centre next spring. And sure enough, the formal-looking letter read:

This is an inquiry about rates and accommodations in your hotel for the March thirteenth concert by the Stars of the Lawrence Welk Show. This is not a confirmation. Do you have seven doubles and seven single rooms with bath for the nights of March 13 and 14? Please fill out the enclosed form.

Richard was just coming down the stairs, preceded by Chris. He was jumping around anxious to get out, Chris that is, not Richard.

"Richard, look what we got in the mail today!"

"Just a minute," he muttered as he opened the east door and watched as the dog bounded away.

"We received an inquiry from the Lawrence Welk Show this morning." I was so excited my voice started to rise.

"Get me a cup of coffee," he said as he rubbed his eyes and came behind the desk. "Where are my glasses?" he asked as he took the letter that I had shoved directly under his nose.

"I'll get them for you. I saw them in the fireplace room last night." I scurried into the restaurant to get his glasses and his cup of coffee.

When I returned to the desk, Richard was already involved in a conversation with several strangers who were asking all sorts of questions about the hotel and Sinclair Lewis.

The phone rang. "Good morning, Palmer House. May I help you?"

"Yes, what is your soup today?"

"Bean with ham," I answered.

"Thank you."

"Who was that?" Richard asked.

"Need you ask?" I replied.

Richard returned to the visitors. "Thank you for stopping," he shouted as they slowly and curiously browsed through the lobby on their way to the door.

Richard read the letter from New York, looked up and said, "We haven't got fourteen rooms with bath. And what do they mean by doubles? I assume a double is two people in a bed. Or would it be two double beds?"

For the past ten years we have wrestled with the definitions of rooms. There are many individual ideas of what constitutes a *double* or a *single*. Most lodging facilities have all the extra conveniences. We do too, except our bathroom is not always located six feet from the bed.

"I'll write them a personal letter explaining our facilities," I explained. "I want them to stay here. You know what a great time the other groups have had."

"Well, if they want all this fancy stuff, they will not be satisfied here," Richard replied.

I am not surprised. Richard takes each room rejection at the Palmer House personally. And well he should. He has stripped the woodwork, chosen the wallpaper and the carpeting. He knows each room intimately. Many times I have seen him crushed when he has shown a room to a couple and they made comments such as, "My, the room is small," or "it's cute, but it has no bathroom!"

"I'll just explain to them that what we lack in convenience, we make up in hospitality," I stated as I headed into the restaurant to get him another cup of coffee.

December 1983

Dear Sir:

Thank you for your inquiry about accommodations at the Palmer House Hotel. We have been "home" for Columbia Artists for the past eight years. Groups like the New Christy Minstrels, Camelot's Harlequin Players and many smaller groups have also stayed with us.

The hotel is a registered historical site, both state and national. We have been in the process of restoring the hotel to give each traveler a piece of Americanna. I give you this background because we are not a luxury hotel. However, we have a personality and a love for the arts.

I gather from your request form that you will have about thirty-three people including the staff. We have twenty private rooms with a double bed, one room with twin beds and private bath, and two rooms with one double bed each and a private bath each. All of the rooms have been restored, many contain antique furniture. They are clean, quaint, and every room has a sink with hot and cold running water. However, most do not have private baths. There are bathrooms and shower rooms down the hallway. These also are private, by that I mean when a guest enters the lavatory or shower room, they can lock the door for privacy.

The hotel is located downtown, within walking distance to six bars, a movie theatre and shopping facilities. Also, it's just nine blocks to the senior high school where the group will be performing.

We can offer the "Stars of the Lawrence Welk Show" both public and private dining facilities on the premises. As an added feature we always throw a cast party in our private banquet room. So to answer your questions on the form, yes, we can accommodate the entire company. Yes, we can compliment one double for the staff. A full-service restaurant is located on the property. Wine and beer are available in the hotel. All rooms are up to fire code and the entire building is protected by an automatic sprinkler system.

Three years ago we had the group for South Pacific in our town. They did not stay with us because they requested all rooms with bath. While in town, some of the cast ate in our restaurant and wondered why they hadn't stayed here with us. The next year Sauk Centre booked the play Camelot! The girl in charge of accommodations had been here the year before and insisted that this time the entire company stay at the Palmer House, even if the rooms did not have private baths. They stayed and many said it was the highlight of their tour. We even received thank you notes from the cast.

Thank you for your inquiry and I hope you do decide to book the company at the Palmer House.

> *Sincerely,*
> *Al Tingley*

Once I put the letter to New York in the mail I had little time to think about the possibility of the group visiting us next spring. We had eighteen Christmas parties booked, three shows of the annual "Breakfast with Santa Claus" and the annual Christmas Gourmet which is my favorite. The holidays were upon us.

The lobby that year was extra special. The stairway was draped in evergreen boughs, and wreaths adored each door. Huge silver snowflakes danced and swirled from the high tin ceilings and miniature lights accented the entrance to the Minniemashie Room, welcoming all who entered the *winter wonderland* within. Inside Santa and his reindeer were flying among the clouds heading for the North Pole. In one corner was the stage, bedecked with Santa's workshop. It takes us weeks to complete the elaborate decorations and each year we try to improve on it.

The Christmas before we purchased the Palmer House, Richard and I visited in Sauk Centre. While shopping, we noticed a store with windows painted like frost. The store seemed to be empty. Yet we saw people entering and leaving with children in tow. "There must be something going on in there," I said to Richard as I tried to keep my ears warm from the cold north wind.

"It certainly isn't a store for shopping," he remarked as we headed toward the door.

Upon entering the building we were shocked. In the middle of the old building was an old folding chair surrounded by a few balloons and a worn leather bag. On the chair was a very emaciated looking Santa, mumbling a feeble, "Ho, Ho, Ho." He was handing bags of candy to several of the children nearby.

"This must be the city's Santa Claus Headquarters?" I exclaimed.

"Is this the best that Sauk Centre can do to help preserve the magic of Christmas?" Richard just shook his head. As we turned to leave the building Santa warbled "Merry Christmas."

Outside, we headed into the north wind and I began planning. If, I promised myself, we should buy the Palmer House, I am going to create a magic land for Santa. "The children of Sauk Centre deserve more than an empty building in which to talk to Santa Claus. I want to create a *Dayton's Auditorium* atmosphere." I was talking to Richard but I don't think he heard me.

And lo it began. Each year the Minniemashie Room is transformed into *Santaland*, regardless of the time and work. And it is a thrill to watch the wide eyes of children and adults as they come to have "Breakfast with Santa." The magic shows, the puppet shows, the sing-a-longs and "Frosty the Snowman" are all part of the excitement of our Christmas special event. It's a far cry from the bare building with the skinny Santa. To me it's another dream fulfilled.

Christmas at the Palmer House lasts for a long time. We start decorating early because we love the atmosphere. Our guests, both in the hotel and the restaurant, pick up on it and everyone seems to be in a more festive mood. When the twelve days of Christmas are over, it's usually thirty more days before all the vestiges of the season have disappeared...

It was late in January when the mail arrived one morning. After waiting for Lester to finish with the letter opener, I opened the letter from Columbia Artists in New York.

We wish to confirm reservations for the "Stars of the Lawrence Welk Show" for the evening of March 13. We will be getting in touch with you in the near future!

"We did it!" I shouted. "They are staying here, even if they do have to go down the hall to the bathroom." I couldn't wait to wake Richard.

* * * * *

March 13 came upon us suddenly but not subtly. As usual, it is difficult to keep a secret in a small town, and the restaurant harbored coffee drinkers all afternoon. They had positioned themselves at the window tables and were anxiously awaiting the first glimpse of the "Stars."

Richard was pacing in the lobby, going from door to door, looking for the bus which was already fifteen minutes late. The rooms upstairs all stood in waiting. He had opened all the doors leaving the key in each one so that they could select their own rooms. Fifteen rooms on each floor, each with a specially prepared fruit basket awaited our special guests. The tension rose moment by moment. What would the first real live glimpse of Joe Feeny be like? Would we recognize Bobby Burgess, Elaine Niverson and Dick Dale? — names that had been household words around Sauk Centre and in many other towns in the United States for many years.

Richard was getting worried. "What if they don't like the rooms?" he said to me as he headed out the east door again to look for the bus.

"They got my letter and they made the reservations. They know what to expect," I called after him as he came in one door and went out the other.

Richard returned to pace behind the front desk. He lighted a cigarette when I pointed out to him that he already had one burning in the ash tray. The chambermaid descended the stairs with a nervous cleaning cloth. She straightened the magazines and gave the hall tables one last polish. You could have cut the tension with a knife.

Two-thirty, they were one half hour late. "What if they drove by the old hotel and decided not to stay here?" Richard suggested as he passed the desk again and headed for the door.

"Relax. We'll have to play it by ear," I answered nonchalantly as he returned. "

"Here comes the bus!"

"The bus is here!"

"They're here!" the customers in the restaurant called out.

Richard and I both lighted up a cigarette and headed out the east door to greet our guests. Richard stood in the street and motioned for the bus to park right alongside the front of our door. When the door to the long awaited bus opened, a tall, young-looking man talked very loudly to the occupants of the vehicle. "You all stay right here and I will go in and check the accommodations."

As he stepped off the bus, Richard moved forward. "Hi, my name is Richard Schwartz. I am one of the owners of the hotel and this is my partner Al Tingley. Welcome to Sauk Centre." Richard shook his hand profusely.

"Hi, I'm Chuck Erdahl, manager of the Stars," came the reply.

"We have all the doors to the rooms open. They can choose their own rooms," Richard stated as we entered the lobby. Richard and I positioned ourselves behind the front desk.

"No, I don't want to do it that way," Mr. Erdahl said. "I would rather assign the rooms. That way there is less confusion. Now, let's go over my list."

"I know what they need for rooms," he continued as he laid a large legal-sized yellow pad on the desk. "Now the Johnson's, that's Elaine Niverson and her husband, will need a large room with two double beds and a bath."

"We don't have a room with two double beds and a private bath," Richard said very nervously.

"What do you mean, no double rooms?" Mr. Erdahl exclaimed.

"Al wrote you a long letter explaining our accommodations," Richard reported as he lighted up yet another cigarette.

"Letter? What letter? I never received a letter."

I felt that I should enter the conversation — to give Richard a little rest. He was visibly shaken. "Sir," I started. "I sent a letter to Mr. Cargin in December explaining how much we would like to have this group stay in our hotel. In that letter I explained that we only had three rooms with private bath but that there are baths down the hall." I moved closer to the desk top, hoping for reassurance.

"What, no bath?"

"There's a bath down the hall."

"Well, a lot of these folks are not married. They don't want to double up. And a bath down the hall! I can't believe it," Mr. Erdahl stammered.

"We have enough rooms so that they each can have their own private room," I answered. "And we do have a room with twin beds and a private bath for Mrs. Niverson and her husband."

"Joe Feeny wants his own room and he has to have a bath," Mr. Erdahl continued.

"Good, we can give him room eight. That has a bath," I said.

"And Amy Barbour has to have her own room with bath," he said, studying his yellow sheet.

"Then we can give her room seven," I said hopefully.

"Does number seven have a bath?"

"Yes," I answered.

"Then I will take that one and Ms. Barbour can have room eight."

He began scribbling on his yellow pad, drawing lines from names to numbers, when Richard reentered the conversation. "Perhaps it would be easier if we went upstairs and showed you the rooms. You might have a better idea of what we have to offer."

"Do you have any rooms on the first floor?" Mr. Erdahl inquired.

"No, none. They are all on the second and third floors," Richard and I answered in unison.

"But I want the Stars on the first floor," Mr. Erdahl replied. He was getting very uptight.

"O.K. Let's go upstairs and look at the rooms," he capitulated as he picked up his scratch sheet and headed for the stairway. He was stopped on the first step by the bus driver who had just entered the lobby shouting, "Sir, the Stars are all getting off the bus."

"Well, tell them to get back on the bus and wait till I come out to talk to them," Erdahl snapped. The driver turned and left.

The three of us continued up the stairs, Richard in the lead. "You will notice the entire building is protected by an automatic sprinkler system, sir," I said, proudly pointing out the sprinkler heads as we climbed the stairs. Mr. Erdahl could have cared less, he was more concerned about the accommodations.

As we headed down the hallway, Mr. Erdahl poked his head into each of the rooms, then brought it back out and shook it. "This will never do!" he muttered.

Richard stopped at room two. "This is the Lorne Greene Room. He stayed here for a week in 1963. It has twin beds and a private bath," Richard pointed out proudly.

Mr. Erdahl continued to shake his head. I quietly left the room as Richard tried desperately to convince the manager of the Stars that what we lacked in facilities we more than made up for in hospitality. Back down at the front desk I quickly looked up the telephone number of the Hillcrest Motel and dialed.

"Hillcrest Motel, may I help you?" a pleasant voice answered.

"This is Al Tingley at the Palmer House. Would you possibly have fifteen rooms with bath open for tonight?" I paused. "You see, the Stars of the Lawrence Welk Show had reservations here but the manager is not pleased about the rooms with no baths."

"Oh, Al, I'm sorry. I know how you must feel," she answered compassionately. "Just a moment."

I could hear her counting rooms aloud, and could almost see her scurrying about the vacancy board looking for rooms, when Richard and Mr. Erdahl entered the lobby.

"I'm going out to inform the group," Mr. Erdahl said as he headed out the door.

"Who are you talking to?" Richard snapped as he came behind the desk.

With one hand over the receiver I said, "Mrs. Tillson at the Hillcrest Motel, just in case they don't stay here."

Richard scrunched out his cigarette and lighted another. "Damn it," he said. "They never received your letter. I was afraid of this." He started pacing back and forth behind the desk like a caged animal. "Why did we ever buy this place anyway? All people want today are rooms with bath, historic site or no historic site," Richard mumbled to himself.

"Oh yes, Mrs. Tillson. You think you can find enough rooms? Great! Okay, the manager is just coming back in. I'll call you right back, Thank you."

Mr. Erdahl quickly approached the desk, "They took a vote whether to stay here or not and the vote was in favor of roughing it for one night." Then he added, "Let's get on with the room assignments."

For the next twenty minutes he and Richard compared notes and scribbled all over the large yellow pad until all rooms had been assigned. I called back to Hillcrest and informed them the Stars would be staying at the Palmer House after all.

It was all hustle and bustle for the next hour. Suitcases, musical instrument cases and garment bags littered the lobby. There was constant movement up and down the stairs and in and out the doors.

"Hi," a silver-haired man said as he stepped up to the desk.

"You're Dick Dale," Richard said as he extended his hand. "Welcome to the Palmer House."

"I really like it here," Mr. Dale said. "It's very homey."

"Hey Joe, come over here," Dick Dale called to a rather short, balding man with a garment bag flung over his arm. "Joe Feeney, this is Richard Schwartz, one of the owners of this fabulous place." I couldn't see if he winked or not.

Shaking hands with Mr. Feeny, Richard the innkeeper reported, "You will be in room eleven. It doesn't have a bath but I think you will like the room." He was beginning to relax. "Dick Seemans, the manager of the New Christy Minstrels stayed in this room. Twice, in fact, in the past four years." Richard nodded proudly. He turned to me and whispered, "Run up and see what they're saying."

Upstairs I heard a guest comment: "Hey look, this room is so small I can tell my friends that I had to sleep standing up."

"Yeah, but at least it has a restaurant."

"It'll do, I guess, except when we all have to fight for the shower," and they laughed.

I knew by their reactions that everything was going to be alright. And just maybe it would really be a fantastic time. I ran downstairs to give Richard the high sign. "We made it." I whispered. "I think it will be fun once the shock is over." He lighted another cigarette and exhaled roughly.

It wasn't long before the restaurant filled with Stars. Exuberantly they gorged themselves on chocolate malts, made from real ice cream and topped with whipped cream and a cherry; burgers and fries, homemade pies and pastries. Many of the locals stood staring — others introduced themselves and were amazed to find the Stars down-to-earth and friendly. Over and over the locals declared that they "had never missed one of their shows," since time began I guess. Then Bobby stood up and thrilled the audience with his original rendition of *Mickey Mouse*. All barriers had been broken. The Stars had satisfied the locals. Suddenly rooms without baths seemed insignificant.

Elaine Niverson noticed one of the welcome banners we had hanging in the lobby. "I want that banner when I leave," she stated. Henry Questa stood nearby signing glossy prints of himself with his famous clarinet in concert. Dick Dale shook the hands of many admirers who never dreamed that in their lifetime they would ever have the opportunity to meet him personally.

At 6:30 the Stars began descending the stairs in their tuxedos and gowns. Amy and Elaine were picture-book beautiful as they left the hotel. "Don't forget, you are all invited to a party in the Minniemashie Room after the show tonight," I called out to our guests as they boarded the bus and headed for the Sauk Centre senior high auditorium.

"And the party is for you, not for all the big wigs in town!" Richard echoed.

"What big wigs?" I questioned.

To get out of the hotel by 8:00 was, for us, like trying to move a mountain. Richard and I have yet to arrive at a concert on time. By the time we find a hotel sitter, make sure the restaurant is closed and the doors are locked, the gas jets lighted, the lights off, and the cash register locked and the one hundred and one other things we just do automatically, we are worn out. We dashed to the van, drove to the senior high school, found a non-parallel parking place and rushed into the concert.

There must have been 2,000 people already gathered in the auditorium. I knew this would be a big concert but I had no idea this many people would turn out. Almost half the city. Personally, I have never been a big fan of Lawrence Welk. I knew that he was on television every Saturday night for umpteen years, but I had never really enjoyed "champagne music." During the concert I was overwhelmed by the personalities performing. Their presence was electric. I was caught up in the excitement being created live before this audience.

Soon I found myself sitting on the edge of my seat. I was transfigured by the interreaction between audience and performers. The audience and the performance overwhelmed me. As the evening progressed I began to appreciate what was happening here. I realized that many evenings these people sat in their living rooms in front of the radio or television, listening to the bubbling music or watching the vibrant dancing of the Stars. And now through the efforts of Pauline and the Community Concert Association, they had a chance to be in the presence of those great Stars who were performing on stage before them.

When Bobby asked if there were any women in the audience who would like to polka with him, grown women screamed and ran to the stage. For them, I suspect it was a dream come true. And then my eyes filled with tears as Joe Feeney stepped off the stage, came into the audience and sang *Danny Boy* to the senior citizens in the front row. He ended with a kiss on the forehead for each of the senior ladies before him. Now I knew why the Lawrence Welk Show had been so successful for so many years. I was thrilled and honored to have been a part of that evening.

As usual, Richard and I left before the encore to return to the hotel to prepare for the reception which was to follow. The wine, the munchies, the veggies and dip were all prepared by the staff and placed in the Minniemashie Room, waiting for the grand entrance of the Stars. We had personally invited twenty-five to thirty people to return for the reception. Nothing formal, just everyday people who would appreciate an opportunity to meet and converse with the Stars.

One of the local bartenders came in and gave us some chits for free drinks at his bar if the group so desired. "We want to make them feel at home in Sauk Centre," he reported.

"Thank you, I'm sure they will appreciate it very much," I said as I took the handful of chits into the Minniemashie Room.

*　*　*　*　*　*

"Wasn't that a magnificent concert?"

"Just perfect."

"I think that was the best concert we have ever had in Sauk Centre."

Those were a few of the comments we heard as the guests began to arrive. Some had their programs in hand ready for autographs. Others had purchased records and were clutching them to their breasts as though they might get away before they were autographed.

The air was charged with excitement. Wine was poured and the opportunity to meet the Stars remained the topic of conversation. Nearly an hour passed as the excited guests awaited their arrival.

"They're here! They're here!" came the cry from the lobby as the first of the band members entered the hotel. Skip Shaffer, the drummer, clad in a full tuxedo, entered first.

"Your guests are impatiently waiting to greet you in the Minniemashie Room," I announced.

"I know. I'm sorry, but we were besieged at the high school. So many people wanted to say hello, shake hands and get autographs. They're all on their way now. I want to go up and change. I'll be right down," he said as he bounded up the stairs.

"We haven't started the food line yet. We'll wait for you," I called after him.

"Great," was the fading reply.

The east door opened and Elaine and Bobby entered, singing and dancing through the doorway. "My, but you seem happy," I commented as Elaine threw her arms around my neck.

"Boy, what a concert! What an audience!" she shouted.

"Your guests are holding their breath waiting to meet you and the food is ready to be devoured."

"Great, I'm starved!" she replied as she headed toward the Minniemashie Room. A round of applause could be heard from within as she entered.

Bobby shook my hand and remarked, "Sauk Centre — What a great audience." He also headed for the reception room to another rousing round of applause. Dick Dale was greeted by Richard and you could see our innkeeper was glowing.

"Do you have any beer?" one of the guests asked as I entered the Minniemashie Room.

"Yes," I answered and I headed for the kitchen. I rummaged through the walk-in cooler. Every time the help cleans out the walk-in they move things around and I never know where anything is. Yesterday it seemed like I was tripping over it, now I couldn't find it. By the time I returned to the Minniemashie Room with the beer, all the Stars had arrived. What a commotion! Everyone was talking at once and the lineup for the food was so long I wondered if there would be enough to go around.

Joe Feeney had been captured by two of the guests and whisked away to a corner. They didn't want to share him with anyone.

"I got my banner," Elaine called out to me as she came in waving the WELCOME sign she had confiscated with our compliments.

Conversation flowed and the easy going warmth of the artists was felt by all present. No one missed getting an autograph. Of all the receptions we have thrown throughout the years, I have never met a more down-to-earth group. They were right at home in small-town, rural America.

The party slowly broke up and some of the Stars headed for various watering holes around town, some with chits in hand. All present agreed it was a real reception with real people. Later, I was told, many partied upstairs until four in the morning and a good time was had by all. This is one of the advantages of owning a small hotel. Often it just becomes a large home.

The next morning the restaurant was again filled with artists and locals, chatting, signing and receiving autographs. The bus was scheduled to leave at 10:00 in the morning. "To think that we almost didn't stay here," Henry Questa remarked to me as I poured myself a cup of coffee.

"I was afraid it was all over when we didn't have enough rooms with bath, especially after Chuck said he hadn't received my letter of explanation," I commented.

"I was one who voted to stay here. I just love places like this. We stayed at a lot of hotels like this in Canada," Henry said as he signed another program which had been placed in front of him.

One by one we shook hands. Ava and Elaine kissed both Richard and I good-bye. Everyone gathered out on the sidewalk to wave good-bye as the bus headed for their next concert. The memory of a night in Sauk Centre will linger long in the minds and hearts of the community. For on that night, the champagne music makers bonded with small town beer drinkers in a spirit of lasting friendship.

A Pair of Boobs!

It started out as an innocent little party, no, not even that, for no party was intended. The head waitress just wanted to do something different to celebrate Richard's fiftieth birthday. It was defiance. For everyone on the staff had strict instructions not to have any surprises or parties. Richard specifically told me, "I don't want a fuss for my birthday. I don't like parties. I think birthdays should be a private business."

"I know, I know," I said. "I hear that every year. But I can't tell the staff to ignore it. They like celebrating. But, I promise I'll do my best."

I came downstairs that morning and found only one waitress, busily running her buns off, in the restaurant. "Where's Jane?" I asked her as she flew by me with two glasses of orange juice and a coffee pot in her hands.

"I don't know. I haven't seen her for the past hour." Her voice definitely showed her anger. I scurried into the kitchen just as the cook was turning down the radio. He had seen me coming through the swinging doors.

"Where's Jane?" I inquired again.

"Making some signs in the Minniemashie Room."

Out the back door and into the Minniemashie Room I ran.

"What are you doing?" I yelled.

"Making a big Happy Birthday sign for the restaurant. You don't have to know a thing about it. I know Richard doesn't want us to celebrate, but he'll get a kick out of it," she stated assuredly.

"Well, they need help in the restaurant. Would you please give them a hand?"

"Certainly," she remarked, and quickly she left the room.

Glancing at the huge Happy Birthday sign, I had to admit, it was artfully done. I left to bus a few tables, then I went to the lobby to stand in line for the mail. There were many birthday cards for Richard. I stacked them on top of those from yesterday which he hadn't even opened. He kept telling me that the big five-0 was not going to bother him, but I could tell from his actions that he wasn't too thrilled with its arrival. I put the mail down and thought of him sleeping upstairs when the phone rang. "Good morning, Palmer House."

"Is this the birthday boy?" the voice asked.

"No, this is Al."

"Well, I called to wish Richard a happy birthday."

"How did you know it was his birthday?"

"They announced it over the radio this morning: 'Today, Richard Schwartz is fifty years old but he doesn't want anyone to know about it' they said."

"Oh boy," I exclaimed, "he isn't going to like that. How'd they find out about it?"

"Someone called in, I guess. Wish him a happy one," the voice ordered.

I had just hung up the phone when it rang again. "Good morning, Palmer House. May I help you?"

"Yes, what is your soup today?" Same familiar faceless soup lady.

"Beef vegetable."

"Thank you."

Immediately the phone rang again. "My god, this is a day for the telephone," I remarked. "Good morning, Palmer House. May I help you?"

"Yes, is this Richard or Al?"

"This is Al."

"Al, this is City Hall calling from the Salvation Army, we have a *knight of the highway here*. Can you help?

Can you help?

In the past few years, we have had contact with a good many of them. Some are so regular we call them by name. They are vagrants who head south in the fall and back north in the spring.

"Could you put this young man up for the night and feed him in the morning?" the voice requested.

"Sure," I answered.

The interesting thing about drifters is that they never seem to have any money for room or board, but invariably they always find enough money for smokes and a bottle of booze. A few years ago, the Salvation Army put up at our hotel a family of five; mother, father, and three children. They claimed their car had broken down and they had to wire home for money. Shortly after they had checked in, the father came up to Richard and asked for cigarette change. He presented a one hundred dollar bill.

Merlin walked past the desk heading for the south door and I called to him. "Merlin, would you come here a minute?" He stopped in his tracks for a moment, then slowly, with military precision, turned about face.

"You talking to me?" he asked.

"Yes, that was City Hall calling."

"City Hall? Who...What?" he muttered as he approached the desk.

"I just got a call from City Hall and they are sending over a man with a Salvation Army slip for meals and a room."

"What? When, Who called?" Sometimes, trying to explain something to Merlin is like talking to a cement wall. So I began again. This time more slowly.

"There is a man coming over. He has a slip from the Salvation Army. If I don't happen to be at the desk, could you have him sign the register and give him room number ten?"

He did another about face and headed for the door. As exasperating as it is, I depend a great deal on Merlin and once he gets the message he is very capable. He stopped. "Oh, I see," he replied. "I'll be right back. I'm just going to mail these letters across the street."

"Al! Al!" The voice was shrill and high and coming from the restaurant doorway. "Al, come quickly! Look at the sign. We put it up."

I locked the dog behind the desk and went into the restaurant. It was full of people out for their morning coffee break. They were all watching our waitress hang a large sign on the wall. 'HAPPY BIRTHDAY, RICHARD,' there was a brief space then an enormous 50 followed. I had to admit, it was a good job, but I also knew Richard would be furious.

I was studying the sign when a thought occurred to me. I turned to the head waitress and asked, "Do you know if the drug store or the discount store has any funeral pieces for sale? Let's get a funeral bouquet and place it right under the fifty." The damage had already been done, I rationalized, so a bit more wouldn't hurt.

I put on my jacket and headed for the stores across the street. The answer was the same wherever I asked. "No, we won't be stocking funeral pieces till next month." My goodness, I wondered, "what do they know that I don't?"

"Would you have any stored in the basement?" I asked again and again.

"No, sorry."

Then I got the bright idea to buy a styrofoam circle and cross. I remembered our basement was loaded with artificial flowers left by the former owners.

Rushing back, I descended into the bowels of the Palmer House. There I found boxes of pathetic plastic flowers and a huge plastic duck with three ducklings which we had used in a scene years ago. I proceeded to drag all my findings upstairs and, before I knew it, the whole restaurant was buzzing about the funeral display around the big "50."

"Now, when Richard comes down, don't anyone look up there," I warned. "I bet he won't even notice it."

The entire staff had gathered around the end of the counter talking excitedly about Richard's party.

"He said he didn't want any celebrations, remember? So nothing more." I ordered.

"I know," one of the waitress lamented, "but we went out and ordered a *Boob Cake* for him. Some of us are coming in just after the restaurant closes to present it to him."

Now, a *Boob Cake* is baked in the shape of that anatomical part of a woman that seems to always catch Richard's eye. So what the heck, I thought, they had already ordered the cake and I had nothing to do with it. I frowned while smiling inside.

"Could I get some more coffee over here?" The voice was rather threatening. As usual, the whole staff was busy talking among themselves. The customers were ignored.

"Hey, get some coffee over there!" I said sternly and the staff suddenly disappeared.

I lighted up a cigarette, and I noticed a rather tall, thin man walk into the lobby. He had on Levis, a denim shirt, and a Buffalo Bill-type suede jacket. On his head he was wearing a cowboy-style straw hat. As I approached the lobby, I thought, well, our *King of the Road* looks like the Marlboro Man, cigarette and all.

Merlin was already behind the desk, handing him a registration card and giving instructions. "Please sign right here. This is the key to room ten. Right up the first flight of stairs and to your right." As he talked, he pointed to the position of the room on the ceiling of the lobby.

"Thank ya. Mighty friendly people you all got around heah," the cowboy said to us as he took the key and headed upstairs. He nodded to me as he passed.

Merlin was putting the guest card in the slot when I joined him behind the desk. "Where's he from?" I asked.

"Here's his card I can't read his last name. First name's Luke, though." I glanced at the card.

Tacoma, Washington, I noticed. Long way from home. Probably put the bite on poor Father Makey. I swear, these guys must have an itinerant guide book that lists the towns and which churches which are the easiest to finagle for a room and a meal.

"He doesn't look deprived to me." I was talking to Merlin until I noticed he had wandered away. Could it be because the telephone was ringing?

I looked at my watch. The hands were straight up.

"Good noon," I answered. Palmer House. May I help you?"

"Yes, what's your special today?"

"Salisbury Steak with mashed potatoes and vegetable for two-seventy-five."

"Could you deliver one to me?"

"Sure could." It was our regular *Meals on Wheels* customer.

The noon rush ended and the coffee hour hadn't begun. I sat down at the end of the counter and lighted a cigarette. Jane had finished for the day. She came over and thanked me for helping with the tables in her section. "By the way," she asked, "what time are we going to give Richard his cake?"

I shrugged my shoulders.

"About 7:30," a voice answered from behind.

"O.K. I'll be here," she announced.

"Wait," I said, suddenly remembering that tonight was Sauk Centre's Conference Championship basketball game. "I'll bet Richard will be going to the game. He said he wasn't going, but about 7:00 he will come up to me and say. 'Do you mind if I go to the game tonight? It's their last conference game.' "

"So what time is the game over?" Jane queried.

"About 9:00 or so. But he won't be back here until 9:30 or 10:00," I answered.

"Then why don't we tell everyone to meet here at 10:00. That way I can play bingo." she stated.

"He isn't going to like this," I muttered.

"You didn't have anything to do with it," she answered.

"I made the funeral wreath, remember?" I mentioned. "Pour me some more coffee, please." And suddenly I wished it was something much stronger.

*　　*　　*　　*　　*

Right on schedule, the coffee table filled up. I again marveled, for it never ceases to amaze me how fourteen men can squeeze around a table made for six. And this afternoon there were more players than usual. A number of them noticed the big sign above the counter. As I watched out of the corner of my eye, I saw Chris heading for the east door. Well, Richard is up and down. His pattern never changes. He lets the dog out first, then if no one is around, he comes into the restaurant for a cup of coffee.

"Happy Birthday to you, Happy Birthday to you," the coffee customer crowd sang as he entered. The look on his face was a sight to behold: it was a mixture of extreme anger, inner-smiling and utter flabbergast. He looked directly at me, and I immediately looked up at the sign on the wall. There I sat, doing the very thing I had warned the others not to do. "Oh, no," Richard commented as he looked up at the sign. "This was your idea wasn't it?" he said to me accusingly.

"No Richard, Jane made the signs and put them up. All I did was add the funeral display."

"Oh Christ, I told you I didn't want to make a big thing out of this."

"But Richard," I said apologetically, "I wasn't going to do a single thing. However when I watched you send one dozen long-stemmed roses and a bottle of Geritol to your classmate who was fifty years old, I decided you deserved similar recognition. Besides, the staff enjoys it."

"Get me a cup of coffee," he muttered as he turned to receive congratulations from several of the coffee table patrons. He bowed, then headed for the door to let Chris in, who was impatiently barking outside while Richard barked inside. I grabbed my coffee and headed into the lobby and stood beside him at the desk.

He had already spotted the Salvation Army slip and the card in box ten. "When did this guy check in?" he asked.

"About 11:30 this morning. City Hall called and requested a room and two meals," I answered as I bent over and patted the dog.

"He's been here before, about three years ago. I recognize the name Luke," he said, studying the slip.

"I don't remember him," I said. "He looks like the Marlboro Man."

"Yes, that's him. He stayed here about three days, in room thirty, remember? I loaned him ten dollars from the Coke fund." Here we go again, Richard and his fantastic memory. I was amazed.

The phone rang and Richard grabbed it, stammering, "goddamn phone!" and "Palmer House" simultaneously.

"Just a minute. I'll get him." Richard laid the receiver down on the desk and then bellowed, "Is John in the restaurant? And bring me some coffee."

When I returned with the coffee, Luke was leaning over the front desk.

"You stayed here two or three years ago, didn't you?" I heard Richard question.

"Ah, don't rightly remember if ah did or not," Luke drawled.

"I could look it up but I think you were in room thirty. It was in the spring of the year. We went out and had a few beers at the Corner Bar, remember?"

Luke scratched his head. "Might be recalling somethin' like that."

"Where are you heading this time?" Richard inquired.

"Got me a chance for a job in Minneapolis. Heerd they was hiring so I thought I'd mosey down an make me some money," he said as he drifted toward the front door.

"Hi Richard, Happy Birthday," a cheery voice greeted.

"How did you know it was my birthday?" he demanded.

"It was on the radio," the voice stated.

"GOD, NO!" He moaned, holding his head in his hands, obviously more than just a little upset.

"Yes," I replied. "Someone called early this morning and had announced it was Richard Schwartz's fiftieth birthday but he doesn't want anyone to know."

"Can't a person have a birthday without the whole town joining in? It makes me mad that everyone wants to get into the act," he stated crossly.

"Well, what do you think your classmate thought when she found the Geritol?" I winked as I walked towards the restaurant.

* * * * *

The clock on the kitchen wall read 3:55 as I slipped on the white cook's jacket and unplugged the radio. I had the evening shift, so I glanced at the steam table to make sure the day cook had left me enough gravy, mashed potatoes, and vegetables. I was right, he had left nothing. Oh, he had boiled up a few potatoes for hash browns and American fries but none had been peeled. It never fails, when I am unprepared, the orders come in. The dishwasher was finishing — I could tell by the banging and slamming of the last few dishes. It's his way of reminding me that he has been working hard all day. Doesn't he know dishes break? But no, he stages a grand finale with the plates taking the place of symbols.

"One-quarter pound fish plate and an English muffin," the waitress called as she entered the kitchen.

"My," I thought to myself, "Ronnie and Rosey are eating early this evening." After ten years in the same kitchen in a small town I can tell who is out front just by the orders. Would you believe there is one woman who has eaten five meals a week at the Palmer House for ten years and has never ordered anything but a hamburger — well done?

I figured we would have a busy evening. A championship basketball game always packs them in. But Richard felt the need to come in and warn me anyway, "Boy, it's filling up early. I'll bet it's because of the game tonight. Do you have enough potatoes peeled?" he asked. He went straight to the walk-in cooler and brought out the unpeeled boiled potatoes and started peeling them. It's unbelievable the thousands of things that Richard does to help me out in the kitchen. And best of all, if I'm still cooking, he often scrubs the pots and pans.

"Do you mind if I go to the game tonight, if the restaurant slows down by 7:00 or so?" he inquired as he dumped the potato peelings in the garbage can.

"No, not at all. I figured you would want to go and watch the *Streeters* play." I placed two hamburgers with fried onions on a plate and rang the bell once for the waitress. "I mentioned that you would want to go."

"To whom?" he asked.

"The kids," I replied smugly.

"Why would they want to know?" he asked sharply. "Now, they're not planning a party or something? You know how I hate parties. Why can't they just leave me alone? I'd like to celebrate my birthday in my own way."

"Now don't get all worked up. I don't think it's a big party, just a little get-together." He sneered and I couldn't help but spill the beans. "I do know, however, that you're getting a boob cake," I added.

By now Richard was up to his elbows in soap suds washing out buckets. "Oh, that stupid boob cake. Remember the one the baker made a few years ago? I think they're gross."

"Be glad it's a boob cake. They were thinking about a dried-out peter cake," I chided.

"Two sirloin strips, medium, with hash browns, one hamburger steak, two reubens and a side of fries," sthe waitress called.

"Boy, it's getting crazy out there," Richard stated, as he wiped his hands and headed into the restaurant. I decided to turn on the second grill.

"Order of fries," the second waitress called out as she slipped the ticket under the message minder above the steam table. She was in such a hurry she knocked several other tickets loose. And sure enough, they landed in the gravy which I had not covered. It's maddening. Naturally it only happens when we are busy, when we don't have to take the time to rewrite them. It usually occurs when the customer is standing by the cash drawer, hollering for his ticket.

Business continued at a hectic pace for an hour and then began to slow. The back door opened and Jane walked in, very angry and wearing a frown. She was carrying a small white cake box. She walked over to the salad table and threw it down. "You wouldn't believe what happened," she stormed.

"Shhhh," I cautioned, "Richard is still here. He's busing tables right now, but he is going to the game tonight."

"Dam." She continued, "I drove all the way to Melrose to pick up the boob cake. It was spectacular! Great big boobies, the likes of which I have never seen before." I laughed. "Richard would have loved it!" she continued.

"What do you mean, WOULD HAVE loved it?" I asked, peeking out the swinging doors to make sure he wasn't coming back into the kitchen.

Jane hid the small white box under the counter. She continued to fume. "Her son carried the cake out to the car. Just as I opened the door, he stumbled and fell right into the cake, smashing the whole thing."

"What?" I asked laughing.

I could just see this kid with his face smashed between the two gigantic boobs looking up at Jane.

"It's not funny," she roared, "I had to rush to the bakery and buy him a plain old cake." She stopped abruptly and smiled as Richard entered the kitchen with a tray of dirty dishes.

"There are three more dirty tables out there. Would someone clear them for me?" he stammered as he placed the full tray near the dishwasher. I grabbed an empty bus tray and headed into the restaurant still laughing at the thought of the bogus boob cake.

*　*　*　*　*

It was 9:45, and the restaurant was dark except for the light above the ice cream freezer. I had been sitting at the counter with the drifter for the past hour, just chatting about guys like him who travel. Oh my, how they specialize in hard luck stories.

Richard had not returned from the game but I knew he would be on cloud nine. The Mainstreeters had won the conference title. The high school gym had been filled to capacity — at least it had sounded like it when I had tuned in the end of the game and had heard the wild excitement as the clock clicked down.

Suddenly people started to arrive. First Jane with some presents under her arm. Then Richard's niece and her husband, and his sister and her husband. They all gathered in the restaurant, wondering if Richard was back from the game. Then the lobby door opened and more friends entered, all wanting to surprise Richard. These guests carried a big, black balloon with gold letters proclaiming OVER THE HILL. As I finished the introductions, Richard entered through the south door and we all piled out into the lobby to sing, "Happy birthday to you, happy birthday to you, happy birthday to dear Richard? Dicky) Dick) R.J.?, happy birthday to you!

Richard stood there, half embarrassed, half smiling, then quietly said, "Thank you, but you know I don't like parties."

As he removed his coat and threw it on the lobby bench, Jane entered from the restaurant carrying a cake, with forty or fifty candles crammed on it. It looked more like a moving campfire than a bithday cake. She set it on the table. Richard took a deep breath and blew out all the candles. A loud cheer went up from the group. Someone else produced a knife, serving forks, and plates. Then I remembered there was left-over orange slush stored in the freezer. As I headed for the kitchen I asked one of the girls to prepare some glasses .

It had been two months since I had last seen the orange slush. As I opened the door I got the *Fibber McGee* closet treatment. Two bags of frozen french fries fell to the floor, followed by a bag of sausages and a pan of cinnamon rolls. Undaunted, I proceeded to look for the pail of slush. By the time I had found it, repacked the freezer, and returned to the lobby, everyone had finished their cake. They were talking about taking Richard over to the bar for a birthday drink. It turned out to be a very good idea, for as I started to pour, I realized I had less slush than and more glasses than I had anticipated. Each guest got one good swallow.

"Who's going to watch the lobby if we all go to the bar!" Richard stated instead of asking.

"I will," his sister replied.

"I will," answered a waitress.

"No, I will," I said. "This is your birthday and your party. I'll watch the desk."

"No Al, I want you to come along," Richard said.

"No, no, we can have a drink any time together. Now out of here, all of you!" I announced, increasing the volume in my voice so that I sounded extremely authoritarian. It was another five minutes before everyone had left and the lobby returned to a quiet state. Suddenly all I could hear was the ticking of the clock. Fifty years, I thought, that's a lot of ticks.

I took my piece of cake and swallow of slush and headed into the dark restaurant. As I entered, I was startled to see the drifter sitting at the far end of the counter with a soft drink can in his hand. "Why didn't you go to the bar with them?" I asked as I approached him.

He said nothing.

"Did you get some birthday cake?"

"Nope."

"Weren't you out in the lobby when Richard came in?"

"Nope."

He was sitting there with both hands wrapped around the can as if he was warming them. I noticed quite a change in his attitude from an hour ago. He was extremely reserved and quiet, where earlier he had been excitedly talkative.

"Would you like some of my cake?" I asked as I pushed it toward him and down the counter. "Or how about a taste of slush?" I said, looking for another glass. "That's all there is, a taste."

"Nope," he answered.

"How about another Coke?" I really had wanted to be left alone and I was fast running out of polite conversation.

"This isn't Coke," he replied, looking at me for the first time. He held the can up to my nose. I winced.

"That's pure booze," I stated in disbelief.

"I've got a lot of things on my mind right now," he answered.

"Well, drinking isn't going to solve anything." I found my old preacher-self coming out, but I really wasn't in the mood to do any counseling, at least not right now.

He reached inside his coat and pulled out a fifth of whiskey. "Would you like a drink?" he offered, holding the bottle up. I looked at the label.

"No, thank you, I drink most anything, but I can't stand whiskey. Brandy, fine, but whiskey, no."

"I can't stand it either," he said as he took one large swig straight from the bottle. I polished off my slush, excused myself, and went into the kitchen to pour a glass of wine. When I returned he was just capping another pull from the bottle.

I sat down just as the telephone rang. I retreated into the kitchen to answer it. "Good evening, Palmer House. May I help you?"

"Yes, could you give me some information on that bus that leaves the hotel for the airport?"

Day and night, people call for information on that bus. I get so tired of being an information agency. And why do we do it, I wondered, for Richard and I get no renumeration for letting the them use our lobby as a depot. However, I still took the time to explain the entire procedure to the caller. The conversation took about fifteen minutes.

I returned to the restaurant to find the drifter had moved to the other end of the counter, closer to the lobby doors. "Guess I'll go upstairs to my room," he announced as he stood up. This time I could tell the alcohol was taking control.

"O.K. I'll walk up with you. Got your key?"

"It's here somewhere."

He started fumbling through his pockets, dropping his bottle. "Here it is," he said joyously, as he pulled it from his back pocket.

As we ascended the stairs, he descended involuntarily. I grabbed on to him as he rocked backwards. Fall down the stairs and we'll have a lawsuit! I thought. Why do we do these things. Why always play the good samaritan.

Down the hallway we went to room ten. He fumbled with the key and the lock until I asked if I could open the door for him. I reached in, turned on the light and said, "Good night, sleep tight." I knew full well he had no choice.

I doubt that I had been upstairs for more than three minutes. I was descending the stairs when Richard was coming out of the restaurant, yelling good and loud, "Where is everyone? Where were you? Who's watching the lobby?"

"I am," I snapped. "I just took that drifter to his room. I haven't been gone two minutes."

"Good lord," he said. "I leave the hotel for one drink and come back and find no one around. It upsets me."

The south door opened and the entire party entered, all talking at once and some of them still singing "Happy birthday to you."

"I hope I'm not going to be stuck with this party all night," Richard grumbled as he threw his coat on the bench.

By now everyone had started lounging around the lobby and it did look like they were going to stay forever. Hoping to get them started toward home I got up and said, "Well, Richard, it's been a great birthday but I have to open in the morning so I had better get to bed. I'll be down about six."

"O.K." Richard replied and positioned himself professionally behind the front desk.

*   *   *   *   *

As I opened the door to the apartment, I was met by Chris. He was all over me as usual, jumping, whining, squeeking, and wagging his tail. You would have thought I had been gone for fifty years. Finally I managed to get through to the den, without stepping on him or tripping over him. I sat down and rubbed his head and ears till he calmed down. I offered him some nibble food which he took and stashed in a pile on the floor. I knew that he would be jumping off the bed, crunching a few, and jumping back on the bed all night long, but I was too tired to care. I was too tired to even turn on the television, but a cool bottle of beer sounded good. I got one from the refrigerator and sat down to relax. It was 1:00 in the morning when I finally crawled into bed. And before I fell asleep I had to chuckle again about the kid with his face buried in the boob cake.

*   *   *   *   *

"ALLAN, ALLAN, WAKE UP!" I opened my eyes to find Richard standing by my bed. The light was on in the living room so I turned to look at my alarm clock. I thought it was after 6:00. "Allan, Allan, Wake up!" Richard kept shouting. I rubbed my eyes.

"What time is it? What's the matter?" I asked struggling for consciousness.

"Allan, we have been robbed!!! Seventy bucks! It's missing from the hotel till and the restaurant cash register."

By now I was fully awake. "What do you mean, robbed? We have never been robbed in all the years we have been here."

"Goddamn birthday party," Richard growled. "In all the commotion someone got to both tills. It had to be that drifter. The guy in room ten," he continued.

I was up now and getting dressed. "How could it be? I took him to his room, remember?"

"He's not there now," Richard said. "I took the pass key and checked the room, first thing. Just a paper bag of clothes and about four empty booze bottles."

I was fumbling for my glasses, "Well, he can't be very far, he hasn't got a car."

"Hurry, come on down and watch the lobby. I'll drive out south of town. He might be hitchhiking or out at one of the truck stops eating." We both ran down the stairs, trying to keep from stepping on or tripping over Chris, who didn't want to miss this extra night-time action.

Downstairs Richard explained as he put on his jacket. "After everyone finally left the lobby, I started to do my book work. I opened the hotel till to check the deposit, and noticed fifteen dollars were missing. You know," he continued. " always have a ten, two fives and five ones in the drawer. Well, the ten and one five were gone." Thinking I had made the wrong change in the restaurant till, I opened it. I noticed right away there wasn't enough money there either. I counted it three times anyway. It was fifty-five dollars short." He stopped at the door turned and said, "this time watch the lobby."

I went into the restaurant and poured a cup of coffee. How could he have gotten in the till? There was someone around all the time. I fought to remember. I had found him sitting in the restaurant alone after everybody had left. But he was sitting at the far end of the counter away from the cash register. As I walked back into the lobby it dawned on me: I had taken a fifteen minute phone call in the kitchen, when I returned Luke was sitting right beside the cash register. He must have hit both tills while I was in the kitchen.

Twenty minutes later a very distraught Richard entered the lobby. "He's gone. I can't find him anywhere. Seventy bucks, just like that. You must have left him alone sometime during the evening."

Now was not the time to explain how I thought it could have happened.

"Seventy bucks! That's just what we need at this time of the year," he said as he lighted a cigarette.

"Well," I said, patting his shoulder, "we got short-changed twice today. First by the baker and then by the burglar. It looks like we're the pair of boobs.

Suggestion Box.

"**N**ow what are you up to?" Richard commented as he decended the stairs.

"Making a suggestion box," I said matter-of-factly. I continued cutting a slit in the top of the cardboard box I had previously covered with white paper.

"A what?" he asked as he walked over to the showcase where I stood performing the surgery.

"A suggestion box. People will see it as they come out of the restaurant. I will leave a note pad beside it so they can drop in suggestions."

"God, you're just asking for trouble," he replied. "Hey I got a suggestion," he continued, "how about getting me a cup of coffee?" He moved to his place behind the front desk, "and let Chris out," he echoed.

Chris was already whining at the door. I opened the door and watched him clear the steps in a single bound. Then I proceeded to get poor Richard a cup of coffee.

When I returned, Richard was opening a bill from the Health Department. "One hundred and fifty dollars. "How come?" Last year it was only forty-five?" He appeared in shock.

"Well," I remarked, "everything goes up."

"No reasons. Not even a warning. It makes me mad! Prices haven't gone up that much."

He continued to stare in disbelief at our latest bill which would soon be added to our pile of already unpaid bills, I continued to cut the slot in the top of the suggestion box.

Over the years we have received many suggestions including a suggestion as to where we should put the suggestion box. Obviously, it's impossible to please everybody. Here are a few suggestions we received that will take some time to accomodate:

Teach Al how to fry eggs.
Please only use Heinz catsup in your restaurant. Thank You.
Toots says, no chips, too fattening lettuce instead.
I'm leaving you!! Petunia.
I'd like to see more of the bosses.
Al, how about a few topless waitresses??????
Summer cold plate - Half as big and alternate meat. Maybe a wiener for a change.
Have a string quartet in the dining room - grinding out Bach.
Free booze.
Get rid of Al!!!!!!
You should have rock-n-roll here.
Coffee too strong!
Take off that oil cloth on the wall, burial paper looks much better.
Tell Al to style his hair!!!
Shut down!!!

Old Josh.

The reliable old regulator clock above the desk showed 8:45.
The mail had arrived early that day and I headed behind the
desk to wait for the letter opener. "Good morning, Merlin. Good
morning, Joe. Morning, Lester. Looks like it might rain." I spoke to
all in the lobby. Josh was already asleep in his regular chair.

Every morning for the past four years, old Josh brought his wife to
the Palmer House so she might join the coffee ladies for their morning ritual. He would sit in the same chair every day and proceed to
fall asleep. Sometimes he slept for two hours before she was ready
to leave. The length of his nap depended on the amount of gossip.

"Good morning, Palmer House. May I help you?"

"I was wondering if you might need help?"

"What kind of help?" I replied.

"You know, dishwashers, waiters or kitchen help," the hesitant
voice replied.

"Are you looking for work?" I asked suspectantly.

"Well, not me sir. I was inquiring for my son. He will be a senior
this year and would like to find a job."

This was not the first time a mother had called looking for employ-
ment for her children. It's crazy! "Why would you want to land a job

for your son?" I asked.

"Well," she confessed, "he is very shy and I don't think he will come in, maybe I could fill out an application for him."

"No, ma'am. We are not hiring at this time. But tell him if he would like to come in person he could fill out an application for himself." Good-bye," I said wondering if she would do his work for him also.

"Hi, Josh," Fred said as he passed through the lobby heading for the restaurant. "Don't you know we charge for sleeping in the lobby?" He didn't answer.

"The light in the third floor bathroom is burned out," Merlin summoned. "Do you want me to pick one up and put it in?

"If you do, don't go to Mirical Hardware. They haven't been in here for a meal in two years," I shouted back.

"Good morning, Al," the voice eminated from one of the businessmen, as he headed for the coffee table. I didn't look up from my mail. I guess I was engrossed in my letter. "Well, aren't you going to say good morning?" came another curt retort, in a voice loud enough to break my concentration.

"Oh, yes. Good morning."

He smiled and headed into the restaurant.

Coffee time was starting to churn. And as they entered the lobby from all walks of life one by one, it was: "Good morning, Al. Good morning, Josh. Good morning, Merlin." The same litany every morning, from the same people.

I got myself a cup of coffee from the restaurant and was back at the desk when the ladies group, the second one, began entering.

They all automatically said hello to Josh even if he was asleep and continued on into the restaurant. It was 9:30. The dice shaking was exceptionally loud this morning. You could hear the pounding of the dice boxes all over the lobby. As one of the coffee ladies arrived a little late, she stopped for a second to speak to Josh. "Josh, Josh." He was not only sound asleep, but he also was hard of hearing. She started to touch him to give him a shake. "My god, I think he's dead." Her voice was shaking and hoarse. I came from around the desk.

"Josh," I called loudly. Then I lifted his hand from the arm of the chair. "He's dead," I repeated as I ran for the telephone. I dialed the police department, "Would you send a policeman to the Palmer House. I believe we have a man in the lobby who is dead. And yes, call the ambulance." Hanging up, I headed back into the restaurant to get Richard's brother-in-law. "I think Josh is dead," I whispered.

"He's what?"

"Dead, I think," I replied, heading back into the lobby.

The Chief of Police rushed through the door. He went directly to Josh and listened for a heartbeat and a pulse, "He's gone alright," he said. "How long has he been here?"

"He was sitting there as usual when I came down an hour ago," I answered.

A small crowd had gathered around. The ambulance siren immediately stopped all the restuarant gossip.

"Has someone told his wife?" I asked, then added, "she's sitting at the coffee table in the back."

The paramedics arrived and I ran upstairs to alert Richard. When I returned, Josh's wife was wailing and moaning very loudly in the lobby. Many people tried to comfort her but it was to no avail. They moved Josh to the ambulance, and escorted his wife home.

"What a way to die," Richard commented as he stood behind the desk. "He falls asleep doing the same thing he has done for years, waiting for his wife to finish coffee."

In a small town, superstitions die slowly. It was almost two months before anyone would again sit in Josh's chair.

God Bless You, Mr. Sito.

The phone bellowed in the lobby as I flew down thestairs to answer it.

"Hello, Al Tingley. May I help you?"

"Al? This is Linda with the International Studies Center at the University of Minnesota."

"Yes, how are you Linda? I haven't seen you in quite a while."

"I know. Been real busy here. Al, I have a big favor to ask of you."

"Go right ahead," I answered positively.

"Well, we just received a message that a Mr. Sito, a professor of American Literature at the University of Tokyo, is in America to study at Yale University. And while in America he would like to visit "Gopher Prairie." She began to giggle. "What's Gopher Prairie?"

"Now Linda, you know that's the name Sinclair Lewis chose for the town in his famous novel, **Main Street**. In reality it's his home town, Sauk Centre, Minnesota," I chided.

"I know, I was only teasing," she laughed. "Anyway, Mr. Sito would like to go to Sauk Centre and present his original Japanese translation of **Main Street** to the Lewis Foundation for permanent display in the Sinclair Lewis Interpretive Center. Would you and your partner, Richard, be interested in volunteering to meet him at the airport and drive him up there? Please?" Her voice augmented her pleading.

"When is he arriving?" I asked.

"This Friday evening at 7:00 on Eastern Flight 709 from New York."

I knew Richard's answer. "Absolutely yes." As a native of Sauk Centre, he is very proud of his community, and its association with Sinclair Lewis. I knew he would be perfectly willing to make the one hundred-mile trip to the Minneapolis-St. Paul airport.

"Sure, Linda, we will do it unless I call you back. By the way, don't be such a stranger."

"Thanks a million. We'll get together soon. Bye now."

*　　*　　*　　*　　*

An area crowded with deplaning passengers makes it difficult to spot anyone, much less one whom you have never met. "Don't worry," Richard assured me. "There can't be too many people from Japan getting off the plane."

Suddenly we spotted a slight, bespectacled gentleman carrying a rather large attache case coming down the ramp. Richard stepped forward, "Mr. Sito, I presume?" he inquired, extending his right hand.

"Yes. Yes, it is." The scholar reached for Richard's hand and shook it enthusiastically, bowing slightly at the same time. The smile on his face was as wide as the Mississippi River.

"This is my partner, Al. Al Tingley, and I am Richard Schwartz. Here, let me take your suitcase."

As Mr. Sito shook my hand he muttered, "Al Tingley. Al Tingley - **Main Street**: Busy place this airport. Almost as bad as Tokyo." He was very soft spoken, so Richard had to lean forward to hear his conversation.

"I am very excited to see Sauk Centre. All my life I dream of coming to America. Lewis is a great American. A great writer."

"Well," Richard said, "we will be in Sauk Centre in about two hours. It's not a very big town, but it does have a hotel downtown called the Palmer House."

"Yes, the Minniemashie House in Gopher Prairie," Mr. Sito smiled and looked at me.

I turned the van out onto the freeway. I was concentrating on driving until that point and I hadn't added much to the conversation.

"I understand you translated **Main Street**," I said.

"Yes, it took three years, and now I am working on **Babbitt**."

"How long have you been in the United States?" Richard asked.

"About nine months. I'll be returning to Japan in three weeks. I was at Yale. Studying Lewis.

"And do you like America?" I asked as I finally pulled out of the Twin Cities traffic and headed north.

"It's nice," he replied with a little hesitation. "But too fast."

"You mean the pace or my driving?" I asked.

"People move too fast. There is no time to reflect. No time to think."

We were now on the highway travelling parallel to the old Great Northern railroad tracks, which prompted Richard to remark, "You see those railroad tracks out there on your right, Mr. Sito?"

Mr. Sito leaned forward and looked out his window. In the headlights one could see the shiny reflection of the tracks.

"This is the same route which Carol Kennicott and Dr. Will travelled on train number seven, on her first trip to Gopher Prairie," Richard continued.

I could feel the emotion as Mr. Sito was mentally reliving that trip described in **Main Street**. I assumed it was a vivid memory, as he had lived with the book for three years while translating it.

"Pretty soon we will go through Winnemaken," Richard noted. "Winnemaken is really St. Cloud, Minnesota."

"I don't believe this is happening to me," Mr. Sito commented. "All my life I have dreamed of coming to America. The two places I have dreamed of visiting in my lifetime are Niagara Falls which I saw just two days ago and Main Street in Gopher Prairie. I can't believe this is happening to me." His voice trailed off as he continued to stare out the window at the hypnotic passing of the shiny railroad tracks.

"Remember, Mr. Sito, when Carol looked at the towns passing by from the train window she remarked 'the towns were as planless as cardboard boxes scattered on an attic floor.' "

Mr. Sito did not answer. All he did was continue to stare and nod his head in the affirmative.

As we drew close to Sauk Centre one could feel the emotion rising within our guest in the front seat. In the next few moments I would witness the most unabashed show of emotion ever in my lifetime. We were about two miles from Sauk Centre when Richard spoke up, breaking the long reverie of the past few miles.

"When we go over the next rise, Mr. Sito, you will see the lights of Gopher Prairie stretched before you."

Even Richard was leaning forward, peering out the front wind-shield. The motor of the automobile hummed with a rhythm that was hypnotic in itself, sweeping along the highway up and down the roll-ing hills of the great midwestern plains. As we climbed the last rise before the city of Sauk Centre, nestled in the Sylvan Valley of the Sauk River basin, I glanced at Mr. Sito to see his reaction. His eyes suddenly not only filled with tears, but literally gushed water as his life long dream unfolded before him. Gopher Prairie. Main Street. Even I could not hold back the mounting emotion. No one spoke, but the feeling was magnetic. It was a bonding across oceans, cultures and time.

Over the years people from all around the world have visited Gopher Prairie to walk Main Street as did Carol Kennicott. I am overwhelmed by the influence of Lewis throughout the world. And as I sit on the corner of Main Street and marvel, I realize that it is a privilege to own a small piece of his history. And somehow, sudden-ly, all the heartaches and headaches associated with ownership of a small town hotel, seem insignificant.

Epilogue

W ell, the truck driver never did pay his bill; however Mary from Fargo eventually sent a check for the entire amount.

In March of 1982, as Richard and I received a great announcement: The Palmer House Hotel was placed on the **STATE AND NATIONAL REGISTER OF HISTORIC PLACES.**

People are still coming to Sauk Centre from all over the world to visit Sinclair Lewis' home town and the entire community is gearing up to celebrate the 100 Birthday of Sinclair — a celebration which begins February 7, 1985.

Here at the Palmer House we are planning on holding a birthday cake decorating contest the week before the celebration. The winning cake will be served at the official celebration. Boob cakes are not allowed.

The Sinclair Lewis foundation is rejoicing in the decision that the United States Post Office is going to issue a Stamp in Lewis's honor February 7, 1985 in Sauk Centre.

The coffee crowd is still shaking dice. The faceless soup lady is still calling — and I am still marveling at people who continue to congregate at the **CORNER ON MAIN STREET.**